RETHINKING SCHOOLS

Rethinking Schools

An Agenda for Change

EDITED BY
David Levine
Robert Lowe
Bob Peterson
Rita Tenorio

THE NEW PRESS
NEW YORK

96 97 98   9 8 7 6 5 4 3

Library of Congress Cataloging-in-Publication Data

Rethinking schools: an agenda for change / edited by David Levine... [et al.].
     p.   cm.
   Includes bibliographical references and index.
   ISBN 1-56584-214-6 (hc)   ISBN 1-56584-215-4 (pbk.)
     1. Public schools—United States. 2. Education change—United States.
3. Education, Urban—United States. 4. Rethinking Schools.
I. Levine, David P.
LA217.2.R48   1995
371'.01'0973—dc20   94-34347
                                                  CIP

Published in the United States by The New Press, New York
Distributed by W. W. Norton & Company, Inc., New York, NY 10110

Established in 1990 as a major alternative to the large, commercial publishing houses, The New Press is the first full-scale nonprofit American book publisher outside of the university presses. The Press is operated editorially in the public interest, rather than for private gain; it is committed to publishing in innovative ways works of educational, cultural, and community value that, despite their intellectual merits, might not normally be "commercially" viable. The New Press's editorial offices are located at the City University of New York.

Book design by Charles Nix

Production management by Kim Waymer

Printed in the United States of America

This book is dedicated to the children of Milwaukee.

Contents

PART V

Building a Community: Teachers, Students, and Parents

Foreword

HERBERT KOHL

The coffee table in the middle of our living room is stacked with books, journals, newspapers, and magazines. It was in one of these stacks that I discovered *Rethinking Schools*. I can't remember how I got my first copy — I might have picked it up at a conference or received it unsolicited through the mail. I just popped it on the pile and it must have sat there for a month or so, getting buried deeper and deeper by a dreary succession of unread educational journals.

It wasn't until my quarterly clean-up-the-table day that I took another look at *Rethinking Schools*. This time my eye was caught by a modified version of Tenniel's drawing of Alice on the cover, under an article by Linda Darling-Hammond entitled "Curiouser and Curiouser: Alice in Testingland." Alice was on my mind those days as I had just finished directing a children's play, which ended up being called *The Three Alices and Their Sister Susie in Wonderland: A Country-and-Blues Musical*. And testing was on my mind as usual, it being one of the greatest impediments to being able to steal the time in school to do productions like *The Three Alices*.

There were two articles on the front page of that issue (January/February 1989, Vol. 3, No. 2). In addition to Darling-Hammond's brilliant dissection of the absurdity of the testing game was an extended discussion of school reform proposals in Milwaukee and their prospects for success. Both articles were well written and provided a depth of analysis and a clarity that I am unaccustomed to encountering in educational journals. I continued reading through the issue and discovered that the quality of writing and depth of analysis was consistent throughout. However, there was more variety in the content than I had anticipated: a teacher's account of the introduction of whole language reading programs in Milwaukee, critical articles on intelligence testing and standardized tests, as well as an account of alternative assessment in a Milwaukee high school. There also was a bibliography of books and articles on issues of testing and evaluation, and finally and delightfully, a back page of student writing.

Educational struggles and successes in Milwaukee are at the center of *Rethinking Schools,* and yet the publication is as national as it is local. The day after reading this issue I subscribed, and whenever it arrives I put it in that small stack of material that simply must be read.

Rethinking Schools is like a good gumbo; it has many distinct flavors that retain their integrity while blending into a tasty and pungent whole. It deals with the concrete and practical aspects of classroom teaching and with particular educational struggles, at the same time that it contains essays that are theoretical and political. It does not neglect current sensitive moral and cultural issues. Much of the writing is done by the editorial staff in Milwaukee, but there are a multiplicity of voices that can be heard in *Rethinking Schools.* These voices range from high school and elementary school students and teachers to better-known writers such as Lisa Delpit and Henry Louis Gates Jr.

Like every good gumbo, there is an underlying flavor, a stock, that pervades the whole and gives it a unique character. For *Rethinking Schools* the stock is moral. Pervading all of the material in the journal and in this anthology, which has been selected from articles published in past issues, is a commitment to equity and social justice. This orientation provides the perspective that unites articles on classroom practice, educational legislation, the politics of education, multiculturalism, race, and gender in the classroom with children's writing, teachers' accounts of their work, lists of resources, book reviews, and editorial comment, transforming them into a coherent whole.

Rethinking Schools displays the variety of tone and content – the humor and anger, the playfulness and seriousness – that characterizes democratic living. Agreement on moral principles does not lead to agreement on particular strategies or analyses. *Rethinking Schools* is a forum for discussion and debate about how equity and social justice are best achieved through education.

Teaching is a moral calling, a craft, and an intellectual occupation. It is often values that bring one to education in the first place. The craft develops through experience and reflection upon that experience. What is hardest to maintain in the midst of the immediate demands of the classroom is the intellectual aspect of teaching, which, though less apparent on an everyday level than the craft issues, still pervades and underlies every good teacher's practice. It has to do with teachers' analysis of how children learn, of the role of ethnicity, gender, and class in learning, of the relationship between school and society, and of the translation of moral values into specific classroom practice.

There is a complex and intimate relationship between theory and practice in the classroom. Theoretical ideas are tested every day by the complex and often unpredictable behavior of students and teachers, and by the constant influence of life outside of the classroom. The immediate translation of theory into practice – finding effective ways to teach reading or manage behavior – is often not possible. Things don't always work out in the classroom, and practicing teachers have to constantly adjust theory based upon their practice. *Rethinking Schools* acknowledges this complex interaction. Both the journal and this anthology serve teachers and other people concerned with education by addressing our moral and intellectual needs. As such, I believe it contains some of the most important writing about education being done today. It is essential reading.

Grateful acknowledgment is made for permission to reprint the following material. Except where otherwise noted, all articles originally appeared in *Rethinking Schools*. Every effort has been made to contact copyright holders. Where the attempt has been unsuccessful, the publisher would be pleased to hear from the copyright holder to rectify any omission.

"Multiculturalism: A Conversation Among Different Voices" by Henry Louis Gates Jr. Vol. 6 , no. 1 (October/November 1991).

"Taking Multicultural, Anti-racist Education Seriously: An Interview with Enid Lee." Vol. 6, no. 1 (October/November 1991).

"How Well Are We Nurturing Racial and Ethnic Diversity?" by Louise Derman-Sparks. Vol. 6, no. 1 (October/November 1991).

"Trouble Over the Rainbow" by Stan Karp. Vol. 7, no. 3 (Autumn 1992).

"Are We Accepting Too Much?" by Foyne Mahaffey. Vol. 6, no. 4 (May/June 1992).

"What Do We Say When We Hear 'Faggot'?" by Lenore Gordon. From the *Bulletin* of the Council on Interracial Books for Children. Vol. 14, no. 3 & 4. Copyright © 1984 by The Council on Interracial Books for Children.

"Building a Vision of Curriculum Reform" by David Levine. Vol. 3, no. 3 (May/June 1989).

"Discovering Columbus: Rereading the Past" by Bill Bigelow. Vol. 4, no. 1 (October/November 1989).

"We Have No Reason to Celebrate an Invasion: An Interview with Suzan Shown Harjo." Vol. 6, no. 1 (October/November 1991).

"What Should Children Learn? A Teacher Looks at E. D. Hirsch" by Bob Peterson. Vol. 8, no. 2 (Winter 1993).

"Why Students Should Study History: An Interview with Howard Zinn." Vol. 7, no. 2 (Winter 1992/1993).

"Distorting Latino History: The California Textbook Controversy" by Elizabeth Martínez. Vol. 7, no. 2 (Winter 1992/1993).

"*The Lorax*: Dr. Seuss Revisited and Revised" by Bill Bigelow. Vol. 4, no. 3 (March/April 1990).

"Whole Language: What's the Fuss? An Interview with Harvey Daniels." Vol. 8, no. 2 (Winter 1993).

"Whose Standard? Teaching Standard English in Our Schools" by Linda Christensen. Vol. 4, no. 2 (December 1989/January 1990).

"Teachers, Culture, and Power: An Interview with Lisa Delpit." Vol. 6, no. 3 (March/April 1992).

"Getting Off the Track: Stories from an Untracked Classroom" by Bill Bigelow. Vol. 7, no. 4 (Summer 1993).

"Is Your Child Being Tracked?" by the National Coalition of Education Activists. From *Maintaining Inequality: A Background Packet on Tracking and Ability Grouping*. Reprinted by permission of the National Coalition of Education Activists.

"Algebra for All: An Equation for Equity" by Barbara Miner. Vol. 8, no. 1 (Autumn 1993).

"Standardized Tests: A Clear and Present Danger" by Terry Meier. Vol. 7, no. 3 (Spring 1993).

"The Perils of Schools Vouchers" by Robert Lowe. Originally published as "The Hollow Promise of School Vouchers" in *False Choices: Why School Vouchers Threaten Our Children's Future*. Special edition (1992).

"Is Public School 'Choice' a Viable Alternative?" by Ann Bastian. *False Choices: Why School Vouchers Threaten Our Children's Future*. Special edition (1992).

"Coming to Terms with Violence in Our Schools" by Pedro Noguera. Vol. 8, no. 1 (Autumn 1993).

"The Hollow Promise of Youth Apprenticeships" by Harvey Kantor. Vol. 8, no. 1 (Autumn 1993).

"Beyond Pizza Sales: Parent Involvement in the 1990s" by the editors of *Rethinking Schools*. Vol. 7, no. 3 (Spring 1993).

"Teachers Through History: The Myth of a Golden Age" by Robert Lowe. Vol. 1, no. 2 (May/June 1987).

"Preparing Teachers for Education in a Diverse World" by Cynthia Ellwood. Vol. 5, no. 3 (March/April 1991).

"Which Side Are You On? The Role of Teachers Unions in School Reform" by Bob Peterson. Vol. 8, no. 1 (Autumn 1993).

"All Children Are Our Children: An Interview with Lola Glover." Vol. 7, no. 3 (Spring 1993).

Rethinking Schools, 1001 East Keefe Avenue, Milwaukee, Wisconsin 53212; tel.: 414-964-9646; fax: 414-964-7220.

Acknowledgments

This book would not have been possible without the help of countless people who, over the years, have contributed to *Rethinking Schools* in myriad ways — from writing articles, to bundling newspapers, to proofreading late into the night. Space prohibits us from mentioning all our wonderful supporters by name. You know who you are. We salute you and thank you.

We would also like to acknowledge the patience and hard work of Jennifer Morales as she shepherded this book through the trials of production.

Introduction

Rethinking Schools made its debut in the fall of 1986 with a lead story entitled, "Surviving Scott Foresman: Confessions of a Kindergarten Teacher." The article, in what became a typical response, was well received by many but hit a raw nerve among teachers and administrators who defended the status quo.

"I'm just telling you to watch out," one elementary school principal told one of the journal editors. "It's like the McCarthy era down there at Central Office."

"We're being called subversives because we are critical of basal readers?" the flabbergasted editor responded.

"All I am saying is, just be careful," the principal said.

Rethinking Schools wasn't particularly careful; it kept publishing and it kept pushing for change. Today, we find ourselves somewhat perplexed that the paper has not only survived but flourished. Nine years ago we had no inkling that *Rethinking Schools* would be nationally recognized as a leading voice for grassroots education reform. At the time, our goal was simply to put out a newspaper to help us organize a reform movement within the Milwaukee Public Schools.

People often ask us, "What exactly is *Rethinking Schools?*" Part of the answer is easy: *Rethinking Schools* is a journal published four times a year, providing a grassroots look at education reform with a particular focus on urban schools.

But we know there is more to it than that. The publication also represents something far more significant but far less tangible. We have been fortunate to have been an integral part of an amorphous but broadly based movement of teachers, parents, and community people deeply concerned about the state of public schools in this country, especially urban schools. In our own way, we have enlisted people in seeing *Rethinking Schools* as a vital part of that movement, as a resource, a home, a place to talk to others about educational equity. Our links with that movement, in turn, have provided a vehicle for comment and criticism and have helped hold us accountable.

When we started, *Rethinking Schools* was little more than a collection of typewritten articles about to be pasted up on a kitchen table at 2 A.M. as we rushed to meet our printer's deadline. We began, literally, without any real budget, kept alive by hours of volunteer help and a few donations from friends and family to pay the printer. Today, we have a modicum of financial stability, a small staff to help with the complexities of publishing a journal, and a circulation of approximately 40,000 copies per issue. We have also published three successful magazine-style special editions: *Rethinking Columbus: Teaching About the 500th Anniversary of Columbus's Arrival in the Americas; False Choices: Why School Vouchers Threaten Our Children's Future;* and *Rethinking Our Classrooms: Teaching for Equity and Justice.*

We didn't have a lot of money when we started, but we believed people can make a difference. We were committed to challenging the racism and inequality in schools and society. We considered good public schools an integral part of our democratic vision for this country. We were dedicated to linking education to the broader effort of building a more humane society. A decade later, we still hold to these principles.

We also had particular ideas about the type of publication we wanted: one that analyzes issues in depth but avoids academic jargon; one that is grounded in classroom practice but also looks at broader policy issues; one that is proudly activist and provides a link for teachers and parents organizing for change.

When we came up with the idea of starting a quarterly journal, we put out a mimeographed call for teachers, parents, and community members to join us. A number of people responded. Over the years a core group developed – people with both the political commitment and time to become the editors, on a volunteer basis, of a quarterly journal. Some made essential contributions but later left the editorial board; founding editor Cynthia Ellwood, in particular, was an invaluable part of *Rethinking Schools* before taking a major administrative position in the Milwaukee Public Schools at the urging of the other editors.

During the past three years, our capacity to produce a well-written publication that reaches a growing audience has been qualitatively boosted through the hard work of a talented and dedicated staff. Managing Editor Barbara Miner, Office Manager Michael Trokan, Editorial Assistant Jennifer Morales, and Administrative Assistant Sharon Matthias have enriched our efforts with top-notch talent, progressive politics, and good humor.

Rethinking Schools has also been fortunate to work with many wonderful volunteers, writers, and friends. In particular you will notice articles written by editorial associates Bill Bigelow, Linda Christensen, and Stan Karp — all of them classroom teachers who scratch out time from their many responsibilities to volunteer with *Rethinking Schools*. Their suggestions and feedback, along with that of editorial associate Larry Miller, are an invaluable part of the *Rethinking Schools* endeavor. Likewise, we have been blessed with a strong network of volunteers and supporters who have helped us proofread articles at all hours of the day and night, who have strained their muscles trudging around bundles of newspapers, and who have helped us celebrate our successes and carry on through our failures.

When people ask us for prescriptions for school reform, we don't have any magical answers. We do know, however, that there are several important factors. One is the need for a constant focus on issues of equity and justice. Another is an understanding that one must change both policy and practice — that one must grapple with policy questions such as vouchers and standardized testing but must also understand that true reform has to affect classroom practice. Finally, one must take a deep breath and commit oneself to organizing for equity not only in the educational arena, but throughout society. In the ongoing struggle for justice, the ultimate aim is not just to understand but to transform.

DAVID LEVINE
ROBERT LOWE
BOB PETERSON
RITA TENORIO
March, 1995

RETHINKING SCHOOLS

Multiculturalism and Antibias Education

In a society marked by great disparities of wealth and power, American schools have often been praised as the pathway to equality. But public education in our country has been marked by a cruel gap between rhetorical commitment to democratic ideals and practices that foster intolerance and inequality. This disparity results from both the failure of schools to educate against prejudice and discrimination that emerge from the larger society, and their active complicity in reproducing unequal relationships. Rigid ethnic, racial, and gender roles and stereotypes have frequently been promoted by school cultures and curricula. All the writers in Part I are searching for ways in which schools can reverse this pattern and actively nurture respect for diversity and antidiscriminatory attitudes and behaviors.

In the first piece, Henry Louis Gates Jr. explains that Anglo-American culture often has been presented as our natural common denominator, and other cultures devalued as parochial intrusions. This perspective slights the need for dialogue between different cultures and the honoring of our plural roots. Gates suggests we instead adopt a commitment to fostering cultural understanding that can help schools promote real democracy.

In the following interview, the African-Canadian educator Enid Lee emphasizes that multicultural education falls into superficiality unless it explicitly confronts racial inequality. She insists that to be truly effective, multicultural education must become an integral element of a school's entire curriculum and should help students confront inequalities in their communities. Lee encourages teachers to bring the voices of silenced groups into the classroom and examine their own attitudes toward those excluded from power.

Because prejudice can have a powerful effect on young children, Louise Derman-Sparks urges early childhood educators to help their students understand and combat stereotypes. She explains the inadequacies of classrooms that center on the dominant culture, adopt a "color-denial" approach, or favor a "tourist-multicultural" curriculum. She also sketches out practical ways to teach about ethnic and racial diversity.

In his piece on a New York City controversy, Stan Karp analyzes the explosive conflict caused by *Children of the Rainbow,* a multicultural guide that includes positive portrayals of gay parents. The strong homophobic backlash to the guide polarized many New York committees and led to heated battles for control of local school boards. Karp argues that it is essential to confront community prejudices through democratic discussion of highly controversial issues.

The effect of gender prejudice is also discussed by Foyne Mahaffey, who is profoundly disturbed by the widespread sexual harassment of girls by the boys at her elementary school. When adults fail to intervene, Mahaffey argues, girls learn to feel powerless and devalued. She urges teachers to help girls express their thoughts about harassment and to consistently challenge unacceptable behavior through direct discussion and appropriate discipline.

In "What Do We Say When We Hear 'Faggot'?" Lenore Gordon sounds a similar theme, focusing on specific ways in which teachers can help elementary and middle school students understand and construct alternatives to antigay attitudes. Gordon notes that homophobic peer harassment promotes prejudice, directly harms children who have homosexual feelings, and cows children into rigid sex roles. In addition to prohibiting harassment in her classroom, Gordon has designed thoughtful ways to build upon each student's own sense of fairness and empathy to critique homophobic ideas and behavior.

At a time when the religious right is mobilizing around social issues and school officials are often reluctant to provoke conservative anger, these accounts are heartening because they show that antibias teaching can draw on strong democratic ideas within American culture, and can use the diversity of our students to enrich learning as it dispels stereotyped thinking.

Multiculturalism: A Conversation Among Different Voices

HENRY LOUIS GATES JR.

What is multiculturalism, and why are they saying such terrible things about it? We've been told it threatens to fragment American culture into a warren of ethnic enclaves, each separate and inviolate. We've been told that it menaces the Western tradition of literature and the arts. We've been told it aims to politicize the school curriculum, replacing honest historical scholarship with a "feel good" syllabus designed solely to bolster the self-esteem of minorities. The alarm has been sounded, and many scholars and educators — liberals as well as conservatives — have responded. After all, if multiculturalism is just a pretty name for ethnic chauvinism, who needs it?

But I don't think that's what multiculturalism is — at least, I don't think that's what it ought to be. And because the debate has been miscast from the beginning, it may be worth setting the main issues straight.

There's no denying that the multicultural initiative arose, in part, because of the fragmentation of American society, by ethnicity, class, and gender. To make it the culprit for this fragmentation is to mistake effect for cause. Mayor Dinkins's metaphor about New York as a "gorgeous mosaic" is catchy but unhelpful, if it means that each culture is fixed in place and separated by grout. Maybe we should try to think of American culture as a conversation among different voices — even if it's a conversation that some of us weren't able to join until recently. Maybe we should think about education, as the philosopher Michael Oakeshott — a self-professed conservative, by the way — has proposed, as "an invitation into the art of this conversation in which we learn to recognize the voices." Common sense says that you don't bracket 90 percent of the world's cultural heritage if you really want to learn about the world.

To insist, then, that we "master our own culture" before learning others only defers the vexing question: what gets to count as "our" culture? What makes knowledge worth knowing? There's a wonderful bit of nineteenth century student doggerel about the great

Victorian classicist Jowett, which nicely sums up the monocultural-ist's claims on this point:

> Here I stand, my name is Jowett
> If there's knowledge, then I know it.
> I am the master of this college:
> What I know not, is not knowledge.

Unfortunately, as history has taught us, an Anglo-American regional culture has too often masked itself as universal, passing itself off as our "common culture," and depicting different cultural traditions as "tribal" or "parochial." So it's only when we're free to explore the complexities of our hyphenated American culture that we can discover what a genuinely common American culture might actually look like. Is multiculturalism un-American? Herman Melville didn't think so. As he wrote, "We are not a narrow tribe, no....We are not a nation, so much as a world." Common sense reminds us that we're all ethnics, and the challenge of transcending ethnic chauvinism is one we all face.

Granted, multiculturalism is no magic panacea for our social ills. We're worried when Johnny can't read. We're worried when Johnny can't add. But shouldn't we be worried, too, when Johnny tramples gravestones in a Jewish cemetery or scrawls racial epithets on a dormitory wall? It's a fact about this country that we've entrusted our schools with the fashioning and refashioning of a democratic polity; that's why the schooling of America has always been a matter of political judgment. But in America, a nation that has theorized itself as plural from its inception, our schools have a very special task.

Ours is a society that simply won't survive without the values of tolerance; and cultural tolerance comes to nothing without cultural understanding. In short, the challenge facing America in the next century will be the shaping, at long last, of a truly common public culture, one responsive to the long-silenced cultures of color. For if we relinquish the ideal of America as a plural nation, we abandon the very experiment that America represents. And that, surely, is too great a price to pay.

Taking Multicultural,
Anti-racist Education Seriously:
An Interview with Enid Lee

The following is condensed from an interview with Enid Lee, a consultant in antiracist education and organizational change, and author of Letters to Marcia: A Teacher's Guide to Anti-Racist Education. *She was interviewed in the fall of* 1991 *by Barbara Miner of* Rethinking Schools.

What do you mean by a multicultural education?

The term *multicultural education* has a lot of different meanings. The term I use most often is *antiracist education*.

Multicultural or antiracist education is fundamentally a perspective. It's a point of view that cuts across all subject areas, and addresses the histories and experiences of people who have been left out of the curriculum. Its purpose is to help us deal equitably with all the cultural and racial differences that you find in the human family. It's also a perspective that allows us to get at explanations for why things are the way they are in terms of power relationships, in terms of equality issues.

So when I say multicultural or antiracist education, I am talking about equipping students, parents, and teachers with the tools needed to combat racism and ethnic discrimination, and to find ways to build a society that includes all people on an equal footing.

It also has to do with how the school is run in terms of who gets to be involved with decisions. It has to do with parents and how their voices are heard or not heard. It has to do with who gets hired in the school.

If you don't take multicultural education or antiracist education seriously, you are actually promoting a monocultural or racist education. There is no neutral ground on this issue.

Why do you use the term antiracist education instead of multicultural education?

Partly because in Canada, multicultural education often has come to mean something that is quite superficial: the dances, the dress, the dialect, the dinners. And it does so without focusing on what those expressions of culture mean: the values, the power relationships that shape the culture.

I also use the term *antiracist education* because a lot of multicultural education hasn't looked at discrimination. It has the view, "People are different and isn't that nice," as opposed to looking at how some people's differences are looked upon as deficits and disadvantages. In antiracist education, we attempt to look at – and change – those things in school and society that prevent some differences from being valued.

Oftentimes, whatever is white is treated as normal. So when teachers choose literature that they say will deal with a universal theme or story, like childhood, all the people in the stories are of European origin; it's basically white culture and civilization. That culture is different from others, but it doesn't get named as different. It gets named as normal.

Antiracist education helps us move that European perspective over to the side to make room for other cultural perspectives that must be included.

What are some ways your perspective might manifest itself in a kindergarten classroom, for example?

It might manifest itself in something as basic as the kinds of toys and games that you select. If all the toys and games reflect the dominant culture and race and language, then that's what I call a monocultural classroom even if you have kids of different backgrounds in the class.

I have met some teachers who think that just because they have kids from different races and backgrounds, they have a multicultural classroom. Bodies of kids are not enough.

It also gets into issues such as what kind of pictures are up on the wall? What kinds of festivals are celebrated? What are the rules and expectations in the classroom in terms of what kinds of languages are acceptable? What kinds of interactions are encouraged? How are the kids grouped? These are just some of the concrete ways in which a multicultural perspective affects a classroom.

How does one implement a multicultural or antiracist education?

It usually happens in stages. Because there's a lot of resistance to change in schools, I don't think it's reasonable to expect to move straight from a monocultural school to a multiracial school.

First there is this surface stage in which people change a few expressions of culture in the school. They make welcome signs in several languages and have a variety of foods and festivals. My problem is not that they start there. My concern is that they often stop there. Instead, what they have to do is move very quickly and steadily to transform the entire curriculum. For example, when we say classical music, whose classical music are we talking about? European? Japanese? And what items are on the tests? Whose culture do they reflect? Who is getting equal access to knowledge in the school? Whose perspective is heard? Whose is ignored?

The second stage is transitional and involves creating units of study. Teachers might develop a unit on Native Americans, or Native Canadians, or people of African background. And they have a whole unit that they study from one period to the next. But it's a separate unit and what remains intact is the main curriculum, the main menu. One of the ways to assess multicultural education in your school is to look at the school organization. Look at how much time you spend on which subjects. When you are in the second stage you usually have a two- or three-week unit on a group of people or an area that's been omitted in the main curriculum.

You're moving into the next stage of structural change when you have elements of that unit integrated into existing units. Ultimately, what is at the center of the curriculum gets changed in its prominence. For example, civilizations. Instead of just talking about Western civilization, you begin to draw on what we need to know about India, Africa, China. We also begin to ask different questions about why and what we are doing. Whose interest is it in that we study what we study? Why is it that certain kinds of knowledge get hidden? In mathematics, instead of studying statistics with sports and weather numbers, why not look at employment in light of ethnicity?

Then there is the social change stage, when the curriculum helps lead to changes outside of the school. We actually go out and change the nature of the community we live in. For example, kids might become involved in how the media portray people and start a letter-writing campaign about news that is negatively biased. Kids begin to see this as a responsibility that they have to change the world.

I think about a group of elementary school kids who wrote to the manager of the store about the kinds of games and dolls that they had. That's a long way from having some dinner and dances that represent an "exotic" form of life.

In essence, in antiracist education we use knowledge to empower people and to change their lives.

Teachers have limited money to buy new materials. How can they begin to incorporate a multicultural education even if they don't have a lot of money?

We do need money and it is a pattern to underfund antiracist initiatives so that they fail. We must push for funding for new resources because some of the information we have is downright inaccurate. But if you have a perspective, which is really a set of questions that you ask about your life, and you have the kids ask, then you can begin to fill in the gaps.

Columbus is a good example. It turns the whole story on its head when you have the children try to find out what the people who were on this continent might have been thinking and doing and feeling when they were being "discovered," tricked, robbed, and murdered. You might not have that information on hand, because that kind of knowledge is deliberately suppressed. But if nothing else happens, at least you shift your teaching, to recognize the native peoples as human beings, to look at things from their view.

There are other things you can do without new resources. You can include, in a sensitive way, children's backgrounds and life experiences. One way is through interviews with parents and with community people, in which they can recount their own stories, especially their interactions with institutions like schools, hospitals, and employment agencies. These are things that often don't get heard.

I've seen schools inviting grandparents who can tell stories about their own lives, and these stories get to be part of the curriculum later in the year. It allows excluded people, it allows humanity, back into the schools. One of the ways that discrimination works is that it treats some people's experiences, lives, and points of view as though they don't count, as though they are less valuable than other people's.

I know we need to look at materials. But we can also take some of the existing curriculum and ask kids questions about what is missing, and whose interest is being served when things are written in the way they are. Both teachers and students must alter that material.

How can a teacher who knows little about multiculturalism be expected to teach multiculturally?

I think the teachers need to have the time and encouragement to do some reading and to see the necessity to do so. A lot has been written about multiculturalism. It's not like there's no information.

You also have to look around at what people of color are saying about their lives and draw from those sources. You can't truly teach this until you reeducate yourself from a multicultural perspective. But you can begin. It's an ongoing process.

Most of all, you have to get in touch with the fact that your current education has a cultural bias, that it is an exclusionary, racist bias and that it needs to be purged. A lot of times people say, "I just need to learn more about those other groups." And I say, "No, you need to look at how the dominant culture and biases affect your view of nondominant groups in society." You don't have to fill your head with little details about what other cultural groups eat and dance. You need to take a look at your culture, what your idea of normal is, and realize it is quite limited and is in fact just reflecting a particular experience. You have to realize that what you recognize as universal is, quite often, exclusionary. To be really universal, you must begin to learn what Africans, Asians, Latin Americans, the aboriginal peoples, and all silenced groups of Americans have had to say about the topic.

How can one teach multiculturally without making white children feel guilty or threatened?

Perhaps a sense of being threatened or feeling guilty will occur. But I think it is possible to have kids move beyond that.

First of all, recognize that there have always been white people who have fought against racism and social injustice. White children can proudly identify with these people and join in that tradition of fighting for social justice.

Second, it is in their interest to be opening their minds and finding out how things really are. Otherwise, they will constantly have an incomplete picture of the human family.

The other thing is, if we don't make clear that some people benefit from racism, then we are being dishonest. What we have to do is talk about how young people can use that from which they benefit to change the order of things so that more people will benefit.

If we say we are all equally discriminated against on the basis of racism, or sexism, that's not accurate. We don't need to be caught up in the guilt of our benefit, but should use our privilege to help change things.

I remember a teacher telling me last summer that after she listened to me on the issue of racism, she felt ashamed of who she was. And I remember wondering if her sense of self was founded on a sense of superiority. Because if that's true, then she is going to feel shaken. But if her sense of self is founded on working with people of different colors to change things, then there is no need to feel guilt or shame.

Where does an antisexist perspective fit into a multicultural perspective?

In my experience, when you include racism as just another of the "isms," it tends to get sidetracked or omitted. That's because people are sometimes uncomfortable with racism, although they may be comfortable with class and gender issues. I like to put racism in the foreground, and then include the others by example and analysis.

I certainly believe that sexism – and ageism and heterosexism and class issues – have to be taken up. But in my way of thinking I don't list them under multicultural education.

For me, the emphasis is race. I've seen instances where teachers have replaced a really sexist set of materials with nonsexist materials – but the new resources included only white people. In my judgment, more has been done in the curriculum in terms of sexism than in terms of racism.

Of course, we must continue to address sexism in all its forms, no question about that. But we cannot give up on the fight against racism either. As a black woman, both hurt my heart.

How can a teacher combine the teaching of critical thinking skills with a multicultural approach?

I don't think there is any genuine multicultural approach without a critical posture. But I am concerned when people say critical thinking, because I am not sure what they mean. I think people sometimes say critical thinking, and all they mean is thinking.

When I say critical thinking, I mean that we help youngsters ask questions about the social state of things, the social origins of things. What interests me are the kinds of questions one asks within the framework of teaching critical thinking skills.

For example, there are situations in which we have the kids thinking about the same old material from the same old Eurocentric point of view. Take the example of kids trying to resolve conflicts. In that process, we never challenge them to think about the unfair treatment, the racism, that may have led to the conflict in the first

place, and that it is the unfairness that has to be changed if the conflict is to be really resolved.

What are some things to look for in choosing good literature and resources?

I encourage people to look for the voice of people who are frequently silenced, people we haven't heard from: people of color,
women, poor people, working-class people, people with disabili-
ties, and gays and lesbians.

I also think that you look for materials that invite kids to seek
explanations beyond the information that is before them, materials
that give back to people the ideas they have developed, the music
they have composed, and all those things that have been stolen from
them and attributed to other folks. Jazz and rap music are two
examples that come to mind.

I encourage teachers to select materials that reflect people who
are trying and have tried to change things to bring dignity to their
lives; for example, Africans helping other Africans in the face of
famine and war. This gives students a sense of empowerment and
some strategies for making a difference in their lives. I encourage
them to select materials that visually give a sense of the variety in
the world.

Teachers also need to avoid materials that blame the victims of
racism and other "isms."

In particular, I encourage them to look for materials that are relevant. And relevance has two points: not only where you are, but
also where you want to go. In all of this we need to ask: What's the
purpose, what are we trying to teach, what are we trying to
develop?

One of the things I haven't talked about much is the outcome of the
educational process. We need to ask ourselves: What is it that the students are experiencing as a result of their interaction with the materials? If the human beings we are working with aren't acquiring skills,
knowledge, and attitudes that help them see themselves in a positive
relationship with other human beings, then we have a problem.

Are we enabling African-Americans and African-Canadians,
Native Americans and Native Canadians, in particular, to find and
create a range of employment opportunities so they have financial
resources and are able to make decisions about their lives? And does
the education encourage them to maintain healthy connections with
their own communities and reject the racist images that are frequently portrayed of them in the media and elsewhere?

What can school districts do to further multicultural education?

Many teachers will not change the curriculum if they have no administrative support. Sometimes, making these changes can be scary. You can have parents on your back, kids who can be resentful. You can be told you are making the curriculum too political.

What we are talking about here is pretty radical; multicultural education is about challenging the status quo and the basis of power. You need administrative support to do that.

In the final analysis, multicultural or antiracist education is about allowing educators to do the things they have wanted to do in the name of their profession: to broaden the horizons of the young people they teach, to give them skills to change a world in which the color of their skin defines their opportunities, where some human beings are treated as if they are just junior children.

Maybe teachers don't have this big vision all the time. But I think those are the things that a democratic society is supposed to be about.

When you look at the state of things in the United States and Canada, it's almost as if many parts of the society have given up on decency, doing the right thing, and democracy in any serious way. I think that antiracist education gives us an opportunity to try again.

Unfortunately, I feel that this educational movement is going to face a serious challenge. The 1980s were marked by very conservative attitudes, and some of the gains of the social change movements in the 1960s and 1970s were rolled back.

A major struggle is taking place in the 1990s to regain those victories of the 1960s and 1970s. I think that antiracist education can help us do that. But the conservative forces are certainly not going to allow this to happen without a battle. So we'd better get ready to fight.

How Well Are We Nurturing Racial and Ethnic Diversity?

LOUISE DERMAN-SPARKS

Teachers of young children have long recognized that we must address issues of diversity and prejudice, a perspective often referred to as multicultural education. It is also time to ask: What exactly are we doing in the name of multicultural education? Are we truly nurturing racial and ethnic diversity?

Teaching diversity is where most early childhood programs score low, according to Sue Bredekamp, Director of the National Academy of Early Childhood Programs, a national accreditation group based in Washington, D.C.

Culture is not an abstraction to young children. It is lived and learned every day through the way family members interact, through language, family stories, family values, and spiritual life; through household customs and the work family members do; and through society's values as transmitted by television and children's books. Too many early childhood programs ignore current research about how children develop identity and attitudes. They also reinforce misinformation and stereotypes – even when that's not the teacher's intention.

Typically, multicultural programs for young children can fall into three traps: a curriculum centered in the dominant culture, a "color-denial" curriculum, or a "tourist-multicultural" curriculum.

It's not that teachers aren't trying. The work we have done represents the best we've known up until now. But it is time to take a careful and critical look at what we are doing in the name of multicultural education. Rather than dwell on self-blame or guilt for our weaknesses, we should focus our energy on learning from our mistakes and moving ahead.

Following are the thee most common problems and how they manifest themselves.

A Curriculum Centered in the Dominant Culture

This shortcoming often crops up in comments like: "I don't see why I have to do multicultural curriculum. My class is all white. We don't have any problems with prejudice like the teachers do in class-rooms that are mixed."

This approach ignores that children are living in a society with ever-increasing diversity. Further, it reflects a lack of awareness of how socially prevailing attitudes shape children's ideas and feelings about other peoples and cultures.

All children are exposed to bias, and from a variety of sources, not just the family. For example, every Thanksgiving there is an explosion of stereotypes about Native Americans, through television specials, greeting cards, decorations, school handouts, children's books, and skits in which children dress up as "Pilgrims" and "Indians."

A curriculum centered in the dominant culture does nothing to counter the biases that children absorb as they go about their daily lives. Consequently, it does not equip them to deal fairly with diversity.

Classroom signs of this approach include:

- A classroom environment in which teaching materials and activities depict only white people and dominant culture beliefs and behaviors.
- Activities in which people are consciously or unconsciously stereo-typed.
- A curriculum in which there is little or no acknowledgment of the differences that exist among members of the dominant culture in terms of family life-styles, specific cultural traditions, and behaviors.

Teachers should also be aware of a variation of this dominant-culture approach that shows itself in statements such as, "My children come from deprived homes. They don't know how to be an American. My job is to teach them how to fit in."

According to educator Carol Brunson Phillips, this argument falsely assumes that if children fail in school, it is due in part, or totally, to their cultural background. It incorrectly assumes that because children are from "different" cultures they are unable to take advantage of "the opportunities for social equity in this country," Phillips says.

There are serious dangers here. Under such a misguided approach, education is used to eliminate cultural differences by teaching children and parents new cultural habits and thereby curing their alleged "cultural deficits." Further, this approach is in direct contrast to a multicultural curriculum that recognizes the positive things that all children bring to school and that encourages children to be proud of their cultural background and identity.

The "Color-Denial" Curriculum

Asked about the racial/ethnic composition of her class, one teacher proudly said, "I don't know what color my children are. I never notice. They are all just children to me. I treat them all alike."

The materials in this classroom — the pictures of nursery rhyme characters decorating the walls, the dolls, the books — were 95 percent white and reflected the dominant Euro-American culture.
One of the three books about "differences" was *The Story of Ping,* a book filled with stereotypic illustrations of how people in China lived.

Yet the children in the class were 75 percent African-American, 15 percent Latino, and 10 percent Caucasian. Despite these figures and her approach, the teacher is sure she is teaching all the children equally.

This is a classic example of the "color-denial" approach. Originally seen as a progressive stance against racial bigotry, it is oblivious to what children can see for themselves and what people of color experience every day. It mistakenly assumes that bias comes from noticing differences, rather than from institutional and interpersonal behaviors that rank differences for economic, political, and social purposes.

By implicitly setting up the dominant culture as the norm, we end up equating "We are all the same," with, "We are all white." Such a curriculum fails to acknowledge or consciously teach about diversity. It reinforces white children's ethnocentrism, and it miseducates children of color by denying their life experiences.

Preschoolers are aware of variations and wonder where they fit in. And they are often fascinated by skin color. Consider the following scenario:

Coloring with brown crayon, three-and-a-half-year-old Donald announces at large, "I'm brown too. I'm about as brown as this crayon."

"Yes," appropriately responds his teacher, "your skin is a beautiful brown."

Positively acknowledging one's skin color is an important step in children's developing concepts of who they are and how they feel about themselves. Another teacher might have said, "Oh, it doesn't matter what color you are; we are all people." This would have diverted Donald's attention from his skin color. It would have been an inappropriate response, based on the mistaken notion that noticing color causes prejudice. In fact, such a response could have taught Donald to think that there is something wrong with his skin color.

In the final analysis, a "color-denial" perspective ends up being a curriculum centered in the dominant culture.

Classroom signs of this approach include:

- An integrated classroom where the environment, materials, and teaching styles do not acknowledge cultural diversity.
- A teacher's belief that young children do not notice differences or are unaffected by society's biases. Some teachers also mistakenly believe that discussing differences with children teaches them prejudice.
- Explicit or implicit expectations that all children should fit into the dominant culture's norms of development, and that child-rearing methods are the same for all.

A "Tourist-Multicultural" Curriculum

This is the most common problem, not only in school curricula but in teacher education courses.

The original intent behind the multicultural curriculum was positive: Let's teach children about each other's cultures so they will learn to respect each other and not develop prejudice. This was a significant improvement from previous thinking, but in practice, such a goal frequently deteriorated into a "visiting" of "other" cultures: a special bulletin board, a multicultural center, an occasional parental visit, a holiday celebration, or even a week's unit on another culture. And then it was back to the "regular" daily activities, which tended to reflect the dominant culture.

This "tourist" approach doesn't give children the tools they need to comfortably, empathetically, and fairly interact with diversity. Instead, it teaches simplistic generalizations that lead to stereotyping rather than understanding. Moreover, "tourist" activities do not foster critical thinking about bias, nor teach children to oppose bias. Moving beyond this approach is key to nurturing diversity.

Signs of this "tourist" approach include:

- Planning multicultural activities at given "special" times in the curriculum rather than integrating them into the teaching environment and all daily activities.
- A patronizing approach that treats "other" cultures as quaint or exotic and disconnects them from children's lives.
- Centering a multicultural curriculum on holidays and disconnecting it from everyday life. Children do not learn about how other

people live, work, and interact, only how they "play" on holidays.
In many curricula, teachers focus on the Chinese New Year as "the"
time to teach about Chinese-Americans. The class builds a dragon
and parents are asked to come to school wearing "Chinese" clothing. The parents, students, and teacher cook a "Chinese" dish, and
the children get to play with chopsticks. This approach trivializes
other cultures. It doesn't deal with real-life daily problems and
experiences of different peoples, but only with surface aspects of
their celebrations.
· Using images and activities of groups based on the past rather than
the present. This misrepresents "other" cultures and makes it seem
as if they have little to do with children's lives.

So as we critique our own programs and identify the problems
we face, the question is: What are we striving for and how do we
get there?

Several books provide concrete information on how to nurture
diversity. A variety of resources are listed in *Anti-Bias Curriculum*
(Louise Derman-Sparks and the ABC Task Force 1989, National
Association for the Education of Young Children).

Some of the components we should strive for are the following:

· Including diversity in all aspects of the classroom environment:
wall posters, photos, art decorations, charts, books, dolls, puzzles,
and math games. We must move beyond tokenism; for example,
having only one African-American doll, or one book about
Japanese-Americans.
· Hiring a staff that reflects different cultures and teaching styles.
· Seeing racial, cultural, gender, and disability diversity as an integral
part of the program, affecting all aspects of the curriculum.
· Fostering bicultural, bilingual development when working with
children who are not part of the dominant culture. While we give
them the skills needed to participate in the dominant culture, we
must also make their home culture, including their language, an
integral part of the curriculum.
· Teaching the children to think about stereotyping; for instance,
noting that there are "unfair" images that hurt people's feelings.
Teachers should discuss stereotypic images and messages that
appear in books.
· When a child teases or rejects another child on the basis of race or
ethnic background, treating it as seriously as physical aggression.
Teachers must also learn how to handle such incidents and help
children learn from them. Take the following example, as noted in
Anti-Bias Curriculum. "Craig's eyes go like this," says 4-year-old
Ruth, pulling her eyes up. "They look funny." Her teacher replies:

"Craig's eyes are not funny; they have a different shape than yours. Craig's eyes are the same shape as his family's eyes, just as your eyes are shaped like your family's. Your eye shape is fine. Craig's eye shape is fine. Both of your eye shapes are good for seeing. It is OK to ask questions about how people look. It is not OK to say they look funny – that hurts their feelings."

• Fostering children's skills to stand up for their rights and the rights of others. Teachers can help students empathize with others, and give suggestions on how to challenge discriminatory behaviors by other children. Teachers can also encourage students to challenge other forms of discrimination such as a lack of books about people of color in the school library, or the lack of handicap-access at the local grocery store, or the fact that there are only white dolls at the toy store.

• Providing opportunities for staff members to discuss issues of diversity and bias with each other and with parents.

This list may seem overwhelming, and nurturing respect for diversity is hard. The important thing is to look on such a list as a guide, and to start on that process of change. (The time line for that change is a decision for each individual and each program.)

As Carol Brunson Phillips notes, "Nurturing diversity through our own variety of multicultural education will require some work – but to start involves only a simple commitment to self-enlightenment. For as we take on the challenge to redesign our institutions based on fuller understanding of the problems within this society, we will do so with a stronger belief in our own power to resolve them. It is my wish that we take on this work and that our teaching will result in the liberation of the human spirit."

Trouble Over the Rainbow

STAN KARP

For former New York City Schools Chancellor Joseph Fernandez there was a pink slip, instead of a pot of gold, waiting at the end of the rainbow. Following a powerful and at times ugly mobilization against a multicultural guide entitled *Children of the Rainbow,* which had urged "respect for the diversity of families" including gay and lesbian parents, the Central Board voted not to renew Fernandez's contract when it expired after a three-year tenure in June 1993.

Fernandez's dismissal threw the city's schools into another round of turmoil, but the implications extended well beyond New York. The curriculum controversy raised crucial questions about exactly what "multicultural education" means, and about how schools should address explosive issues of prejudice in an increasingly diverse and divided society. It also posed questions about what role parents will play in efforts to remake a public school system that remains in crisis in many parts of the country.

The fierce fight over *Children of the Rainbow* took many by surprise. The guide was compiled to implement mandates from the Central Board, which in 1989 had sought to counteract discrimination against students, parents, or school personnel on the basis of race, color, religion, national origin, gender, age, sexual orientation, or handicapping condition. An Office of Multicultural Education was created, reflecting a national trend toward multicultural reform.

In general, this trend has been more a delayed reaction to events than a radical innovation. Demographic changes in public school populations, which will raise the number of minority students to 40 percent by the end of the 1990s, are pushing schools to more accurately reflect in their curricula the changes occurring in their classrooms. The trend is also an aftershock of the civil rights and social struggles of the 1960s and 1970s. Social movements for the rights of African-Americans, women, disabled people, gays and lesbians, and others have already forced changes in cultural sensibilities and federal and state law. Several decades of academic scholarship have revised traditionally narrow versions of literature and history. Lumbering school bureaucracies, which have rarely been on the cutting edge of change, are simply trying to catch up by taking a closer look at their textbooks, course outlines, and bulletin boards.

At another level, however, multicultural education is a potentially explosive issue. Racial tensions increased in the 1980s, with the administrations of Reagan, Bush, and, in New York, Mayor Ed Koch all contributing. Police murders of young black men and other racially charged confrontations are familiar features of the nightly news. Blacks and Jews continue to clash on several fronts, and while the gay community has attained new visibility and political influence, religious institutions and sizable portions of popular opinion remain stubbornly resistant to their inclusion. New York City police record 500 bias incidents a year, with thousands of others unreported.

Against this background, a broad, if superficial, consensus developed that promoting harmony among the city's nearly 1,000 schools and 1 million students was crucial. *Children of the Rainbow* was an attempt to address this issue in a comprehensive, if somewhat bureaucratic, fashion. Conceived more as a resource guide for teachers than a formal curriculum for students, it was produced by central office personnel with review by a twenty-five member advisory board. The book is filled mostly with strategies for developing academic and social skills appropriate for first graders. There's an emphasis on celebrating diversity, building self-esteem, and encouraging constructive group interaction. The 440 pages that were largely ignored during the heated controversy are typically devoted to methods for setting up classroom learning centers, instructions for making Chinese New Year's scrolls, and the words and music to the *Animal Nonsense Song*.

One section on "societal concerns" speaks directly to the pressures growing numbers of kids face early on. It gives teachers suggestions for dealing with homeless students, "latch-key" children, physically or emotionally abused kids, those touched by the HIV/AIDS epidemic, and so on. It's here that three pages on "Understanding family structures to meet children's needs" mentioned the special circumstances of students with gay or lesbian parents. The section was drafted by a lesbian first-grade teacher who was added to the curriculum project after gay rights advocates, with the help of then-Mayor David Dinkins's office, succeeded in getting access to Fernandez and raising their concerns about the climate of hate and gay-bashing in the city.

In the fall of 1991, the curriculum guide was adopted by the chancellor's office with little notice. Even most gay-rights advocates, parent's groups, and education activists had their attention focused elsewhere, including a contentious debate over the chancellor's HIV/AIDS curriculum and condom distribution policies for the high schools. (Fernandez's opponents wanted an AIDS curriculum that preached abstinence instead of safe sex, and wanted condoms made available only with parental consent. Fernandez prevailed after bitter battles, although the HIV/AIDS curriculum was weakened by a Central Board resolution requiring all consultants hired from outside the school system to emphasize abstinence.) Like the city's racial climate, debate over school policy was becoming highly polarized.

Bigotry Explodes

Children of the Rainbow was sent to the district boards for use in the schools. Like others before it that had embodied good intentions, the thick manual might ordinarily have collected dust on the shelf while teachers coped with the daily crisis of survival in New York public schools. The extensive program of staff training, resources, and administrative support necessary to put the curriculum guide into practice was not in place. Most schools and teachers never heard about *Children of the Rainbow* until Community School Board (CSB) 24 in Queens used it to light a fire in the spring of 1993.

District 24 was routinely described in the press as "conservative, heavily Catholic, and middle class." But more than 70 percent of the 28,000 students in the district's public schools are children of color. The area has the fastest-growing immigrant population in the city and some of the most overcrowded schools. The nine-member community school board, however, was all white. One member was a priest. Six had sent their children to private schools.

Mary Cummins, the board president who became the symbol of resistance to *Children of the Rainbow,* was elected with 346 votes in local board elections that drew about 7 percent of eligible voters in 1989. Cummins ran the board in authoritarian fashion and was no champion of grassroots parent involvement. District 24 had been the only local board to file suit against new regulations that sought to expand parental participation in the selection of principals and administrators. Parent groups inside the district publicly complained about the local board's high-handed ways.

Cummins and her board were already angry at the chancellor over his AIDS and condom policies, though there was little they could do directly to block them, since high schools fall under the jurisdiction of the central rather than district board. Church leaders, including Cardinal John O'Connor, encouraged District 24's opposition, eventually providing legal and other assistance. When Cummins received the *Rainbow* curriculum, she reportedly consulted with Howard Hurwitz of the right-wing Family Defense Council, who "immediately recognized it as part of the homosexual movement. It was gay and lesbian propaganda."

CSB 24 rejected *Children of the Rainbow* out of hand. Using at least $7,000 in public funds, Cummins began a campaign of letters and mailings attacking the guide, contending it contained "dangerous misinformation about sodomy."

"We will not accept two people of the same sex engaged in deviant sex practices as 'family,'" she wrote. Tapping into the furor over the AIDS curriculum, she added, "The victims of this AIDS scourge are homosexuals, bisexuals, intravenous users of illicit drugs and the innocent people they infect by exposing them to their tainted blood and other bodily fluids....[Fernandez] would teach our kids that sodomy is acceptable but virginity is something weird."

For many people inside and outside the schools, news reports of District 24's snarling response to *Children of the Rainbow* was the first they heard of the curriculum. This ensured that a complicated debate about how schools should handle sensitive, controversial issues would take place under the glare of sensational media attention against a backdrop of foaming antigay bigotry.

The central office process that produced *Children of the Rainbow* had excluded most district board members, parents, and teachers. Chancellor Fernandez's twenty-five-member advisory board and the review process at the board's Brooklyn headquarters were no substitute for an inclusive debate that might have created support for the curriculum before it arrived in the mail from 110 Livingston Street. (At the very least, as one district board member pointed out, more local input would have let Fernandez know what he was in for.) Even gay activists later acknowledged that they had relied too heavily on lobbying Central Board personnel while Catholic, Pentecostal, and other church groups were mobilizing antigay sentiment in the boroughs.

When he returned to his native New York in 1990, Fernandez had brought with him a somewhat heavy-handed reputation from Miami. Though he won support from progressives for his AIDS and condom policies, for initiatives to create new, smaller high schools, and for being an effective advocate for public education, he was still, in the eyes of some critics, "a man with a plan and a two-by-four."

As a matter of principle, the chancellor deserved support for insisting that "at some time in the elementary school grades," schools must deal "proactively with the issue of same sex families." But when it comes to public schools, support for teaching progressive views on sexual, racial, or similar issues needs to be carefully mobilized as part of a democratic debate. Public schools almost by definition are obligated to act as mediators and conciliators in the face of controversy. Schools are highly vulnerable to emotional posturing, particularly when it comes from parents or "taxpayers," and they can easily be immobilized by polarizing crises. Where prejudice or bigotry exists, it absolutely needs to be challenged and exposed and, if necessary, restrained by central authorities from depriving minorities of their right to be represented and protected in public life. But top-down administrative measures, no matter how well-intentioned, have decidedly limited and mixed impact.

Progressive curriculum policies emanating from the top within large public school systems may be likened to federal civil rights laws passed in the 1960s. After much grassroots struggle, federal laws attempted to codify democratic impulses and transform deeply rooted practices like segregation. Yet just as civil rights laws ran into "states' rights" bigotry tinged with populist resentment, so too progressive education policies endorsed at the top may run into righteous resistance from conservative parents and local communities. In the final analysis, the added rounds of education, organizing, and political struggle it takes to turn progressive policy into actual practice must occur at the school and community level. Administrative support for such campaigns can be crucial to their success. But bureaucratic directives alone, imposed from the top, won't get the job done.

In the case of *Children of the Rainbow,* the defiance of CSB 24 touched a chord of populist resentment against a traditionally heavy-handed educational bureaucracy. This helped lift it above the realm of Cummins's crackpot bigotry and turn it into an angry cry that resonated in many parts of the city. When the chancellor suspended the district's board after its deliberately provocative rejection of the *Rainbow* curriculum, he reinforced dictatorial impressions – so much so that the Central Board ultimately reversed the suspension and undercut the chancellor's position.

But a populist rallying cry against the central administration wasn't the only weapon that opponents of *Children of the Rainbow* had. There were some dubious aspects of the curriculum itself. It was unusual in explicitly suggesting that teachers initiate discussion of gay and lesbian issues with first graders. The guide urged teachers to "include references to lesbians/gay people in all curricular areas" and promote "actual experiences via creative play, books, visitors, etc., in order for them to view lesbians/gays as real people to be respected and appreciated." Exactly what this means for five- and six-year-olds with no clear notions of adult sexuality is problematic.

Certain sections also provided unnecessary ammunition to critics intent on alarmist distortion. While the guide's aim was clearly to promote tolerance and respect for same sex families, the controversial section that discusses gay households is titled "Fostering positive attitudes toward sexuality." However related, positive attitudes toward sexuality and tolerance of gay and lesbian families are different issues. Similarly, even some who worked on the curriculum later acknowledged that it was a mistake to include books like *Heather Has Two Mommies* or *Gloria Goes to Gay Pride* in a list for first graders. The books are too hard for first graders to read, and they raise issues more appropriate for older children. Instead of clarifying the intent of the curriculum, the books became red flags for opponents eager to appeal to the worst fears of straight parents.

Gays and lesbians understandably view AIDS education, homophobia, and the bigotry that drives disproportionate numbers of gay youth to suicide as matters of survival. But first-grade classrooms are not necessarily the place to address these issues except in the most general ways. Collapsing issues of sexual orientation with issues of tolerance for all people including gays and lesbians can even reinforce what *Village Voice* writer Donna Minkowitz described as "the tendency...to think of gays and lesbians in sexual terms – not in terms of culture, history, romances and families."

The few debatable features of the curriculum in no way justified the hysterical distortions Cummins and company raised about "teaching sodomy" or "recruiting children to the homosexual lifestyle." Nevertheless, they did put *Rainbow* supporters on the defensive, and they stand as a caution about the care necessary to unite the broadest possible consensus around progressive approaches to teaching about topics like sexual or cultural identity. Democratic process and clear guidelines are essential.

If the response to *Children of the Rainbow* showed how complicated it is to put multicultural education into classroom practice, it also showed what a reservoir of bigotry and hatred its opponents have to draw on. As District 24's campaign continued into the fall, it spread to other districts, leading to at least two threats on Fernandez's life, police protection for several local school boards, and outbreaks of violence at several public meetings. "A curriculum that was designed to promote tolerance has instead revealed an astonishing level of homophobia," noted Ron Madison, a member of the Gay and Lesbian Teachers Association.

Subsidized busloads of parents and angry residents descended on community school board meetings to condemn the curriculum. Conservative whites who had opposed civil rights, affirmative action, and bilingual education made common cause with religious Latino communities. Gay rights advocates were baited as the representatives of an elite, white agenda that had never been concerned about other racial or ethnic minorities. Sharp class divisions surfaced between gay professionals and black, Latino, and white working-class constituencies.

Brooklyn's District 15, a Latino, African-American, white working-class, and Catholic area that also has a sizable gay and lesbian community, reflected all these tensions. Norm Fruchter, CSB 15 president and a long-time parent advocate and education activist, recalls, "From the first meeting in September, it was very clear that there was a very large, incredibly aggravated, almost panic-stricken group of people, predominantly Latino, who were mobilized around the curriculum issue." Progressive members on the local board wanted to counter distortions of the curriculum and limit the extent of the growing polarization. Working with the more conservative members, they settled on a series of meetings that would give the community the sort of input they hadn't had earlier.

It seemed like a good place to start. Heather Lewis, a parent activist and District 15 board member, remembers the November hearing as "a model of what democracy should be. It was difficult because there were very strong feelings on both sides, but democracy is messy." More than ninety people spoke and many were "incredibly moving." But while this was exactly the sort of process needed to create a constituency for tolerance, it also exposed the depth and complexity of the tensions involved.

Most of those who spoke in support of the curriculum were white and, in many cases, professional or middle class. "I'm gay and I'm a homeowner," some speakers asserted in the course of impassioned pleas for their rights, as if their mortgages somehow lent legitimacy to their status. (Conversely, the newspapers rarely failed to call *Rainbow* supporters "activists," while its opponents were usually "parents.") Still, as Fruchter saw it, many gay advocates, given their own anger and pain, found it difficult to recognize the fears and resentments of the groups that had been maneuvered into opposition against them: "I'm not sure how many people saw the class aspects of it at all. I think what many people saw were opponents, and sometimes they saw people acting only out of ignorance. Those perceptions didn't help."

Most of those who spoke against the curriculum were Latino, along with black or white working-class parents. While their opposition to the curriculum was undoubtedly heavily motivated by religious views, there were other concerns at work as well. "The schools aren't teaching kids to read and write," some complained. "Why don't schools leave this personal stuff to the families and concentrate on the basics?" Such arguments, even if disingenuous, struck a chord. School failure is a desperate issue in many communities. If antibias education is to win broad support it has to be integrated at the school level in the overall context of effective educational programs, rather than introduced as isolated statements of political policy.

Even in District 15, which had pioneered several antibias initiatives and had significant progressive leadership, reasoned debate was overwhelmed by the passions unleashed by the organized campaign against the *Children of the Rainbow*. A group called Concerned Parents for Educational Accountability circulated videotapes linking the curriculum to "the homosexual conspiracy." Lillian Lopez, another parent and district board member, recalls parents "in different neighborhoods saying the same thing," as if they'd been coached. Heather Lewis says, "It became almost like a witch-hunt." Parents would make wild claims about what might happen and declare, "I can't rest at home if I know that one teacher in the district may do this."

Things Turn Ugly

When it came time to make a decision, things turned ugly. Lopez recalls the session at which District 15 adopted its compromise resolution: "It wasn't a discussion; it was the most horrible display of human intolerance and bad behavior and the ugly side of people. Anybody that got up to speak for the curriculum was told to shut up, sit down, go home. There were more than enough obscenities yelled out. By the time it came down to vote, people were on their feet yelling at us, and all we could do was yell out our vote. The only one who had any chance to say anything was the one board member who voted against it. The police had to escort us out. It was particularly humiliating, one of the most humiliating things I was ever a part of. We could not reason, at any moment."

District 15's resolution called for using *Children of the Rainbow* to support first-grade teachers in their efforts to promote multiculturalism and reduce bias. It also reaffirmed the board's "belief that the most effective curricula are developed at the district and school levels rather than at the Central Board" and called for meetings at every school to discuss how "the district's goals of respect for family and cultural diversity, tolerance, bias awareness, and conflict resolution" were being addressed. In response to critics' claims and parents' fears, the resolution stated that "there will be no specific references to sexuality in first grade" and that schools should disregard any "specific reference to teaching about sexual orientation." Some gay and lesbian activists complained that this retreated too far, but since the real intent of the *Rainbow* curriculum was to teach tolerance, not sexuality, CSB 15 members argued that the resolution effectively undercut the opposition while preserving the goal of promoting respect for all groups, including gays and lesbians. The resolution passed 7 to 1.

Throughout the controversy the media gave disproportionate coverage to the *Rainbow's* opponents. For example, the lone District 15 member voting against the curriculum was the only one quoted in the next day's papers. Later, progressives were able to present students, parents, and others at a press conference on the steps of board headquarters where they gave moving testimony about the importance of antibias education. But media sensationalism continued to cloud issues and polarize public opinion.

Progressives responded in several other ways. People About Changing Education (PACE), a multiracial activist group that publishes a citywide paper on school issues called *School Voices,* initiated a broad-based Campaign for Inclusive Multicultural Education, which enlisted hundreds of individuals and organizations in support of the *Rainbow* curriculum. Through news releases, press conferences, and public forums, it helped raise the profile of progressive Latino, African-American, and Jewish groups that spoke up for multicultural inclusion in the very communities that the right had mobilized against it.

Ultimately, more than half of the local boards responded to protests by delaying mention of gays and lesbians until the fifth or sixth grade or otherwise modifying the guide. Fernandez readily accepted these changes and also ordered several of the most controversial passages in the guide rewritten. "Heather" and her two moms were taken off the reading list. But CSB 24 remained completely hostile to the curriculum and refused repeated invitations to submit an alternative. To die-hard opponents, the wording and the details were almost beside the point. They were looking for ways to sharpen the confrontation, not defuse it.

The Opt-out Option

A number of people, including writer and gay advocate Richard Goldstein, supported proposals to let parents "opt-out" of curriculum units they deemed inappropriate by pulling their kids out of class. When "two powerful commitments – like gay rights and parental rights – collide," Goldstein argued, opt-outs make sense. "What is at stake here has less to do with discrimination than with the power of central authorities to determine educational standards without parental consent. That's a battle progressives have been waging for decades against these same authorities."

But while it may sometimes make tactical sense to propose such provisions as a way to limit resistance to teaching about homosexuality and other topics like abortion, opt-outs really beg the issue. For one thing, the antibias intentions of the *Rainbow* curriculum are not confined to particular units that parents could exempt their kids from. The point is to promote a pervasive and systematic approach to reducing prejudice in all areas. The methods proposed by the *Rainbow* curriculum apply as much to everyday classroom practice and unanticipated situations as they do to a particular set of lessons.

More fundamentally, the issue is one of how to make and carry out democratic education policy. Every parent should have a right to participate in the making of public school policy in a meaningful way. But individual parents don't have a right to unilaterally impose their own version of it on teachers and schools. Should prejudiced parents, as matter of school policy, be able to pull their kids out of black history programs? Should anti-Semitic parents be able to avoid lessons on the Holocaust? Parents have the right to teach their beliefs to their children, but public school is where students are taught what society thinks of itself. What that vision should be continues to be a matter of sharp struggle, but it should remain a collective, rather than an individual, process. Students should be exposed to values and norms of behavior that presumably give everyone a stake in making social institutions work democratically. In the process, hopefully they will learn mutual respect and the critical skills needed to make their own judgments about what both their schools *and* their parents tell them.

There's also another issue: "choice." Extending the logic of opt-outs, some have seized on the *Rainbow* controversy as yet another argument for a system of public school "choice." The *Wall Street Journal* asserted that the entire *Rainbow* controversy "all adds up to more fuel for the burgeoning school-choice movement." In the *New York Times,* Richard Vigilante of the Center for Social Thought wrote that "choice" is "a successful and honorable way to avoid the culture wars that threaten our schools....In a true school choice program *Heather Has Two Mommies*...would be read by children whose parents chose the schools that accepted the textbook. Overnight, the fight over the *Rainbow* Curriculum, like all such fights for control over 'the system' would become moot."

The "choice" scenario, here applied to curriculum issues, envisions an educational market system that would remain "public" only in its provision of public funds to individual schools. Such a system could be quite friendly to pockets of educational privilege and prejudice. Allowing parents or students to escape any contact with democratically achieved guidelines on social policy or racial and cultural differences is, in fact, not democratic at all. Such proposals reinforce suspicions that the real goal of "choice" plans is to undermine public education as a democratic social institution and to preserve class and racial inequalities.

In this connection, it's worth noting that the focus on same sex families in the campaign against *Children of the Rainbow* masks a deeper resistance to other forms of multiculturalism. While progressive educators are trying to expand multicultural education to include real recognition of diversity and programs that actively fight bias, others want to keep it confined to superficial versions of melt-ing pot myths and exclude whole categories of people. "Multicultur-alism does not include life-styles," said one district board member, as if it applied only to those willing to adopt conventional modes of behavior and belief. Similarly, Michael Petrides, a member of the Central Board from Staten Island, complained that "educators are now picking off voting blocs like politicians, to make sure voting blocs are represented in the curriculum. We are dissecting every-thing into what is special and different, rather than what we have in common."

Such claims — which are wildly exaggerated — reflect the discom-fort historically privileged groups feel in the face of demands for inclusion and more democratic versions of the curriculum. In most schools, multiculturalism hasn't even begun to go beyond food fes-tivals and superficial celebrations of holidays. It hasn't begun to explain why some "differences" translate into access to wealth and power, while others become a source of discrimination and injus-tice. Opponents want to limit multicultural initiatives before they develop into more substantive pluralist and antiracist efforts. Attacking tolerance for gay families is a way of attacking multicul-tural education at its perceived weakest link.

What Role for Parents?

With the board and much of the city deeply divided following Fer-nandez's ouster, the search for a replacement was protracted and difficult. In the midst of the process, a new round of school board elections was held. Churches and conservative groups ran an unprecedented number of candidates using AIDS, condom, and cur-riculum controversies as the basis of their campaigns. PACE, along with other groups, helped organize slates of progressive candidates that offered not only forthright support for the *Rainbow* curriculum, but also comprehensive proposals for school change. All the atten-tion on the school board elections helped to double turnout over 1989, but still only about 15 percent of those eligible cast ballots. Right-wing anti-*Rainbow* candidates tended to win in districts that were already conservative, while progressives made gains in several areas, preserving or winning majorities in some key districts (including Brooklyn's District 15) and securing the election of the first openly gay board members. Overall, there may be a few more polarized boards, but there was no dramatic shift in power.

After some messy public maneuvering, the conservative majority on the Central Board hired Ramon Cortines, formerly head of San Francisco schools. Cortines sidestepped the *Rainbow* controversy calling it "a tempest in a teapot." Instead, he was immediately confronted with a long-brewing scandal over unreliable asbestos inspections that frightened and enraged parents and delayed the start of the new school year. Cortines also quickly became mired in another round of steep budget cuts imposed by new Republican Mayor Rudolph Giuliani (who had benefited from the *Rainbow* controversy in his successful race against David Dinkins, the city's first black chief executive).

In the wake of the city's latest school wars, it seemed that there was at least one point of broad agreement: the current school governance structure is unworkable. As it now stands, the mayor appoints two of the seven Central Board members, and the five borough presidents each appoint one. This arrangement produces a body with little coherence or accountability. "Long term, " argues CSB 15 president Norm Fruchter, "there's a major problem with governance in New York City schools. And it's not only governance, but bureaucratic layers that impede anything real happening at the school level." Despite this, reform proposals continue to languish in the state legislature.

In the final analysis, however, the deeper issues raised by the struggle over *Children of the Rainbow* have less to do with the politics of New York's school bureaucracy than with the role the majority of public school parents will play in transforming an educational system that is failing their children. Across the country, there is evidence of a concerted national campaign by far-right groups to mobilize parents and target school board seats. The liberal lobby People for the American Way identified nearly 100 school board candidates in 1992 in just two southern California counties who were associated with radical rightist groups. Almost a third of them won. The report quotes Ralph Reed, executive director of the Christian Coalition, on the importance of such candidates hiding their organizational affiliations. "Stealth was a big factor in San Diego's success," said Reed. "But that's just good strategy. It's like guerrilla warfare. If you reveal your location, all it does is allow your opponent to improve his artillery bearings. It's better to move quietly, with stealth under cover of night." Echoes of these tactics were heard across New York City throughout the *Rainbow* curriculum struggle.

Aided by homophobia and racial tension, the forces of the right are trying to mobilize parents, including large numbers of Latinos, Asians, and African Americans, behind conservative "family values" and racial/cultural backlash. How to counter this effort and enlist parents in campaigns for more democratic schooling remain among the unfinished lessons of the *Rainbow* curriculum.

Are We Accepting Too Much?

FOYNE MAHAFFEY

The bell signals the start of the school day. Doors open and lines file into the building, up stairways and through the halls. I see two boys run their open hands across the faces of girls as they walk past them. The look at each other and smile.

"We didn't touch any girls," they protest, anticipating my disapproval. "We were just playing." They stomp away like angry victims.

These kinds of incidents are not extraordinary anymore. In fact, "girls are experiencing sexual harassment by boys at an increasing rate," according to a recent study by the American Association of University Women (AAUW).

I recently talked with a group of eight- to twelve-year-old girls about such issues, and their stories infuriated and saddened me. Most disturbingly, I knew their stories were not unique. As you read some of their words below, ask yourself: How long would you, as an adult, be able to work effectively under the situations these girls are talking about? And what are we, as teachers, doing about it? How do girls' experiences in the early elementary grades — even issues that seem trivial, such as boys kicking girls under the table — help set the stage for problems that crop up later, such as a sense of powerlessness about resisting abuse?

The "might-makes-right" lesson that too many girls learn in school often begins on the playground. It is the first place where girls realize that "power" is not distributed equally. Some people have more of it than others. Teachers, by and large, don't challenge that power distribution. Unfortunately, I know that by experience.

As I walked my assigned area of the playground on a recent Monday, I looked out at boys playing basketball on the far end and the girls huddled or walking in small groups along the sides. No one was fighting or swearing, so I figured it was a good day.

And then I caught myself. No, all was not well. Because I knew that some of those girls huddled in groups like to play basketball. So why weren't they playing? And what was I doing about it? Why did I allow a "might-makes-right" playground, where the boys decide where they will play and with whom — which in practice means no girls on the basketball or soccer teams? What was the hidden message I was giving to the girls on the playground? That the boys decide, and that's that?

For some girls, the problems are much worse than not being able to play soccer or basketball. This is what one girl had to say: "I always feel fear in the hallways. People ahead of you will beat up on you because you're younger. Because I'm short, they think they can beat up on me. Boys mostly. They come up and get you against the wall. You get up against the wall and they hit you with a backpack. They pretend it's an accident. Even if you tell a teacher, they make it like it's an accident. If you push back, they get mad and get you worse the next time."

One eleven-year-old reported the following incident to me that she had witnessed. "——— was in the coatroom getting ready to go to computer. He pushed up against ——— and touched her chest and rubbed her thigh and she didn't like it."

Perhaps one of the most important messages in such incidents comes next. What do we, as teachers, do in these situations? In this incident, the boy was suspended and warned that police might become involved if there were another infraction. The girls were listened to.

But that's not always the case. In one situation I am familiar with, the administrator has a pattern of handslapping and then sending back to class boys who make lewd remarks to female students, grabbing them and harassing them. One teacher concluded, based on both the boys' and administrator's behavior, "Men don't give good examples and boys don't see consequences."

As girls get to middle school, there is more shoulder shrugging about the sexual behavior of students. Some teachers conclude that the children are merely reflecting the conduct that is seemingly allowed in today's society. "Look at how they dance, what they watch on TV, and what they listen to," one teacher said.

Some girls conveyed disturbing messages to me about the powerlessness they feel in combatting harassment. They said things like: "We can't do anything, probably nobody will listen to us"; "I told my mom and she says I just have to put up with it"; "We don't want to get in trouble." Anita Hill has no doubt heard from thousands of women echoing those same feelings.

I ask myself, Are we accepting too much? Are we even talking to children about what sexual harassment is and why it is wrong?

To many teachers, incidents of improper touching, innuendo, humiliation, and intimidation seem to be increasing at an uncontrollable rate. The perceived inability to control such antisocial behavior is leading some otherwise responsible staff members to ignore it. Yet such unchecked harassment teaches students something, even though it's not a lesson we would be proud of.

As the AAUW report notes, "When sexual harassment is treated casually, as in 'boys will be boys,' both girls and boys get a dangerous, damaging message: 'girls are not worthy of respect and that appropriate behavior for boys includes exerting power over girls.'"

I know that many female teachers are frustrated with the quiet acceptance of harassment. "Last week," a colleague recently confided, "I saw this boy humping against a girl, right in her face, and he was laughing. He was transferred over here because of a sexual assault on another girl."

"What did you do about it?" I asked.

Painfully and sadly, she admitted, "I was tired, tired after a whole day of it. Tired of seeing it, yelling about it. I am tired. I didn't do anything."

Fortunately, there are teachers who are doing something. Sometimes it's on a one-on-one level, immediately confronting boys when they harass girls. Sometimes it's on a broader level, initiating discussion in the class on issues of gender inequality and harassment. Sometimes it's raising consciousness among fellow teachers.

The girls spoke highly of those teachers who encourage personal communication through journal writing and who provide a way for the girls to talk about these issues. They applaud teachers with high standards who are not afraid to hold direct conversations or confront issues related to gender and harassment.

To those teachers who have taken this stance, the girls know who you are and they appreciate your efforts. Maybe someday they will tell you themselves.

What Do We Say
When We Hear 'Faggot'?

LENORE GORDON

Alice is eleven. She walks down the school halls with her arm around her best friend, Susan. During lunch, they sit on the floor holding hands or combing each other's hair. Lately, Alice has been called "dyke," and boys have been told not to be her friend.

Brian refuses to take part in a fight on his block. As he makes his way home, he hears cries of "faggot" and "sissy." Suddenly he begins to run, realizing that the other children may now attack him.

Carl is gifted musically; he would like to join the elementary school chorus. Although he hesitates for several weeks, the music teacher persuades him to join. One morning soon after, he enters the classroom tense and angry after chorus, muttering that several boys have called him "gay."

Some children play a "game" called "Smear the Queer," in which one child suddenly attacks another, knocking him to the ground. The attacker shouts "Fag!" and then runs away.

Homophobic name-calling is pervasive. Even first graders are now using such terms as "faggot" to ridicule others, and such name-calling is increasingly common in the older grades. Homophobic name-calling is devastating to young people experiencing homosexual feelings. For youngsters who are not gay, such name-calling creates or reinforces hostility toward the gay and lesbian population. And it forces all children to follow strict sex-role behaviors to avoid ridicule.

Because homosexuality is such a charged issue, teachers rarely confront children who use homophobic name-calling to humiliate and infuriate other children. Many teachers do not realize that this sort of name-calling can be dealt with in much the same way as other kinds of bigotry and stereotyping.

Teaching children to be critical of oppression is teaching true morality, and teachers have the right, indeed the obligation, to alert

Adapted from an article that appeared in the *Bulletin* of the Council on Interracial Books for Children, Vol. 14, Nos. 3–4.

their students to all forms of oppression. Educating children not to be homophobic is one way to show the difference between oppressive and nonoppressive behavior.

Challenging homophobic name-calling by teaching children nonjudgmental facts about homosexuality and by correcting myths is also intrinsically connected to antisexist educational values, since homophobia is used to reinforce rigid sex roles. Furthermore, if adults criticize other forms of name calling but ignore antigay remarks, children are quick to conclude that homophobia is acceptable because gay men and lesbians deserve to be oppressed.

Boys are far more likely to be the object of homophobic name-calling than girls, perhaps because sex roles for boys remain, to some extent, more rigidly defined. A boy involved in a traditional "female-only" activity such as sewing or cooking risks out-and-out contempt from his peers, as well as the possibility of being called "faggot" or "sissy." Girls are more able to participate in activities that have traditionally been for boys, such as sports or shop, without loss of peer approval.

At the late elementary and junior high school levels, physical affection between girls is far more acceptable than between boys, but a girl will be called a "dyke" if she does not express, by junior high, a real interest in pleasing boys or in participating with other girls in boy-centered discussions.

As an elementary school teacher, I have made an awareness of oppression and of the concept of "majority" and "minority" a focus of current events, history, and social studies. Throughout the year we discuss those who are not in the majority in this country: Native Americans, Puerto Ricans, blacks, Chicanos, disabled people, older people, and many others. We also discuss women, a generally powerless majority.

If oppression is being discussed, it is impossible to ignore lesbians and gay men as a group that faces discrimination. Children in the middle grades have a strong sense of justice, and they can understand the basic injustice of people being abused because they are different from the majority. They can also identify with the powerlessness of oppressed groups because children themselves are often a verbally and sometimes a physically abused group.

Types of Name-Calling
When initiating a discussion of name-calling, teachers can explain that there are two kinds of name-calling. One, which is unrelated to

any particular group, is often scatological or sexual (i.e., the four-letter words). The other is group-biased; it uses the name of the group — "nigger," "chink," "Polack," — as the insult and implies that there is something wrong about being a member of that group.

Group-biased name-calling can be handled in a variety of ways. Sometimes children do not truly understand why a word is offensive. If a teacher simply takes the time to tell the class that a particular word insults or demeans a group of people, children will often stop using the word. (Occasionally, children do not even know what a term means. One New York City ten-year-old who frequently called others "faggot" told me that the word meant "female dog." A twelve-year-old said that a lesbian is a "Spanish Jew.")

Discussions about the meaning of homophobic words can often be quite consciousness-raising. When I hear a child use the word "faggot," I explain that a faggot, literally, is a stick used for kindling. I also explain that gay people used to be burned in medieval times simply for being gay, and they had to wear a bundle of sticks on their shirts to indicate that they were about to be burned. (At times, gay men were used as the kindling to burn women accused of witchcraft.) After the discussion that ensues from this revelation, I make it clear to my students that the word is not to be used again in my classroom, and it rarely is.

When I mention the words "lesbian" and "gay man," there is always a stir of discomfort, so I ask what those words mean. I am usually told that a gay man is an "effeminate" man. We discuss the stereotyping inherent in that myth, as well as the fact that "effeminate" means "behaving like a woman," and the class begins to realize that "behaving like a woman" is viewed negatively.

When asked what it really means to be called a "faggot" and why it is insulting for a boy to be called "gay," students will often respond that saying a boy is like a girl is the worst insult imaginable. At this point, girls are likely to sense that something unjust has been touched upon, and they will often take up their own defense, while simultaneously having their own consciousness raised.

Before we go on with the lesson plan, I usually attempt to reach a consensus on definitions. Here are some that have seemed acceptable: "Someone who loves someone of the same sex, but can be close to people of the opposite sex if they want to" and "Someone who romantically loves someone of the same sex." We added the word "romantically" in one class after a boy commented in a confused tone, "But I love my father...." When discussing definitions, it is important to tell children that gays and lesbians are as different from one another as are heterosexual men and women. There is no such thing as a "typical" lesbian or gay man.

Imagining Names

As part of the lesson plan, I ask students to imagine being called names as they walk with a close friend of the same sex; they describe feeling "different," "dumb," "weird," "afraid," and "embarrassed." (One very different response was, "I'd feel loved, because the main thing would be walking with someone I loved.") When asked how they would feel as one of the name-callers, children usually admit that they "would feel like part of the group."

Suggested responses to homophobic attacks have included, "It's my choice," "We like each other, and for your information, we're not homosexual," "I'm not ashamed," "I'm just as different as you are," "I don't care," and "So what!"

I have also used the music of Holly Near to teach about oppression. Song are an effective tool in reaching children, and they seem to retain information presented in this way more easily. Near sings about the oppression of many different groups, and her songs help students make linkages between their struggles.

Another way to combat homophobia – particularly for older students – is to invite a speaker from a gay organization to talk to the class. Listening to a gay or lesbian who is also a living, breathing human being – someone who has parents, siblings, and looks a little nervous in front of a group – is often a decisive factor in breaking down homophobic stereotypes.

Homophobic attitudes can also be countered in discussions about sex roles. Students can be asked, "What does a boy have to do to 'act like a girl?'" (and vice versa). The stereotypic behaviors that are mentioned can usually be quickly discounted by asking children to consider their own home lives. Many children, particularly those with single or divorced parents, have seen their mothers working and their fathers cleaning the house. Boys are often relieved to argue that a boy can read, sing, or clean up without losing respect. However, these same boys will worry that other children will continue to believe in sex-role myths. These fears are often strong enough to keep children in traditional sex roles even when they become aware of the unjust nature of these roles.

Another classroom activity is to ask students to look in any standard dictionary or thesaurus for the definitions of "male" and "female," "masculine" and "feminine," "husband," "wife," et cetera. The definitions are often so blatantly offensive and stereotypic that they create a small sensation when read aloud, thus challenging children to rethink their own definitions.

Discussing homophobic concepts is one thing; enduring homophobic name-calling is an entirely different matter. The pressure to conform is especially overwhelming within the school/peer structure, and it is vital that teachers try to instill the courage needed to function independently when one is the object of ridicule.

I attempt to teach my students to be willing to defend not only their own rights but the rights of others. Because name-calling is so common among children, and because it embodies the bigotry learned from adults, it is a good place for educators to begin.

Recommended Resources

Multiculturalism and Antibias Education

Freedom's Plow: Teaching in the Multicultural Classroom

edited by Theresa Perry and James Fraser, New York: Routledge, 1993. Many ideas and activities offered by teachers about antiracist, multicultural classrooms.

Affirming Diversity: The Sociopolitical Context of Multicultural Education

by Sonia Nieto, White Plains, NY: Longman, 1992. How personal, social, political, cultural, and educational factors interact to affect the success or failure of students.

Teaching Multicultural Literature in Grades K–8

edited by Violet Harris and Christopher Harris, Norwood, MA: Christopher Gordon, 1992. Excellent essays and bibliographies on many racial groups.

Anti-Bias Curriculum: Tools for Empowering Young Children

by Louise Derman-Sparks and the ABC Task Force, Washington, D.C.: National Association for the Education of Young Children, 1989. An excellent book for the early child/primary level on how to teach about all forms of bias.

Valuing Diversity

by Janet Brown McCracken, Washington, D.C.: National Association for the Education of Young Children, 1993. One of the few books that offer both practical suggestions for classroom activities and strategies to challenge one's own thinking.

Teaching Strategies for Ethnic Studies (5th ed.)

by James A. Banks, Boston: Allyn & Bacon, 1991. A readable summary of the histories of the major ethnic groups in the U.S.; good teaching ideas.

Flirting or Hurting? A Teacher's Guide on Student-to-Student Sexual Harassment in Schools (Grades 6 through 12)

by Nan Stein and Lisa Sjostrom of the Wellesley College Center for Research on Women, published by the National Education Association, 1994. (Order from the Center for Research on Women, Publications Dept., Wellesley College, 106 Central St., Wellesley, MA 02181-8259.) A new lesson guide to combat sexual harassment.

Videos

California Newsreel, 149 9th St., #420, San Francisco, CA 94103; 415-621-6196; and *Third World Newsreel,* 335 38th St., 5th Floor, New York, NY 10018; 212-947-9277. Two excellent sources for videos for multicultural education.

Rethinking Our Classrooms

edited by Bill Bigelow, Linda Christensen, Stan Karp, Barbara Miner, and Bob Peterson, Milwaukee, Wis.: Rethinking Schools, 1994. A curriculum guide focusing on equity and social justice in the K-12 classroom.

Teaching Tolerance

400 Washington Ave., Montgomery, AL 36104; 205-264-0286; fax 205-264-3121. A semi-annual anti-bias magazine mailed free to teachers.

Project 21

Gay and Lesbian Alliance Against Defamation, San Francisco Bay Area, 514 Castro Street, Suite B, San Francisco, CA 94114; 415-861-4588. Information on curriculum resources to bring the history and achievements of gay, lesbian, and bisexual people into the classroom.

California Tomorrow

Fort Mason Center, Building B, San Francisco, CA 94123; 415-441-7631. Information on the multiracial, multiethnic and multicultural population of California, including reports on immigrant children and education of Limited English Proficiency students.

PART II

Rethinking the Curriculum

In the opening chapter in this section, teacher David Levine urges that we approach schooling as an experiment in democracy, where teachers collaborate to equip students to develop the values and knowledge needed to be full participants in society. Unfortunately, as Levine points out, an alternative vision often holds sway, a vision of schools as "knowledge factories," with teachers as technicians, transmitting a predetermined body of information.

Both practically and theoretically, the chapters in this part elaborate on how schools might succeed as these experiments in democracy. They critique the traditional curriculum as well as new curricular reforms that share antidemocratic premises. Beyond just offering criticism, the pieces provide concrete examples of how to transform classroom practice and school culture.

In "Discovering Columbus: Rereading the Past," Bill Bigelow describes several lessons he uses to enlist students as "textbook detectives" to critique versions of history that justify racism and colonial domination. Using the Columbus myth as a point of departure, Bigelow shows step by step how students can be encouraged to read for bias and omission – to "talk back" to the text. On a similar theme, in "We Have No Reason to Celebrate an Invasion," Suzan Shown Harjo criticizes the "cotton-candy version of history" delivered to U.S. children, especially those that condone the subjugation of Native Americans.

Bob Peterson dissects the influential E. D. Hirsch books to reveal their Eurocentric bias. Peterson argues that embedded in Hirsch's so-called cultural literacy is a conservative curricular paradigm, one that demands rote memorization. This "superficial familiarity with facts" stands in opposition to a teaching methodology that encourages deep questioning. Peterson contrasts critical literacy with "cultural literacy." In one example, he compares Hirsch's approach to *Robinson Crusoe* – children should memorize its plot line – with one that asks students to raise "fundamental issues about justice and equality."

In his interview with Barbara Miner, the historian Howard Zinn argues that the curriculum should not be aimed at coercing students to memorize a fixed body of information, but at engaging students in a search for answers to fundamental social problems: war and peace, wealth and poverty, racial division. The curriculum must encourage students to ask the big questions of right and wrong. Zinn says that the history curriculum has always been partisan, traditionally looking at the world through the eyes of the powerful: presidents, generals, and industrialists. He argues that it's time we listened to the voices of those whose stories have been systematically excluded.

Elizabeth Martínez, in "Distorting Latino History: The California Textbook Controversy," targets the Houghton Mifflin series adopted by the state of California, textbooks that label slavery a "life-style." Her article raises fundamental questions about the "immigrant America" framework central to the country's U.S. history courses. Martínez cautions against counting "multicultural" pages in books — and, by implication, hours of study or course titles — as a way of measuring equity. She suggests that an ersatz multiculturalism can actually camouflage a fundamentally Eurocentric approach, and asks readers to "de-imagine" the United States and re-imagine it as a "'world': a community of communities relating on the basis of mutual respect and integrity."

In "*The Lorax:* Dr. Seuss Revisited and Revised," Bill Bigelow shows how even "progressive" children's literature may carry ambiguous messages. He encourages his students to "read deep between the lines" to develop a critical literacy. Bigelow also contends that a vital component of this critical literacy requires inviting students to imagine alternatives. Included are excerpts from several students' rewrite of Dr. Seuss's *The Lorax,* as they confront tough questions about the causes of, and solutions to, environmental degradation.

In his interview with Barbara Miner, Harvey Daniels describes what "whole language" is and is not, and warns against its co-optation by corporate interests that seek to profit from every curricular twist and turn. Daniels agrees with David Levine that curriculum reform is not a thing, but a process. Whole language, he says, has a classroom dimension — most important, children exercise more choice — but also has a strategic dimension: it must be grassroots, teacher-driven, democratic. Right wingers oppose whole language, according to Daniels, because they want schools devoid of ideas, thinking, debate, meaning.

As Linda Christensen points out in "Whose Standard? Teaching Standard English in Our Schools," a rethought curriculum does not aim only at a livelier classroom, more student talk, or more choice, but also asks students to reflect on the broader society that helps shape and often limit who they are. Christensen tackles the thorny issue of Standard English to demonstrate that there is no contradiction between teaching "skills" and critical literacy. She draws on examples from her own life as well as her long classroom experience to discuss how students can learn simultaneously to use the rules of Standard English and to question them. Without a critical component, Christensen argues, "we condition [students] to a pedagogy of consumption where they will consume the knowledge, priorities, and products that have been decided and manufactured without them in mind."

Lisa Delpit, in her interview with Barbara Miner, appends a "not so fast" to discussions of curriculum rethinking. She states clearly that there is no inherent conflict between students acquiring skills and developing critical capacities. But Delpit reminds us that the race and cultural/economic background of reform-minded teachers are often quite different from those of the people they hope to serve. She offers examples of the arrogance of white teachers who think they know how best to teach children of color. She strongly cautions that teaching other people's children requires humility and a willingness to listen.

As David Levine emphasizes in his introductory article to this section, curriculum reforms can be no better than the social vision on which they're premised. In different ways, all of the writers in this section insist on a rigorous democratization of the curriculum. They demand, and they demonstrate, that schools can begin to prefigure a more just, more equitable society than the one that currently exists.

Building a Vision
of Curriculum Reform

DAVID LEVINE

The restless spirit of curriculum reform stalks the educational land-scape. It is conjured up from the cries of battle-weary teachers, from parents whose children aren't learning, from business people worried about their future work force, from legislators alarmed at the growth of an economic underclass. This spirit of reform calls into question current goals, methods, content, and means of evalua-tion; in short, the totality of the present school curriculum.

The promise of reform is heartening, but we must remember that reforms can only be as sound as the vision upon which they are constructed. And while exciting experiments in curricular reform have popped up here and there, many educational policymakers and managers still remain most comfortable with approaches that treat schools as knowledge factories and teachers as technicians. As long as this is the case, meaningful reform is unlikely to be widespread.

Not that these people nakedly extol an industrial model of educa-tion. Educational jargon has acquired smoother, more refined vocabulary since the days when Franklin Bobbitt urged educators to adapt the methods of industrial production to schools. But under modern phraseology we can find ongoing practices and proposals that reflect a production-line mentality. Consider:

1. The disheartening popularity of "systems management" approaches, which seek to set in place elaborate lists of objectives, rigid sequential instruction in isolated skills, and standardized tests as "teacher-proof" mechanisms for guaranteed, easily quantifiable results. These management techniques flood schools as commer-cially produced learning systems or are constructed by school system officials under such labels as "curriculum alignment" or "out-come-based education."

2. The tyranny of the standardized test, which continues to distort curriculum. When multiple-choice tests hold sway as the most hon-ored means of "quality control," the pressures to trivialize, teach isolated skills, and neglect higher-order skills are tremendous.

3. The enduring commitment to forms of school organization and instruction which treat children as raw material to be processed by teachers into educationally finished products. Many parents, teachers, and administrators still think of schooling as the "transmission" of a static body of knowledge from teachers to students, with little opportunity for young people to play an active role in their own education. Walk the halls of any modern high school and you are likely to pass classrooms in which the predominant forms of student activity remain listening to the teacher, giving short-answer oral or written responses, reading a text book, and cramming for a test. This traditional pattern is reinforced by pressure to "cover the curriculum," to produce acceptable test results, and to manage large numbers of students with little preparation time.

Of course, there have always been teachers, inspired by their love of learning and children, who have gone beyond the basics to fill their classrooms with innovative and enlivening learning experiences. But such teachers remain embattled, torn between their sense of what constitutes good teaching and the constraints of a bureaucratized and isolating system that does little to encourage initiative and experimentation.

If we want good teaching to flourish, we must create contexts in which such teachers feel comfortable, and all teachers are encouraged to consistently examine, discuss, and improve their work. Such a context can only be created by taking a comprehensive look at the underlying notions and typical practices that characterize school curricula and being willing to explore profoundly different ideas about the structure and function of schools.

I think the best way to challenge the depressing (though largely unacknowledged) reality of "school as factory" is with metaphors that seek to express our own countervision of what schools should be. I would like to suggest two: In the place of "school as factory," I propose "school as an experiment in democracy"; in place of "teacher as technician," I propose "teacher as artist."

Since these two metaphors depart from traditional educational language, some explanation is in order. By "experiment in democracy," I mean to suggest a commitment to helping all students develop the values, skills, and knowledge they will need to succeed in a democratic society. Teachers committed to such a goal would be willing to actively confront the effects of racism, sexism, and class bias on student achievement. They would be willing to explore and develop student-teacher relations and curriculum content that promote high expectations, cooperation, and student initiative. A school that is an experiment in democracy would be characterized by ongoing debate and reflection among students and staff about these issues, governed by the idea that constant evolution is the sign of a healthy institution.

Since teaching for democracy means helping students become highly competent, sensitive, and independent human beings, it is a complex undertaking beyond the ability of teacher as technician. It requires the effort of a teacher who is aspiring to treat her or his profession as an art. In *The Educational Imagination,* Elliot Eisner explains, "Teaching is an art in the sense that teachers, like painters, composers, actresses, and dancers, make judgments based largely on qualities that unfold during the course of the action. Qualitative forms of intelligence are used to select, control, and organize classroom qualities, such as tempo, tone, climate, pace of discussion, and forward movement. The teacher must 'read' the emerging qualities and respond with qualities appropriate to the ends sought or the direction he wishes the students to take. In this process, qualitative judgment is exercised in the interest of achieving a qualitative end."

In Eisner's framework, the "work of art" on which each teacher labors consists of the process of teaching itself and the relationship between teachers and students out of which learning grows. Teaching conceived as a democratizing art subverts the mold of standardization. It celebrates diversity of style and content. At the same time, I think this kind of approach strongly suggests certain core qualities that are desirable in a curriculum.

Student-centeredness

This approach would relate the universe of knowledge to the issues, experiences, and contradictions each child confronts in his or her own life. This implies much more than using a fragment of personal interest to hook a child into a prefabricated curriculum. It means conceiving the curriculum as a means through which students make sense of their own experience, encounter the world beyond their immediate lives, and put these two elements of reality together into a meaningful whole. For example, a social studies unit on law might draw out what students know about crime, drug use, and police-community relations in their own neighborhood and use this knowledge to explore questions concerning how the criminal justice system works and the conflicting rights of the individual and society.

Such an approach would challenge students to expand their understanding through reading, discussion, and interviews, and to inte-
grate new knowledge into the web of understanding they bring to
the classroom.

The starting presumption of a student-centered teacher is that
each child brings to the classroom a unique set of perceptions and
abilities that can be cultivated to expand understanding, sharpen
skills, and increase motivation. A student-centered classroom is a
place where students are encouraged to explore their own interests,
and to view school not as the imposition of an alien agenda, but as
an organized means to articulate their own.

Since a student-centered approach is respectful of the students
and their world, of necessity it celebrates the language and culture
that each child brings to the classroom. It is incumbent upon the
teacher to consider a multicultural classroom not as an impediment
but as an opportunity to explore and appreciate the rich variety of
human experience.

Interactiveness

Learning is a social process most effectively accomplished with the
active engagement of the learner. Although lectures can be a valid
and stimulating mode of instruction, a classroom overwhelmingly
dominated by teacher talk stifles the capacity of students to be active
learners. Dialogue, performance, experimentation, debate, questioning, and collaboration all tend to enliven students. Research in
"cooperative learning" has shown how the explicit cultivation of
social skills can help students learn to work together and increase
the achievement of children of varying abilities.

An interactive approach subverts the normal hierarchy that iso-
lates students from each other and sets them into competition for
the attention and approval of the teacher. Practiced well, it promotes tolerance, the ability to listen and respond, and respect and
appreciation for the views of others.

The Encouragement of Real Intellectual Work

Real intellectual work is marked by rigor, depth, and intrinsic
meaning. It enables students to simulate, as closely as possible,
activities that take place in the world outside of school. It favors the
integration of several skills into the coordinated performance of a

meaningful action. If we hold these qualities in mind, they suggest that some classroom practices are likely to be more valuable than others. For example:

- In the place of the basal reader, students should be encouraged to read whole books.
- In the place of grammar and spelling drills, students will best master writing through producing, editing, and publishing their own essays, stories, poems, and plays.
- In the place of answering questions at the end of the chapter, students will better learn to think like scientists by conducting and explaining their own experiments.
- In the place of completing multiple-choice and short-answer tests, students will better learn to think like historians by conducting their own interviews and writing their own research papers.

Real intellectual work can also be fostered by cutting through the trivia that dominates many courses. Grant Wiggins, former director of research for the Coalition of Essential Schools, argues that instead of parading students through a broad and superficial survey of topics in a given field, it is more effective to identify "essential questions" that have sparked debate among actual practitioners of knowledge — writers, scientists, historians — and structure learning around serious inquiry into these questions. According to Wiggins, essential questions "go to the heart of a discipline. They can be found in the most historically important (and controversial) problems and topics: What 'causes' the major events of history? Is light a particle or a wave? Are social and moral habits 'natural'? Is *Death of a Salesman* a tragedy? What is a 'great' book or work or art? What is adequate 'proof' in each field of inquiry?" As Wiggins contends, such questions encourage critical and original thinking.

The Welcoming of Controversy

Schools are highly political institutions. How could they not be, given that one of their main charges is to reproduce within the next generation values and social relations deemed appropriate for the continuation of civilization? When teachers pose as "objective" and "neutral" purveyors of a collection of value-free skills they are merely obscuring a large part of what their interaction with students is all about.

Politics exist in schools not only in the content of the curriculum, but in the social relations that characterize classrooms and the school as a whole — what has been called the "hidden curriculum." The arrangements of power and authority, teacher expectations of how students will behave and achieve, and the tracking of students all involve value judgments made either consciously or reflexively.

And then there is the content itself. Here teachers act as political beings through the opinions they express, their framing of discussions and issues, the questions they ask, the topics they address or ignore, and the materials they choose to use.

If we want school to encourage the artful cultivation of democracy, we will acknowledge the value-laden nature of education and seek responsible ways to let conflict and discussion unfold in our classrooms. In part, this means helping students reflect critically on their own thoughts and feelings about big issues: racism, sexism, ecology, violence, distribution of wealth, the role of the United States around the world. But it also means sharing our own opinions on these issues with students, not as the final arbiters of truth, but as what we are in reality — thinking and feeling human beings with our own impulses and obligations to stand up for what we believe. The advantages of accepting the political nature of schools are twofold. First, we give ourselves the chance to think about and discuss with our colleagues responsible ways to express our own values in the classroom. Second, we realize that the politics inherent in school life, whether they involve issues that students encounter outside the school or issues embedded in the "hidden curriculum" of schools' social relations, are a great source of discussion and projects that can unleash the creativity and enthusiasm of students.

The Path to Reform

If the practices described above are to become the norm rather than the exception in our schools, comprehensive reform is essential. A good starting point for such reform would be a clear and sound delineation of the ways in which teaching can and cannot be "scientific." Teaching can be scientific in the sense that it can be informed and guided by knowledge or appropriate learning research, and in the sense that it is good for a teacher to proceed "experimentally," to form hypotheses about how children learn, to try out ideas based on these hypotheses, and to evaluate the results. But it cannot be scientific in the sense used to describe technical fields such as chemistry or physics, in which exact and quantitatively verifiable conclusions can be spelled out. Nor can it be scientific in the sense of industrial scientific management, based on the idea that a precise and unvarying technique for producing the most efficient results can confidently be established.

Since teaching is not a science or a precise technical procedure, but, at its best, an artful endeavor, curriculum should demand rigor without being narrowly proscriptive or dominated by formulaic commands. As Elliot Eisner explains, "Rationality includes the capacity to play, to explore, to search for surprise and effective novelty. Such activities are not necessarily contrary to the exercise of human rationality; they may be its most compelling exemplification. What diminishes human rationality is the thwarting of flexible human intelligence by prescriptions that shackle the educational imagination."

Unshackling the educational imagination means understanding that at its heart good teaching is an act of creative intelligence, and that it can best flourish when teachers are given the freedom and responsibility to construct and critique their own curriculum. We need to popularize the notion that effective curriculum development involves constant cycles of teaching practice, discussion, reflection, and evaluation. In place of "educational prescriptions," teachers need broad curricular goals and outcomes for which they are held accountable, and a working environment that encourages them to consult with their peers and experiment with a broad array of materials and activities within their own classrooms. Good teachers are constantly tinkering with their curriculum: searching for new materials, trying out new activities, designing new challenges and means of assessment for their students. Healthy curricular reform would include removing all that constrains such practices and providing structures and training that encourage them.

Time and Teaching Load

At present, a great deal of "curriculum development" energy is absorbed by such activities as revising lists of objectives and choosing new texts. But the impact of such activities on what happens inside the classroom will be negligible unless we change how the time and energy of teachers are spent. Teachers are not given enough time to plan or to consult with their colleagues, and their energy is spread too thinly over large groups of students. Structural changes are needed to remedy these problems.

There are several ways that adequate preparation time could be provided: a paid two-week period at the start of the school year, one day each month set aside for planning, or longer planning time built into each day. This additional preparation time should be structured in ways that allow teachers to plan on their own and, just as important, to meet with their colleagues. At present, teachers operate in debilitating isolation. Professional consultation must often be squeezed into a rushed hallway conference or a few words exchanged at the end of an exhausting work day. We need opportunities to meet in relatively relaxed settings to discuss common problems, learn about each other's successes, and debate the merits of different goals, techniques, and curricular materials.

Structural changes that provide for more adequate preparation time should be accompanied by reforms that reduce the number of students each teacher is responsible for. Consider the dilemma of a high school teacher who wants to teach creatively. Her class sizes range from twenty-six to thirty-three students and her total student load is between 130 and 170. She may be able to memorize all her students' names, but she won't have the time to get an in-depth understanding of their individual strengths and weaknesses. Nor will she have the time to implement the kind of labor-intensive activities and assessment essential to good teaching. Against her idealistic aspirations, she will be drawn by the practical constraints of her situation into the mass-production techniques of overreliance on the textbook and standardized tests.

There is no reason to consider the present teacher-student ratios to be immutable. Some schools have decided to cut down on their total number of course offerings and have instituted interdisciplinary courses as ways of substantially reducing the student-teacher ratio. The Coalition of Essential Schools recommends a student-teacher ratio of no more than eighty to one, and has helped schools move toward this goal without extravagant increases in budget.

But just providing more time and improved student-teacher ratios is not enough. It's harder to be a teacher as artist than a teacher as technician. Many teachers would find the idea of designing their own curriculum or seriously sharing problems with their colleagues both daunting prospects. Guidance and training are needed to help all teachers struggle with the difficult tasks of thinking independently and self-critically about their own teaching, and being willing to talk with others about their own successes and failures. One effective way to encourage these skills is to have groups of teachers design curricula together, and then meet periodically to discuss their own efforts to implement what they've created. Another approach, "peer coaching," has been used as a nonthreatening way for teachers to receive both affirmation and constructive criticism from each other.

The defenders of the "teaching as a science" model might argue that to move out of the world of curricular blueprints and omnipresent standardized tests is to inevitably move into the world of pedagogical sloppiness and subjectivity. But ironically, it is their approach to education that is sloppy and subjective, because it loses sight of the fundamental qualities of good teaching. In actuality, when we demand that teachers learn to think for themselves and to talk seriously to each other about teaching, that they help students master real skills instead of mindless drills, that they constantly challenge and rework their own classroom practice, we make possible a level of rigor and accountability now missing from most schools. If our schools are to emerge from the widely acknowledged crisis that now grips them, it will be by taking paths that lead away from teaching as a technology and toward teaching as a democratizing practice that aspires to artistry.

Discovering Columbus: Rereading the Past

BILL BIGELOW

Most of my students have trouble with the idea that a book — especially a *textbook* — can lie. That's why I start my U.S. history class by stealing a student's purse.

As the year opens, my students may not know when the Civil War was fought or what James Madison or Frederick Douglass did; but they know that a brave fellow named Christopher Columbus discovered America. Indeed, this bit of historical lore may be the only knowledge class members have in common.

What students don't know is that their textbooks have, by omission or otherwise, lied to them. They don't know, for example, that on the island of Hispaniola, an entire race of people was wiped out in only forty years of Spanish administration.

Finders, Keepers

So I begin class by stealing a student's purse. I announce that the purse is mine, obviously, because look who has it. Most students are fair-minded. They saw me take the purse off the desk so they protest: "That's not yours, it's Nikki's. You took it. We saw you." I brush these objections aside and reiterate that it is, too, mine and to prove it, I'll show all the things I have inside.

I unzip the bag and remove a brush or a comb, maybe a pair of dark glasses. A tube of lipstick works best: "This is my lipstick," I say. "There, that proves it *is* my purse." They don't buy it and, in fact, are mildly outraged that I would pry into someone's possessions with such utter disregard for her privacy. (I've alerted the student to the demonstration before the class, but no one else knows that.)

It's time to move on: "OK, if it's Nikki's purse, how do you know? Why are you all so positive it's not my purse?" Different answers: We saw you take it; that's her lipstick, we know you don't wear lipstick; there is stuff in there with her name on it. To get the point across, I even offer to help in their effort to prove Nikki's possession: "If we had a test on the contents of the purse, who would do better, Nikki or I?" "Whose labor earned the money that bought the things in the purse, mine or Nikki's?" Obvious questions, obvious answers.

I make one last try to keep Nikki's purse: "What if I said I *discovered* this purse, then would it be mine?" A little laughter is my reward, but I don't get any takers; they still think the purse is rightfully Nikki's.

"So," I ask, "Why do we say that Columbus discovered America?"

What Is Discovery?

Now they begin to see what I've been leading up to. I ask a series of questions that implicitly link Nikki's purse and the Indians' land: Were there people on the land before Columbus arrived? Who had been on the land longer, Columbus or the Indians? Who knew the land better? Who put their labor into making the land produce? The students see where I'm going — it would be hard not to. "And yet," I continue, "What is the first thing that Columbus did when he arrived in the New World?" Right: he took possession of it. After all, he had discovered the place.

We talk about phrases other than "discovery" that textbooks could use to describe what Columbus did. Students start with phrases they used to describe what I did to Nikki's purse. He stole it; he took it; he ripped it off. And others: He invaded it; he conquered it.

I want students to see that the word "discovery" is loaded. The word itself carries a perspective, a bias. "Discovery" is the phrase of the supposed discoverers. It's the invaders masking their theft. And when the word gets repeated in textbooks, those textbooks become, in the phrase of one historian, "the propaganda of the winners."

To prepare students to examine textbooks critically, we begin with alternative, and rather unsentimental, explorations of Columbus's "enterprise," as he called it. The admiral-to-be was not sailing for mere adventure and to prove the world was round, as I learned in fourth grade, but to secure the tremendous profits that were to be made by reaching the Indies.

Mostly I want the class to think about the human beings Columbus was to "discover" — and then destroy. I read from a letter

Columbus wrote to Lord Raphael Sanchez, treasure of Aragón and one of his patrons, dated March 14, 1493, during his return from the first voyage. He reports being enormously impressed by the indigenous people:

> As soon...as they see that they are safe and have laid aside all fear, they are very simple and honest and exceedingly liberal with all they have; none of them refusing anything he *[sic]* may possess when he is asked for it, but, on the contrary, inviting us to ask them. They exhibit great love toward all others in preference to themselves. They also give objects of great value for trifles, and content themselves with very little or nothing in return....I did not find, as some of us had expected, any cannibals among them, but, on the contrary, men of great deference and kindness.[1]

But, on an ominous note, Columbus writes in his log, "should your Majesties command it, all the inhabitants could be taken away to Castile [Spain], or made slaves on the island. With 50 men we could subjugate them all and make them do whatever we want."[2]

I ask students if they remember from elementary school days what Columbus brought back from the "New World." Students recall that he returned with parrots, plants, some gold, and a few of the people he had taken to calling "Indians." This was Columbus's first expedition and it is also where most school textbook accounts of Columbus end — conveniently. What about his second voyage?

I read to them a passage from Hans Koning's fine book, *Columbus: His Enterprise*:

> We are now in February 1495. Time was short for sending back a good "dividend" on the supply ships getting ready for the return to Spain. Columbus therefore turned to a massive slave raid as a means for filling up these ships. The [Columbus] brothers rounded up fifteen hundred Arawaks — men, women, and children — and imprisoned them in pens in Isabela, guarded by men and dogs. The ships had room for no more than five hundred and thus only the best specimens were loaded aboard. The Admiral then told the Spaniards they could help themselves from the remainder to as many slaves as they wanted. Those whom no one chose were simply kicked out of their pens. Such had been the terror of these prisoners that (in the description by Michele de Cuneo, one of the colonists) "they rushed in all directions like lunatics, women dropping, and abandoning infants in the rush, running for miles without stopping, fleeing across mountains and rivers."
>
> Of the five hundred slaves, three hundred arrived alive in Spain, where they were put up for sale in Seville by Don Juan de Fonseca,

the archdeacon of the town. "As naked as the day they were born," the report of this excellent churchman says, *"but with no more embarrassment than animals..."*

   The slave trade immediately turned out to be "unprofitable, for the slaves mostly died." Columbus decided to concentrate on gold, although he writes, *"Let us in the name of the Holy Trinity* go on sending all the slaves that can be sold." (Koning's emphasis)[3]

Certainly Columbus's fame should not be limited to the discovery of America: he also deserves credit for initiating the trans-Atlantic slave trade, albeit in the opposite direction than we're used to thinking of it.

Looking Through Different Eyes

Students and I role-play a scene from Columbus's second voyage. Slavery is not producing the profits Columbus seeks. He believes there is gold in them thar hills and the Indians are selfishly holding out on him.

   Students play Columbus, I play the Indians: "Chris, we don't have any gold, honest. Can we go back to living our lives now and you can go back to wherever you came from?"

   I call on several students to respond to the Indians' plea. Columbus thinks the Indians are lying. Student responses range from sympathetic to ruthless: OK, we'll go home; *please* bring us your gold; we'll lock you up in prison if you don't bring us your gold; we'll torture you if you don't fork it over.

   After I've pleaded for awhile and the students-as-Columbus have threatened, I read aloud another passage from Koning's book describing Columbus's system for extracting gold from the Indians:

> Every man and woman, every boy and girl of fourteen or older, in the province of Cibao...had to collect gold for the Spaniards. As their measure, the Spaniards used...hawks' bells....Every three months, every Indian had to bring to one of the forts a hawk's bell filled with gold dust. The chiefs had to bring in about ten times that amount. In the other provinces of Hispaniola, twenty-five pounds of spun cotton took the place of gold.
>
>   Copper tokens were manufactured, and when an Indian had brought his or her tribute to an armed post, he or she received such a token, stamped with the month, to be hung around the neck. With that they were safe for another three months while collecting more gold.
>
>   Whoever was caught without a token was killed by having his or her hands cut off....

There were no gold fields, and thus, once the Indians had handed in whatever they still had in gold ornaments, their only hope was to work all day in the streams, washing out gold dust from the pebbles. It was an impossible task, but those Indians who tried to flee into the mountains were systematically hunted down with dogs and killed, to set an example for the others to keep trying....

During those two years of the administration of the brothers Columbus, an estimated one-half of the entire population of Hispaniola was killed or killed themselves. The estimates run from one hundred and twenty-five thousand to one-half million.[4]

The goal is not to titillate or stun, but to force the question: Why wasn't I told this before?

Reexamining Basic Truths

I ask students to find a textbook, preferably one they used in elementary school, and critique the book's treatment of Columbus and the Indians. I distribute the following handout and review the questions aloud. I don't want them to merely answer the questions, but to consider them as guidelines.

- How factually accurate was the account?
- What was omitted – left out – that in your judgment would be important for a full understanding of Columbus? (Some examples might be his treatment of the Indians, slave taking, his method of getting gold, the overall effect on the Indians.)
- What motives does the book give to Columbus? Compare those with his real motives.
- Who does the book get you to root for, and how is that accomplished? (For example, are the books horrified at the treatment of Indians or thrilled that Columbus makes it to the New World?)
- How do the publishers use illustrations? What do these communicate about Columbus and his "enterprise"?
- In your opinion, *why* does the book portray the Columbus-Indian encounter the way it does?
- Can you think of any groups in our society who might have an interest in people having an inaccurate view of history?

I tell students that this last question is tough but crucial. Is the continual distortion of Columbus simply an accident, or are there social groups who benefit from children developing a false or limited understanding of the past?

The assignment's subtext is to teach students that text material, indeed all written material, should be read skeptically. I want students to explore the politics of print — that perspectives on history and social reality underlie the written word, and that to read is both to comprehend what is written, but also to question *why* it is written. My intention is not to encourage an "I-don't-believe-anything" cynicism,[5] but rather to equip students to analyze a writer's assumptions and determine what is and isn't useful in any particular work.

For practice, we look at excerpts from a California textbook that belonged to my brother in the fourth grade, *The Story of American Freedom,* published by Macmillan in 1964. We read aloud and analyze several paragraphs. The arrival of Columbus and crew is especially revealing — and obnoxious. As is true in every book on the "discovery" that I've encountered, the reader watches events from the Spaniards' point of view. We are told how Columbus and his men "fell upon their knees and gave thanks to God," a passage included in virtually all elementary school accounts of Columbus. "He then took possession of it [the island] in the name of King Ferdinand and Queen Isabella of Spain."[6] No question is raised of Columbus's right to assume control over a land that was already occupied. The account is so respectful of the admiral that students can't help but sense it approves of what is, quite simply, an act of naked imperialism.

The book keeps us close to God and the Church throughout its narrative. Upon returning from the New World, Columbus shows off his parrots and Indians. Immediately following the show, "the king and queen lead the way to a near-by church. There a song of praise and thanksgiving is sung."[7] Intended or not, linking church and Columbus removes him still further from criticism.

Students' Conclusions

I give students a week before I ask them to bring in their written critiques. Students share their papers with one another in small groups. They take notes toward what my co-teacher, Linda Christensen, and I call the "collective text": What themes recur in the papers and what important differences emerge? What did they discover about textbook treatments of Columbus? Here are some excerpts:

Matthew wrote:

As people read their evaluations the same situations in these textbooks came out. Things were conveniently left out so that you sided with Columbus's quest to "boldly go where no man has gone before"....None of the harsh violent reality is confronted in these so-called true accounts.

Gina tried to explain why the books were so consistently rosy:

It seemed to me as if the publishers had just printed up some "glory story" that was supposed to make us feel more patriotic about our country. In our group, we talked about the possibility of the government trying to protect young students from such violence. We soon decided that that was probably one of the farthest things from their minds. They want us to look at our country as great, and powerful, and forever right. They want us to believe Columbus was a real hero. We're being fed lies. We don't question the facts, we just absorb information that is handed to us because we trust the role models that are handing it out.

Rebecca's collective text reflected the general tone of disillusion with the textbooks:

Of course, the writers of the books probably think it's harmless enough — what does it matter who discovered America, really; and besides, it makes them feel good about America. But the thought that I have been lied to all my life about this, and who knows what else, really makes me angry.

Why Do We Do This?

The reflections on the collective text became the basis for a class discussion. Repeatedly, students blasted their textbooks for giving readers inadequate, and ultimately untruthful, understandings. While we didn't press to arrive at definitive explanations for the omissions and distortions, we tried to underscore the contemporary abuses of historical ignorance. If the books wax romantic about Columbus planting the flag on island beaches and taking possession of land occupied by naked red-skinned Indians, what do young readers learn from this about today's world? That might — or wealth — makes right? That it's justified to take people's land if you are more "civilized" or have a "better" religion? That white people have an inherent right to dominate people of color?

Whatever the answers, the textbooks condition students to accept inequality; nowhere do they suggest that the Indians were sovereign peoples with a right to control their own lands. Furthermore, if Columbus's motives are mystified or ignored, then students are less apt to question U.S. involvements in, say, Central America or the Middle East. As Bobby, approaching his registration day for the military draft, pointed out in class: "If people thought they were going off to war to fight for profits, maybe they wouldn't fight as well, or maybe they wouldn't go."

It's important to note that some students are troubled by these myth-popping discussions. One student wrote that she was "left not knowing who to believe." Josh was the most articulate in his skepticism. He had begun to "read" our class from the same critical distance from which we hoped students would approach textbooks:

> I still wonder...If we can't believe what our first-grade teachers told us, why should we believe you? If they lied to us, why wouldn't you? If one book is wrong, why isn't another? What is your purpose in telling us about how awful Chris was? What interest do you have in telling us the truth? What is it you want from us?

They were wonderful questions. Linda and I responded by reading them (anonymously) to the entire class. We asked students to take a few minutes to write additional questions and comments on the Columbus activities or to imagine our response as teachers — what *was* the point of our lessons?

We hoped students would see that the intent was to present a new way of reading, and ultimately, of experiencing the world. Textbooks fill students with information masquerading as final truth and then ask students to parrot the information in end-of-the-chapter "checkups." The Brazilian educator Paulo Freire calls it the "banking method": students are treated as empty vessels waiting for deposits of wisdom from textbooks and teachers.[8] We wanted to tell students that they shouldn't necessarily trust the "authorities," but instead need to participate in their learning, probing for unstated assumptions and unasked questions.

Josh asked what our "interest" was in this approach. It's a vital question. Linda and I see teaching as political action: we want to equip students to build a truly democratic society. As Freire writes, to be an actor for social change one must "read the word and the world."[9] We hope that if a student maintains a critical distance from the written word, then it's possible to maintain that same distance from one's society: to stand back, look hard and ask, "Why is it like this? How can I make it better?"

We Have No Reason
to Celebrate an Invasion:
An Interview with
Suzan Shown Harjo

Suzan Shown Harjo is president and director of the Morning Star Foundation in Washington, D.C. The foundation sponsored the 1992 Alliance, formed to provide an indigenous peoples' response to the 500th anniversary of Columbus's arrival in the Americas. Harjo, a Cheyenne-Creek, agreed to answer questions about why some people did not want to celebrate the anniversary. She was interviewed in the fall of 1991 by Barbara Miner of *Rethinking Schools*.

Why aren't you joining in the celebration of the Columbus quincentenary?

As Native American peoples in this red quarter of Mother Earth, we have no reason to celebrate an invasion that caused the demise of so many of our people and is still causing destruction today. The Europeans stole our land and killed our people.

But because the quincentenary is a cause célèbre, it provides an opportunity to put forth Native American perspectives on the next 500 years.

Columbus was just "a man of his times." Why are you so critical of him? Why not look at the positive aspects of his legacy?

For people who are in survival mode, it's very difficult to look at the positive aspects of death and destruction, especially when it is carried through to our present. There is a reason we are the poorest people in America. There is a reason we have the highest teen suicide rate. There is a reason why our people are ill-housed and in poor health, and we do not live as long as the majority population.

That reason has to do with the fact that we were in the way of Western civilization and we were in the way of westward expansion. We suffered the "excesses" of civilization such as murder, pillage, rape, destruction of the major waterways, destruction of land, destruction and pollution of the air.

What are those "positive" aspects of the Columbus legacy? If we're talking about the horse, yeah, that's good. We like the horse. Indians raised the use of the horse to high military art, especially among the Cheyenne people and the tribes of the plains states.

Was that a good result of that invasion? Yes. Is it something we would have traded for the many Indian peoples who are no longer here because of that invasion? No.

We also like the beads that came from Europe, and again we raised their use to a high art. Would we have traded those beads for the massacres of our people, such as the Sand Creek massacre [in which U.S. soldiers massacred hundreds of Native American men, women, and children at San Creek, Colorado, in 1864]? No.

Why do we focus on Columbus rather than any number of U.S. presidents who were also responsible for the death and destruction of Indian people? Because it's his 500 years; it's his quincentenary.

Isn't criticism of Columbus a form of picking on the Spaniards? Were they any worse than other Europeans who came to America?

In my estimation, the Spaniards were no worse than any number of other Europeans. The economy of slavery and serfdom that existed in northern Europe — how do you measure that in cruelty and in long-term effects against the Spanish Inquisition?

I view the issue more as the oppressive nature and arrogance of the Christian religions. And that continues today.

Our Indian religions are not missionary religions. We are taught to respect other religions. It was a shock when we were met with proselytizing zealots, especially those who thought that if your soul can't be saved, you're better off dead — or if your soul can be saved, you should be dead so you can go to heaven. And that's the history of that original encounter.

How does that arrogance and ignorance manifest itself today?

How? Well, for example, the Catholic Church has said that 1992 is a time to enter into a period of grace and healing and to celebrate the evangelization of the Americas. My word, how can you be graceful and healing about the tens of thousands of native people who were killed because they would not convert to a religion they didn't understand, or because they didn't understand the language of those making the request?

It's difficult to take seriously an apology that is not coupled with atonement. It's as if they're saying, "I'm sorry, oops, and we'll be better in the next hemisphere." That doesn't cut it. We've had empty platitudes before.

The combination of arrogance and ignorance also results in making mascots of Indian people, of dehumanizing and stereotyping them – in the sports world, in advertising, and in society at large. The Washington Redskins football team is an excellent example.

There is no more derogatory name in English for Indian people than the name Redskins. And the Redskins is a prominent image right here in the nation's capital that goes by unnoticed. Because we are an invisible population, the racism against us is also invisible for the most part.

You don't see sports teams called the White Trash, the Black Chicks, the Jew Boys, or the Jack Mormons. And if we did see that, it wouldn't be for long, you can be sure of that.

Why can't we use the Columbus quincentenary to celebrate American diversity and the contributions of all, Europeans and Native Americans alike?

There will be lots of people who will be putting forth the perspective of rah-rah Columbus, rah-rah Western civilization. Our perspective is putting forth native peoples's views on our past and present. We also want to get into the public consciousness the notion that we actually have a future on this planet. This is something missed by even what is hailed as the most progressive of American movies, *Dances with Wolves.*

We're more interested in the 500 years before Columbus and what will go on in the next 500 years. The truth of the intervening 500 years is really known in the hearts of people worldwide, even though the particulars have been obscured by a cotton-candy version of history.

Aren't some of the criticisms of Columbus just substituting Native-centrism for Eurocentrism?

Oppressed people need to be centered within themselves. Racism and centrism become a problem if you are in the dominant society and are subjugating other people as a result of your centrism. I don't accept the question. I think it's an empty argument.

Aren't criticisms of Columbus just another form of ensuring "political correctness?"
The Eurocentric view, having been exposed for its underlying falsehood, now wishes to oppose any other view as either equally false or simply the flip side of reality: a secondary or dual reality.

Feelings are usually dual realities; perspectives are dual realities. But there are some things that don't have a dual reality. For example, if we look at who has polluted all of our water, causing a whole lot of death and a whole lot of illness in this country alone, then we have a bit of a clue where the problem might rest. We have a clue whose reality might expose the truth and whose reality might obscure the truth.

It's about time for the people who are the true historic revisionists, who are on the far right side of this whole political correctness debate, to stop lying to themselves, to their readership, and to their students. They must stop their silly ivory-tower kinds of debates about whether multiculturalism should be used, and so forth.

What is the true history? Just start dealing with some indisputable realities. The world is a mess. This country is a mess. The people who fare the worst in this country are poor, nonwhite children and poor, nonwhite old people. Societies that do not care for their young people and old people are decadent, decaying societies.

I think there are a lot of good minds that are reflecting that decadence and decay when they choose to spend their time on these kinds of ivory-tower debates. There are things about which they can do much, and they are doing nothing.

What are the key struggles that native people face today?
We need, in the first instance, basic human rights such as religious freedom. Or how about life, liberty, and the pursuit of happiness, and other things that many people in the United States view as standard fare but are out of reach for Indian people?

There is also the issue of land and treaty rights. We have property that we don't own and we should, and we have property that we own but don't control and we should.

We have treaties with the United States that are characterized in the U.S. Constitution as the supreme law of the land. Yet every one, without exception, of nearly 400 treaties signed between native peoples and the U.S. government has been broken. Every one of them.

A good place to start would be for the United States to live up to every treaty agreement. It's also the way you get at resolving some of the problems of poverty, alcoholism, unemployment, and poor health.

If we don't handle the big things, we can't get to the manifestations of the problem. We have to go to the basic human rights issues, the basic treaty rights issues.

If we don't resolve these issues, then all people in this country are going to be complicit in the continuing effort to wipe out our Indian people. It's as simple as that.

What Should Children Learn?:
A Teacher Looks at E. D. Hirsch

BOB PETERSON

As a fifth-grade teacher I use a variety of resources to provide my students information that is, I hope, comprehensible, yet challenging. I use anything – yellowed newspaper clippings, old textbooks, audio tapes from National Public Radio. Often a student will want more information than our classroom or school library can provide, so in the evening I poke around my dusty basement files or go to the public library. It was one such incident that introduced me to E. D. Hirsch.

A group of students had been interested in mountains – high ones, of course – and wanted help finding more information. That evening I went to a local bookstore and a huge display of Hirsch's books greeted me as I entered. I decided to check them out. Upon paging through a book – *What Your Fourth Grader Needs to Know* – I found a section on mountains. Out came my plastic and for $20 plus tax I had a new textbook.

The next day I photocopied the section for my students. While the factual information was correct – as corroborated by cross-checks by my students – we uncovered two troubling passages.

In describing the highest mountain of Africa, Mount Kilimanjaro, Hirsch writes that it "was known to local people as the 'Mountain of Cold Devils' because of its snow-capped peaks. The news of a snow-capped mount so near the equator was not believed for many years after its discovery in 1848 by two missionaries."

"What's odd about that passage?" I asked my students. Initially they thought the name a bit odd. But their second response was that two missionaries could not have "discovered" the mountain because Africans had already been there and, as even Hirsch acknowledged, had named it. "That's like saying Columbus discovered America," said one student.

The account of Mount Everest was equally troublesome, highlighting the cultural biases in even seemingly neutral subjects such as geography. "In 1852, a British surveyor excitedly burst into the office of his superior and announced: 'Sir, I have discovered the highest mountain in the world.'"

That night I questioned whether I should have used the material. I decided yes, because with questioning and discussion, it can help children see the European bias that is woven throughout such passages. It reminded me of one of the few things I like about school textbooks – they're useful in getting students to critique bias.

My use of Hirsch's fourth-grade book roused my curiosity, inspiring me to read the other books in the series. Rather than easing my fears, however, my investigation left me even more concerned. I came away convinced that the project is fundamentally flawed and that, because of its wide notoriety, has the potential to negatively affect education in the United States.

Hirsch's "cultural literacy" project is problematic on a number of levels. First, Hirsch misdiagnoses what ails American education, arguing that a lack of emphasis on "content" has left our children "culturally illiterate." Second, he defines knowledge in a way that equates learning with memorization and teaching with the transmission of information. Third, his definition of "core knowledge" attempts to institutionalize a curriculum that focuses almost exclusively on contributions and perspectives of mainstream European Americans – albeit with a slight nod toward a more multicultural perspective. In this regard, he is smart enough to try to co-opt what he can't defeat.

Hirsch also makes some valuable points, however. He raises the issue of unequal access to knowledge and literature in our stratified society. And he argues that schools have a responsibility to ensure that all members of society have sufficient "intergenerational" knowledge so they can participate in the economic and political affairs of our nation. That his solution to these problems is off base does not negate the validity of this concern for equity.

Hirsch's Growing Popularity

E. D. Hirsch is a professor of English at the University of Virginia. His big splash on the educational scene came in 1987 with the publication of *Cultural Literacy: What Every American Needs to Know*. Combining theoretical analysis with entertaining anecdotes about illiteracy and a list of 5,000 things that "culturally literate" Americans need to know, Hirsch's book climbed to the top of the *New York Times* best-selling list.

Funded in part by the Exxon Education Foundation, Hirsch then began a publishing project that started with the immodestly titled *What Your First Grader Needs to Know.* He continued with each grade until, by the fall of 1993, he had reached *What Your Sixth Grader Needs to Know.* He has also published other books, including *A First Dictionary of Cultural Literacy: What Our Children Need to Know.* According to its less than humble introduction, the dictionary contains "what American children should acquire by the end of 6th grade."

Hirsch also founded the Cultural Literacy Foundation, which later was called the Core Knowledge Foundation. The foundation, based in Charlottesville, Virginia, publishes a newsletter, promotes its *Core Knowledge Sequence Curriculum* and other materials, conducts training, advises schools free of charge, and boasts of having 100 schools in twenty-five states using its curriculum.

Hirsch's perspective strikes a popular chord. It has been endorsed by a range of people including Albert Shanker, president of the American Federation of Teachers, James P. Comer, noted African-American psychiatrist, and William Bennett, former secretary of education under Bush.

Some people find Hirsch appealing because he is an articulate champion of mainstream Western European heritage. He holds more appeal in this area than his late contemporary Allan Bloom, author of *Closing of the American Mind,* who stridently opposed efforts to acknowledge this country's multicultural history.

Other people find Hirsch appealing because his ideas mesh all too nicely with a conservative analysis of the problems with American schools and society. Hirsch argues that students' achievement in reading and writing are declining – and poverty is increasing – because schools have stressed skills instead of content and do "not give children a specific core of shared knowledge in early grades." He offers a low-cost, straight-forward solution – all students should obtain "core knowledge" – and conveniently ignores the all-too important issue of equity in funding and resources.

Still others find Hirsch appealing because he directly confronts a central question that runs throughout controversies about multiculturalism, outcomes-based education, and textbook adoptions: What do our kids need to know?

In critiquing Hirsch, it is essential to note that the debate over his views is part of a broader controversy in American society sparked by shifting demographics, the civil rights and feminist movements, increased immigration by people of color, and the changing global economy and rising prominence of Asia, Africa, and Latin America. As historian Ronald Takaki, author of *A Different Mirror,* has noted: "What is fueling this debate over our national identity and the content of our curriculum is America's intensifying racial crisis."

In response, Hirsch, Bloom, Bennett, and others have "attempted to create an ideological consensus around the return to traditional knowledge," according to Michael Apple, University of Wisconsin professor of education. They believe that the "'great books' and 'great ideas' of the 'Western tradition' will preserve democracy... increase student achievement and discipline, increase our international competitiveness, and ultimately reduce unemployment and poverty."

This "return to tradition" perspective contrasts sharply with those who in recent decades have pushed for a more inclusive definition of American culture and school curriculum. For instance, Theresa Perry and James Fraser point out in their book *Freedom's Plow: Teaching in the Multicultural Classroom,* "If there is to be democracy in the 21st century, it must be multiracial/multicultural democracy.... The debate is about the United States of America, and what its definitive values and identity will be in the next century."

The debate over Hirsch, then, is about far more than culture and education; it strikes at the core of our vision of this country's future. The irony is that Hirsch, in his attempt to define the twenty-first century American identity, relies on educational methods and content that dominated the nineteenth century.

Hirsch and Culture

My criticisms of Hirsch's perspective fall into two categories: his definition of "national culture" and his definition of knowledge.

Hirsch writes about a "single national culture" that all literate people share. He argues that middle-class children acquire mainstream literate culture "by daily encounters with other literate persons" and that "disadvantaged" children don't. Schools, he argues, should provide an "antidote to [the] deprivation" of "disadvantaged" children by making "the essential information more readily available." As he writes in *Cultural Literacy,* "We will be able to achieve a just and prosperous society only when our schools ensure that everyone commands enough shared background knowledge to be able to communicate effectively with everyone else."

Hirsch admits that multicultural education is "valuable in itself" but then goes on to add an all-important caveat that it "should not be allowed to supplant or interfere with our schools' responsibility to ensure our children's mastery of American literate culture." Equal access to culture is an undeniably worthwhile concern and Hirsch's care for equity should be commended. But a deeper look at his assumptions and limitations reveals that implementation of his ideas would more likely marginalize instead of enfranchise those students Hirsch says he wishes to help.

There are several related issues here involving complex questions of culture in a changing society. One needs to look not just at Hirsch's rhetoric of concern, but also at his definition of "traditional culture," his neglect of "nonmainstream" cultural histories and traditions, and his dismissal of the need to teach children to think critically.

First of all, what is Hirsch asking children to learn? After reading eight books by Hirsch it is clear that his view of "American literate culture" is overwhelmingly European-American based. Moreover, while he talks about the "classless character of cultural literacy" he virtually ignores the history, tradition, and literature of and about the working class and other marginalized groups and their conflicts with dominant society. He knows better than to dismiss the contributions of women completely, but recognizes them in a way that doesn't question the status quo.

I have no problem with children learning "American literate culture" if it includes *all* Americans and the competing, often conflicting, views from the many peoples that make up this diverse nation. Hirsch's "core knowledge," however, is little more than a distillation of that which already dominates most textbook series and what kids have been getting for decades. Before looking at this issue more completely, let's examine Hirsch's books.

A First Dictionary of Cultural Literacy is divided into sections such as literature, mythology, and history. The section on literature has 201 entries, 24 of which are literary terms. Of the remaining 166 entries, 154 (94 percent) are of European-American origin. Of the remaining 11, 6 deal with stories from *The Arabian Nights,* 1 deals with Native Americans (Hiawatha, with a reference to the poem by Henry Wadsworth Longfellow) and 4 refer to African-Americans (Maya Angelou, Richard Wright, and the stories of B'rer Rabbit and Uncle Remus). There are no references to Latino or Asian-Americans. The only entries dealing with working-class life or struggle are two works by Charles Dickens and "The Village Blacksmith" by Henry Wadsworth Longfellow. In the chapter on mythology, all 80 references are to European myths. There is not a single reference to racism, sexism, or prejudice in the entire 271-page book – not even at the level of words that his young readers should know. To claim that this dictionary "outlines the knowledge" that elementary children need to know is offensive to anyone who believes in justice and equality. Because of similar criticisms, Hirsch modified his "lists" of knowledge for both adults and children. But the fundamental problem remains.

A statistical analysis of his series of books *What Your First [through Sixth] Grader Needs to Know* shows that 82 percent of the pages devoted to literature and poetry have Euro-American selections. Of those that deal with non-European cultures, 37 percent have animals as main characters, compared to 11 percent of the Euro-American selections. The not-so-subtle message is that stories about non-European cultures are not as serious.

There is a question of more than European culture, however. Hirsch, for example, is concerned that children learn the traditional fairy tales such as Snow White and Cinderella. But nowhere does he question the biases in many of those fairy tales. As educator and writer Herb Kohl noted in a review of the books written for the first and second grade, the literature sections include "tales of royalty and wealth filled with passive or wicked females, evil stepparents, pure and handsome princes....Young women need to be rescued from older women, purified for marriage into royalty or sacrificed to save their fathers." By contrast, I try to promote values in my classroom that include respect for all types of families, cooperative, nonhierarchical approaches to working together, and equality of the sexes and all races.

One could argue that *What Your First [through Sixth] Grader Needs to Know* is meant for parents and shouldn't be held to such standards of criticism. However, similar problems permeate a curriculum for schools published by Hirsch's Core Knowledge Foundation. The curriculum, *Core Knowledge Sequence Grades 1–6,* is designed explicitly for schools. Further, Hirsch advocates that the sequence "should be taught as recommended, with no omissions or rearrangement of content to a different grade level." The fourth-grade literature sequence, for example, calls for the students to read ten "stories." Seven of them are Euro-American: *A Voyage to Lilliput, The Legend of Sleepy Hollow, Rip Van Winkle, Little Women, Robinson Crusoe, Treasure Island,* and *Little House on the Prairie.*

For some unexplained reason, there is a particular emphasis on *Robinson Crusoe*. This emphasis is typified in *A School's Guide to Core Knowledge: Ideas for Implementation* by Constance Jones. Principal of the Three Oaks School in Fort Myers, Florida — the country's first "Core Knowledge" school — Jones twice mentions that students read *Robinson Crusoe*: once as an example of how students "practice the skills of recognizing the main idea in a passage," and second as part of a Cross-Disciplinary Unit on Christopher Columbus and "discovery." During the discovery unit, children read *Robinson Crusoe* as a class, and everyone keeps a daily journal "about the adventures he/she would have if he/she were marooned on an island." The *Core Knowledge Sequence Grades 1–6* suggests that teachers may want to purchase class sets of *Robinson Crusoe*.

Robinson Crusoe, written by Daniel Defoe in 1719–1720, is an interesting choice. Often considered one of the first true novels ever written in English, it has an undeniable place in the literary canon. But the book also uncritically mirrors the racial, religious, and imperialist biases that dominated English culture at the time. As Edward Said, professor of comparative literature at Columbia University, notes in his book *Culture and Imperialism, Robinson Crusoe* is "the prototypical modern realistic novel" in which the protagonist "is the founder of a new world, which he rules and reclaims for Christianity and England." [1]

Hirsch says he is concerned that "disadvantaged" children be enfranchised by acquiring "cultural knowledge." Yet how can an uncritical look at a novel that constantly refers to nonwhite people as "savages" and is infused with a belief in the inherent superiority of white people help so-called disadvantaged children?

One might counter that the study of such a book would be valuable if it were done in the context of a study of colonialism and imperialism. Unfortunately, Hirsch instead has students read *Robinson Crusoe* as part of a unit that explicitly equates "discovery" with "adventure," not with colonialism.

Which gets me into my other criticism of Hirsch's approach to culture: he not only neglects the cultures of those who have been traditionally silenced in school textbooks, such as working-class whites and people of color, but even when emphasizing "traditional culture," he has children do so uncritically. Would it be too much to ask that students study competing narratives of people in history in order to understand the complexity of social phenomena? Couldn't they be taught to question Defoe's use of the term *savages* as a way of exploring the social dynamics of the time?

Hirsch seems content that students know who wrote *Robinson Crusoe* and when, and understand its plot line and major characters. This kind of "just the facts ma'am" approach may produce people good at playing Trivial Pursuit but doesn't produce critical thinkers. Instead, I believe a teacher should help students read such literature critically and set it in a broader context that raises fundamental issues about justice and equality.

A teacher, for example, might have students write from the perspective of Friday, Crusoe's "servant." Or they could locate the events in the novel as part of the African slave trade, which might cast Crusoe in a less than heroic light. (Crusoe shipwrecks while on a voyage to West Africa to capture slaves.)

I'm not suggesting that children shouldn't learn what some would call "traditional" American history and culture, only that it be done critically and broadened to include all the peoples who have shared the North American continent and who have shaped our history. Even within the "European-American" tradition there is a rich history of social and ideological conflict, which is usually omitted in school textbooks. Hirsch's materials continue this long-standing American tradition of silencing those voices. In the process, he sends a powerful message that one culture, the dominant culture, is more valuable than others.

It's true that students need to know that mainstream culture is more *valued* in our society, but that should not be equated with what is more *valuable*. Yes, students need to know that they will be at a disadvantage in the world of politics, education, and the humanities if they don't learn about the dominant culture. But that's not enough.

To function effectively within future society, students will need much more than what Hirsch suggests. Cultural literacy is far more fluid and complex than his approach outlines. And it's not just a question of a dominant or nondominant culture. His very approach to "knowledge" assumes that students "receive" and succumb to knowledge and the values and institutions it represents, rather than viewing knowledge critically and challenging its underlying assumptions.

Promotional rhetoric aside, the *Core Knowledge Sequence* is not substantially better, and perhaps worse, than many basal social studies, science, and literature series. In fairness, it should be noted that both Hirsch and his Core Knowledge Foundation say that this planned sequence should only consume 50 percent of the teaching time in a school. Yet when I read the dozens of things that are to be covered, I was incredulous. The history sections alone – if done well – would require a significant portion of the school day.

It should also be recognized that many good teachers are used to dealing with lock-step curriculum programs and won't passively accept such scripted materials. Just as teachers select a few interesting poems and stories from basal readers, they may do the same with Hirsch's materials.

Hirsch and Knowledge

The only conceivable way that a teacher could "cover" the amount of material prescribed by the Core Knowledge Foundation in the suggested time is if one defined learning as superficial acquaintance with "facts" – elevating word recognition to the status of knowledge. Although the *Core Knowledge Sequence* says it is "not a list of facts to be memorized," practical realities will push in that direction.

In analyzing Hirsch's books, it's clear that his definition of knowledge is synonymous with a superficial familiarity with facts and relies on rote memorization and the acquisition of disconnected bits of information. In fact, Hirsch himself admits that his lists will almost certainly lead to "the trivialization of cultural information." Moreover, it is likely that Hirsch's "core knowledge" curriculum might serve as fertile ground for a new crop of standardized tests that rely on "facts" rather than knowledge.

In an age where technological advances have led to what is uniformly acknowledged to be an "information glut," Hirsch stands firmly in a nineteenth century approach and boldly states that "only a few hundred pages of information stand between the literate and illiterate, between dependence and autonomy." And in many cases, Hirsch implies, it's not necessary to understand *why* something is important; one must just know that it *is* important.

When meeting with college-level English teachers from the National Council of Teachers of English and the Modern Language Association in 1987, Hirsch was criticized for the "narrowing of national culture" and the teaching of small bits of information. "A telling moment came when he [Hirsch] said it wasn't so important to read Shakespeare or see performances of the plays themselves – plot summaries or 'Lamb's Tales' would do fine," according to

Peter Elbow, a professor of English at the University of Massachusetts at Amherst. Ultimately, Hirsch's emphasis on the transmissions of disconnected facts – what he calls "core knowledge" – directly contrasts with the need for students to think, analyze, critique, and understand their world.

Even if the facts that Hirsch promoted were completely multicultural, his approach would be flawed by his definition of knowledge. Students need more than facts. They need to understand the relationships between "facts" and whose interests certain "facts" serve. They need to question the validity of the "facts," to ask questions such as "why" and "how." They need to know how to find information, to solve problems, to express themselves in oral and written language so their opinions can be shared with, and have an influence on, broader society. It is only through such an approach that students can construct their own beliefs, their own knowledge.

In his sections on the American Revolution and the Constitution, for example, Hirsch essentially dismisses as irrelevant the pro-slavery, antiwoman assumptions of our Founding Fathers. No mention is made that about 40 percent of the delegates to the Constitutional Convention were slave owners, that Washington himself had slaves, and that in 1779 he ordered that U.S. troops launch an expedition against the Iroquois Confederacy and seek the "total destruction and devastation and the capture of as many persons of every age and sex as possible....Parties should be detached to lay waste all settlements around, with instructions to do it in the most effectual manner, that the country may not be merely overrun, but destroyed."

A teacher should not shy away from presenting a complete picture of Washington, and should encourage students to grapple with such facts. A teacher might, for example, have students write a dialogue poem between Washington and one of his slaves. Or do a fictional role play of a Constitutional Convention in which disenfranchised people speak and advocate for themselves. Or have students imagine they were members of the Iroquois Confederacy in 1779.

It is only when students compare, analyze, and evaluate information that they can go beyond memorization and construct meaning. As Michael Hartoonian, head of social studies for the Wisconsin Department of Public Instruction, writes: "Information provided by a teacher or textbook is generally, and wrongfully, perceived as knowledge....[Instead] knowledge is something created through a process of personal involvement that allows for complex relationships between the learners (including the teacher) and the text and context of the classroom, even when the classroom includes the larger community."

The National Council of Teachers of English was even more explicit in its critique of Hirsch's approach. In a 1988 resolution just shortly after Hirsch hit the national limelight, the council passed a resolution underscoring its concern with "curricula that reduce literature to lists of information." The resolution went on to note that reducing literature "to an accumulation of particular facts such as titles, names, phrases, and dates negates its very integrity."

Hirsch and Teaching

Embedded in Hirsch's viewpoint on culture and knowledge is his approach to teaching. First, rather than calling upon students to study less but understand more, he advocates a more-the-merrier approach — regardless of whether children understand what is presented to them. Second, he distorts the relationship between content and skills, criticizing what he claims are current emphases on "mental skills," "learning-to-learn skills," and "critical thinking skills."

On the issue of more versus less, good teaching requires a precarious balance between exposing students to lots of information and studying a few topics in depth. While Hirsch alludes to this balance, ultimately he advocates pumping as much information as possible into students. This stands in sharp contrast to the fine work of many teachers — whether in groups such as the Coalition of Essential Schools or as part of national curriculum groups such as the National Council of Teachers of English — who hold that "less is more" and encourage in-depth projects by students.

The question of content versus skills is a bit more complicated. Hirsch emphasizes content over skills largely on the grounds that students will understand what they read only if they have sufficient "relevant prior knowledge." Likewise, he argues that broader thinking skills also depend on a wealth of "relevant knowledge."

Like any good teacher, Hirsch recognizes that there is an important relationship between content and skills. No good teacher would deny the importance of prior knowledge in the educational process or that adults have important information to share with children. Hirsch, however, distorts this relationship by overemphasizing content to the degree that the teaching of skills all but disappears from the curriculum.

Despite Hirsch's rhetoric of giving children what they need to seek meaning from reading, his prescriptions make it likely that reading will become a mechanical process dependent on calling up what one has memorized. But isn't reading a more complicated process? Doesn't it also involve learning strategies to understand and critique what one has read? Further, students need to be taught how to read difficult texts that may go beyond previously learned "relevant knowledge" – otherwise they'll rarely venture into and understand new areas of knowledge. Rather than adopt Hirsch's approach, we should establish classrooms where children are encouraged to take responsibility for their learning, to become independent writers, readers, thinkers, and speakers, and to take an active role in creating a more just society.

I also disagree with Hirsch's basic premise that teachers throughout America underemphasize content and overemphasize skills. Hirsch charges that the main problem in U.S. schools is "educational formalism," that is, there is an overemphasis on teaching "mental skills" and that to the degree there is content, it is fragmented. My experience, however, is that too few teachers are concerned with mental skills and too many follow content-heavy basal systems in a lock-step manner. John Goodlad, author of *A Place Called School,* found in his research that "not even 1 percent of the instructional time in high school was devoted to discussion that requires some kind of response involving reasoning or perhaps an opinion from students."

The problem is not that students don't get the "core knowledge" and facts that Hirsch holds dear. Rather, the problem is that they are being bombarded with thousands of bits of disconnected information and rarely write, discuss, or read things that are meaningful to their lives.

What Should Kids Learn?

One of Hirsch's major arguments is that there needs to be a collective discussion about what children learn. I agree. We just disagree on what and how. Hirsch's work, for instance, has many omissions. He says little about racism and sexism. History from the perspective of working people is virtually an unknown. The issue of the mass media and its biases is nonexistent. Other key problems in society – violence, the environment, rapid technological change – are ignored. Hirsch addressed some controversies, such as bilingualism and multilingualism, but mainly to oppose them.

Instead of opposing multilingualism and bilingualism and ignoring issues of racism and prejudice, it would be better to figure out how to prepare our children to live in a multicultural, technological, ever-changing world. Children need to develop cross-cultural literacy, critical abilities, and respect for different viewpoints and experience. They also need to learn social responsibility and their individual role in the collective struggle against discrimination, prejudice, and inequality. Shouldn't such issues be at least as important in our "core knowledge" as learning the plot line of *Robinson Crusoe?*

In attempting to answer the question, "What should our kids learn?" the list approach should be discarded and a different framework adopted. One such effort is the K–12 Reform in the Milwaukee Public Schools. The core of this systemwide curricular reform is ten "Teaching and Learning Goals" developed by parents, educators, and community members. The goals, in turn, are detailed in more specific age-appropriate "performance indicators."

For example, the first goal is, "Students will project anti-racist, anti-biased attitudes through their participation in a multi-lingual, multi-ethnic, culturally diverse curriculum." Implicit in the goal, and explicit in the performance indicators, is a sense that students have a social responsibility to act upon what they have learned. This is radically different from Hirsch's approach, which not only views students as passive recipients of facts, but also as passive members of society.

The K–12 reform effort differs from Hirsch's not just in content but in approaches to teaching. While Hirsch explicitly states that his core sequence does not require any specific teaching method, the K–12 reform effort openly advocates teaching styles that are student-centered and activity-based, use heterogeneous groupings, and promote deep thinking and problem solving.

Hirsch and School Reform

Never humble, Hirsch argues that his approach is the solution to our country's educational crisis. Even more astounding, he also maintains it is key to economic reform and the reduction of poverty.

Hirsch says that reform must be based on an approach that teaches children "a specific core of knowledge in each of the first six grades." Such a low-cost proposal undoubtedly appeals to some policymakers. Unfortunately, it ignores institutional causes of inequity, which have been eloquently summarized by Jonathan Kozol in *Savage Inequalities*. These include inadequate and unequal funding for decent and safe facilities, lower class size, adequate technology, teacher training, and programs for children with special needs.

Hirsch's stance also dovetails with the tendency to scapegoat our schools for all our country's economic problems. He writes: "The great scandal of the American school system during the past 10 years is that poverty has increased in a rising economy. This misfortune is mainly due to a lack of economically useful skills among the poverty class, a lack created by the unequal education of our students."

Like many of his conservative counterparts, Hirsch wants to blame poverty on the schools and suggests that there are educational solutions to fundamental economic problems, such as the massive global restructuring that has led to the elimination of hundreds of thousands of jobs as multinational companies seek out ever-cheaper sources of labor and production. The subtext in this approach is obvious: no fundamental economic or political change is necessary to ensure equity in our schools or society. One would hope that such silliness would speak for itself. But unfortunately, Hirsch's views on literacy and curriculum are already affecting classroom practice and parental perspectives.

For kids in my class who briefly read Hirsch's article on high mountains, or for the hundreds of thousands of others who are daily bombarded with facts either through Hirsch's series or one of several basal programs, the issue is not whether they will be able to recall 50, 500 or even 5,000 core facts. The issue is whether they will be in classrooms where they are respected and challenged — not only to understand the world but to develop the cross-cultural perspectives, critical skills, and moral courage needed to deal with the vast racial, gender, class, and ecological problems that their tomorrow will bring.

Bibliography

APPLE, MICHAEL. *Official Knowledge: Democratic Education in a Conservative Age,* New York: Routledge, 1993.

BRAGAW, DONALD, AND H. MICHAEL HARTOONIAN. "Social Studies: The Study of People in Society," in *Content of the Curriculum, 1988 ASCD Yearbook,* edited by Ronald S. Brandt.

CHRISTENBURY, LEILA. "Cultural Literacy: A Terrible Idea Whose Time Has Come," *English Journal,* January 1989.

CORE KNOWLEDGE FOUNDATION. *A School's Guide to Core Knowledge: Ideas for Implementation,* Charlottesville, VA: Core Knowledge Foundation, 1991.

ELBOW, PETER. *What Is English?* New York: Modern Language Association/National Council of Teachers of English, 1990.

FRASER, JAMES W., AND THERESA PERRY. *Freedom's Plow: Teaching in the Multicultural Classroom,* New York: Routledge, 1993.

GOODLAD, JOHN. *A Place Called School,* New York: McGraw-Hill, 1984.

HIRSCH, E. D. *A First Dictionary of Cultural Literacy: What Our Children Need to Know,* Boston: Houghton Mifflin, 1989.

HIRSCH, E. D. *Cultural Literacy: What Every American Needs to Know,* New York: Vintage Books, 1988.

HIRSCH, E. D. *What Your First [through Sixth] Grader Needs to Know,* New York: Doubleday, 1991–1993.

KOHL, HERBERT. "Rotten to the Core," *The Nation,* April 1992, pp. 457–61.

SAID, EDWARD. *Culture and Imperialism,* New York: Knopf, 1993.

TAKAKI, RONALD. *A Different Mirror: A History of Multicultural America,* Boston: Little, Brown, 1993.

Why Students Should Study History: An Interview with Howard Zinn

The following is condensed from an interview with Howard Zinn, who has taught history and political science at Spelman College in Atlanta and at Boston University. He is the author of *A People's History of the United States, The Politics of History, Declarations of Independence,* and, most recently, *You Can't Be Neutral On a Moving Train: A Personal History of Our Times*. He was interviewed in the winter of 1992 by Barbara Miner of *Rethinking Schools*.

Why should students study history?

I started studying history with one view in mind: to look for answers to the issues and problems I saw in the world about me. By the time I went to college I had worked in a shipyard, had been in the air force, had been in a war. I came to history asking questions about war and peace, about wealth and poverty, about racial division.

Sure, there's a certain interest in inspecting the past and it can be fun, sort of like a detective story. I can make an argument for knowledge for its own sake as something that can add to your life. But while that's good, it is small in relation to the very large objective of trying to understand and do something about the issues that face us in the world today.

Students should be encouraged to go into history in order to come out of it, and should be discouraged from going into history and getting lost in it, as some historians do.

What do you see as some of the major problems in how U.S. history has been taught in this country?

One major problem has been the intense focus on U.S. history in isolation from the world. This is a problem that all nations have — their nationalistic focus on their own history — and it goes to absurd lengths. Some states in this country even require a year-long course in the history of that state.

But even if you are willing to see the United States in relation to world history, you face the problem that we have not looked at the world in an equitable way. We have concentrated on the Western world, in fact on Western Europe. I remember coming into my first class in Spelman College in Atlanta in 1956 and finding that there was no required course in black history, or Asian or African history, but there was a required course in the history of England. And there on the board was this chart of the Tudors and the Stuarts, the dynasties of England.

For the United States, emphasis has been particularly glaring in terms of Latin America, which is that part of the world closest to us and with which we've had the most to do economically and politically.

Another glaring problem has been the emphasis in teaching American history through the eyes of the important and powerful people, through the presidents, the Congress, the Supreme Court, the generals, the industrialists. History textbooks don't say, "We are going to tell the story of the Mexican War from the standpoint of the generals," but when they tell us it was a great military victory, that's exactly what they are doing.

Taking that as an example, if one were to have a more inclusive view of the war with Mexico, what would be some of the themes and perspectives one would include?

The Mexican War is an example of how one event raises so many issues. You'd have to see the war first of all as more than a military action. So often the history of war is dominated by the story of battles, and this is a way of diverting attention from the political factors behind a war. It's possible to concentrate upon the battles of the Mexican War and just to talk about the triumphant march into Mexico City, and not talk about the relationship of the Mexican War to slavery and to the acquisition of territories that might possibly be slave territories.

Another thing that is neglected in the Mexican War is the viewpoint of the ordinary soldiers. The soldiers who had volunteered for the Mexican War — you didn't need a draft because so many people in the working classes were so destitute that they would join the military on the promise of a little bit of pay and mustering-out money and a little bit of prestige — the volunteers went into it not really knowing the bloodshed it would involve. And then so many of them deserted. For example, seven regiments of General Winfield Scott deserted on the road to Mexico City.

You should tell the story of the Massachusetts volunteers who went into the Mexican War. Half of them died, and the half who returned were invited to a homecoming party, and when a commanding officer got up to address the gathering, they booed him off the platform.

I think it's a good idea also to do something that isn't done anywhere so far as I know in histories in any country, and that is, tell the story of the war from the standpoint of the other side, of "the enemy." To tell the story of the Mexican War from the standpoint of the Mexicans means to ask, How did they feel about having 40 percent of their territory taken away from them as a result of the war? How did they view the incident that President Polk used as a reason for the beginning of the war? Did it look real or manufactured to them?

You'd also have to talk about the people in the United States who protested against the war. That would be the time to bring up Henry Thoreau and his essay, "Civil Disobedience."

You'd have to look at Congress and how it behaved. You'd have to look at Abraham Lincoln, who was in the House of Representatives during the Mexican War. You'd learn a lot about politicians and politics because you'd see that Abraham Lincoln on the one hand spoke up against the war, but on the other hand voted to give money to finance the war. This is so important because this is something that is repeated again and again in American history: the feeble opposition in Congress to presidential wars, and then the voting of funds for whatever the president has initiated.

How do you prevent history lessons from becoming a recitation of dates and battles and congresspersons and presidents?

You can take any incident in American history and enrich it and find parallels with today. One important thing is not to concentrate on chronological order, but to go back and forth and find similarities and analogies.

You should ask students if anything in a particular historical event reminds them of something they read in the newspapers or see on television about the world today. When you press students to make connections, to abstract from the uniqueness of a particular historical event and find something it has in common with another event, then history becomes alive, not just past but present.

And, of course, you must raise the controversial questions and ask students, "Was it right for us to take Mexican territory? Should we be proud of that, should we celebrate that?" History teachers often think they must avoid judgments of right and wrong because, after all, those are matters of subjective opinions, those are issues on which students will disagree and teachers will disagree.

But it's the areas of disagreement that are the most important. Questions of right and wrong and justice are exactly the questions that should be raised all the time. When students are asked, "Is this right, is this wrong?" then it becomes interesting, then they can have a debate, especially if they learn that there's no simple, absolute, agreed-upon, universal answer. It's not like giving them multiple choice questions where they are right or wrong. I think that's a tremendous advance in their understanding of what education is.

Teachers must also address the problem that people have been miseducated to become dependent on government, to think that their supreme act as citizens is to go to the polls and vote very two years or four years. That's where the history of social movements comes in. Teachers should dwell on Shay's Rebellion, on colonial rebellions, on the abolitionist movement, on the populist movement, on the labor movement, and so on, and make sure these social movements don't get lost in the overall story of presidents and Congresses and Supreme Courts. Emphasizing social and protest movements in the making of history gives students a feeling that they as citizens are the most important actors in history.

Students, for example, should learn that during the Depression there were strikes and demonstrations all over the country. And it was that turmoil and protest that created the atmosphere in which Roosevelt and Congress passed Social Security and unemployment insurance and housing subsidies and so on.

How can teachers foster critical thinking so that students don't merely memorize a new, albeit more progressive, set of facts?

Substituting one indoctrination for another is a danger and it's very hard to deal with. After all, the teacher, no matter how hard she or he tries, is the dominant figure in the classroom and has the power of authority and of grades. It's easy for the teacher to fall into the trap of bullying students into accepting one set of facts or ideas. It takes hard work and delicate dealings with students to overcome that.

The way I've tried to deal with that problem is to make it clear to the students that when we study history we are dealing with controversial issues with no one, absolute, godlike answer. And that I, as a teacher, have my opinion and they can have their opinions, and that I, as a teacher, will try to present as much information as I can but that I may leave out information. I try to make them understand that while there are experts on facts, on little things, on the big issues, on the controversies and the issues of right and wrong and justice, there are no experts and their opinion is as good as mine.

But how do you then foster a sense of justice and avoid the trap of relativity that, "Well, some people say this and some people say that"?

I find such relativity especially true on the college level, where there's a great tendency to indecisiveness. People are unwilling to take a stand on a moral issue because, well, there's this side and there's that side.

I deal with this by example. I never simply present both sides and leave it at that. I take a stand. If I'm dealing with Columbus, I say, "Look, there are these people who say that we shouldn't judge Columbus by the standards of the twentieth century. But my view is that basic moral standards are not different for the twentieth century or the fifteenth century."

I don't simply lay history out on a platter and say, "I don't care what you chose; they're both valid." I let them know, "No, I care what you chose; I don't think they're both valid. But you don't have to agree with me." I want them to know that if people don't take a stand, the world will remain unchanged, and who wants that?

Are there specific ways that teachers can foster an antiracist perspective?

To a great extent, this moral objective is not considered in teaching history. I think people have to be given the facts of slavery, the facts of racial segregation, the facts of government complicity in racial segregation, the facts of the fight for equality. But that is not enough.

I think students need to be aroused emotionally on the issue of equality. They have to try to feel what it was like, to be a slave, to be jammed into slave ships, to be separated from your family. Novels, poems, autobiographies, memoirs, the reminiscences of ex-slaves, the letters that slaves wrote, the writings of Frederick Douglass – I think they have to be introduced as much as possible. Students should learn the words of people themselves, to feel their anger, their indignation.

In general, I don't think there has been enough use of literature in history. People should read Richard Wright's *Black Boy;* they should read the poems of Countee Cullen; they should read the novels of Alice Walker, the poems of Langston Hughes, Lorraine Hansbury's *A Raisin in the Sun*. These writings have an emotional impact that can't be found in an ordinary recitation of history.

It is especially important that students learn about the relationship of the United States government to slavery and race.

It's very easy to fall into the view that slavery and racial segregation were a southern problem. The federal government is very often exempted from responsibility for the problem, and is presented as a benign force helping black people on the road to equality. In our time, students are taught how Eisenhower sent his troops to Little Rock, Arkansas, and Kennedy sent troops to Oxford, Mississippi, and Congress passed civil rights laws.

Yet the federal government is very often an obstacle to resolving those problems of race, and when it enters it comes in late in the picture. Abraham Lincoln was not the initiator of the movement against slavery but a follower of a movement that had developed for thirty years by the time he became president in 1860; it was the antislavery movement that was the major force creating the atmosphere in which emancipation took place following the Civil War. And it was the president and Congress and the Supreme Court that ignored the Thirteenth, Fourteenth, and Fifteenth Amendments after they were passed. In the 1960s it wasn't Johnson and Kennedy who were the leaders and initiators of the movement for race equality; it was black people.

In addition to focusing on social movements and having a more consciously antiracist perspective, what are some other thematic ways in which the teaching of history must change?

I think the issue of class and class conflict needs to be addressed more honestly because it is ignored in traditional nationalist history. This is true not just of the United States but of other countries. Nationhood is a cover for extreme conflicts among classes in society, in our country, from its founding, from the making of the Constitution. Too often, there's a tendency to overlook these conflicts and concentrate on the creation of a national identity.

How does a teacher deal with the intersection of race, class, and gender in terms of U.S. history, in particular that the white working-class has often been complicit, consciously, or unconsciously, in some very unforgivable actions?

The complicity of poor white people in racism, the complicity of males in sexism, is a very important issue. It seems to me that complicity can't be understood without showing the intense hardships that poor white people faced in this country, making it easier for them to look for scapegoats for their condition. You have to recognize the problems of white working people in order to understand why they turn racist, because they aren't born racist.

When discussing the Civil War, teachers should point out that only a small percentage of the white population of the South owned slaves. The rest of the white population was poor and they were driven to support slavery and to be racist by the messages of those who controlled society — that they would be better off if the Negroes were put in a lower position, and that those calling for black equality were threatening the lives of these ordinary white people.

In the history of labor struggles, you should show how blacks and whites were used against one another, how white workers would go out on strike and then black people, desperate themselves for jobs, would be brought in to replace the white workers, how all-white craft unions excluded black workers, and how all this creates murderously intense racial antagonisms. So the class and race issues are very much intertwined, as is the gender issue.

One of the ways of giving some satisfaction to men who are themselves exploited is to make them masters in their own household. So they may be humiliated on the job, but they come back home and humiliate their wives and their children. There's a wonderful short story by a black woman writer, Ann Petry, "Like a Winding Sheet" that should be required reading in school. It's about a black man who is humiliated on the job and comes home and, on the flimsiest of reasons, beats his wife. The story is told in such a way as to make you really understand the pent-up anger that explodes inside a family as a result of what happens out in the world. In all these instances of racial and sexual mistreatment, it is important for students to understand that the roots of such hostility are social, environmental, situational, and are not an inevitability of human nature. It is also important to show how these antagonisms so divide people from one another as to make it difficult for them to solve their common problems in united action.

How can we explain the roots of this complicity in racism and sexism by white working-class people without falling into the trap of condoning it?

That's always a problem: how do you explain something without justifying it? That issue, as a theoretical issue, needs to be explained because it's a common confusion. You need to make the point again and again that trying to understand why people do something is not the same as justifying it. And you need to give specific historical examples of that problem, or, as I suggested, literary examples.

How can you teach white students to take an antiracist perspective that isn't based merely on guilt over the things that white people have done to people of color?

If such a perspective is based only on guilt, it doesn't have a secure foundation. It has to be based on empathy and on self-interest, on an understanding that the divisions between black and white have not just resulted in the exploitation of black people, even though they've been the greatest victims, but have prevented whites and blacks from getting together to bring about the social change that would benefit them all. Showing the self-interest is also important in order to avoid the patronizing view of feeling sorry for someone, of giving somebody equality because you feel guilty about what has been done to them.

At the same time, to approach the issue merely on the basis of self-interest would be wrong, because people should learn to empathize with other people even where there is no visible, immediate self-interest.

In response to concerns about multiculturalism, there's more lip service to include events and perspectives affecting women and people of color. But often it's presented as more facts and people to learn, without any fundamental change in perspective. What would be the approach of a truly antiracist, multicultural perspective in U.S. history?

I've noticed this problem in some of the new textbooks, which obviously are trying to respond to the need for a multicultural approach. What I find is a bland eclecticism where everything has equal weight. You add more facts, you add more continents, you add more cultures, you add more people. But then it becomes a confusing melange in which you've added a lot of different elements but without any real emphasis on what had previously been omitted. You're left with a kind of unemotional, cold combination salad.

You need the equivalent of affirmative action in education. What affirmative action does is to say, look, things have been slanted one way for a long time. We're going to pay special attention to this person or to this group of people because they have been left out for so long.

People ask me why in my book *A People's History of the United States* I did not simply take the things that I put in and add them to the orthodox approaches so, as they put it, the book would be better balanced. But there's a way in which this so-called balance leaves people nowhere, with no moral sensibility, no firm convictions, no outrage, no indignation, no energy to go anywhere.

I think it is important to pay special attention to the history of black people, of Indians, of women, in a way that highlights not only the facts but the emotional intensity of such issues.

Is it possible for history to be objective?

Objectivity is neither possible nor desirable.

It's not possible because all history is subjective, all history represents a point of view. History is always a selection from an infinite number of facts, and everybody makes the selection differently, based on their values and what they think is important. Since it's not possible to be objective, you should be honest about that.

Objectivity is not desirable because if we want to have an effect on the world, we need to emphasize those things that will make students more active citizens and more moral people.

One of the problems for high school history teachers is they may have five periods and thirty kids in each class, and before you know it they're dealing with 150 students. What types of projects and approaches can they use?

The most important thing is to get students to do independent reading and research. Tell the students, "Pick something that interests you, pick out a person that interests you." Your job as teacher is to present them with a wide spectrum of events and people, and not just the usual heroes of history but all sorts of people or incidents that they may never have heard of but that might intrigue them. I find that when students have a research project of their own, they can get excited about it – especially if they are allowed to choose from a complex set of possibilities.

How can a progressive teacher promote a radical perspective within a bureaucratic, conservative institution? Teachers sometimes either push the limits so far that they alienate their colleagues or get fired, or they're so afraid that they tone down what they really think. How can a teacher resolve this dilemma?

The problem certainly exists on the college and university level. People want to get tenure, they want to keep teaching, they want to get promoted, they want to get salary raises, and so there are all these economic punishments if they do something that looks outlandish and radical and different. But I've always believed that the main problem with college and university teachers has been self-censorship. I suspect that the same thing is true in the high schools, although you have to be more sympathetic with high school teachers because they operate in a much more repressive atmosphere. I've seen again and again where college and university teachers don't really have a problem in, for instance, using my *People's History* in their classrooms, but high school teachers always have a problem. They can't get it officially adopted, they have to get permission, they have to photocopy parts of it themselves in order to pass it out to the students, they have to worry about parents complaining, about what the head of the department or the principal or the school superintendent will say.

But I still believe, based on a lot of contact with high school teachers over the past few years, that while there's a danger of becoming overly assertive and insensitive to how others might view you, the most common behavior is timidity. Teachers withdraw and use the real fact of outside control as an excuse for teaching in the orthodox way.

Teachers need to take risks. The problem is how to minimize those risks. One important way is to make sure that you present material in class making it clear that it is subjective, that it is controversial, that you are not laying down the law for students. Another important thing is to be extremely tolerant of students who disagree with your views, or students who express racist or sexist ideas. I don't mean tolerant in the sense of not challenging such ideas, but tolerant in the sense of treating them as human beings. It's important to develop a reputation that you don't give kids poor grades on the basis of their disagreements with you. You need to create an atmosphere of freedom in the classroom.

It's also important to talk with other teachers to gain support and encouragement, to organize. Where there are teachers unions, those are logical places for teachers to support and defend one another. Where there are not teachers unions, teachers should always think how they can organize and create a collective strength.

Teachers don't always know where to get those other perspectives. Do you have any tips?

The orthodox perspective is easy to get. But once teachers begin to look for other perspectives, once they start out on that road, they will quickly be led from one thing to another to another.

So it's not as daunting as people might think?

No. It's all there. It's in the library.

Distorting Latino History: The California Textbook Controversy

ELIZABETH MARTÍNEZ

When we read a social studies test for fifth graders that refers to slavery as a "life-style," we might think it's some book from the 1940s or 1950s. Alas, such descriptions can be found in the glossy series published by Houghton Mifflin and adopted for California schools in 1990–91. Even worse, this series was supposed to mark a major break with the longtime Eurocentric textbook tradition.

California had invited publishers to submit new histories for grades K–8 as part of an overall effort to upgrade its instructional materials and methods. Houghton Mifflin was the only house that submitted books for all those grades. It also was the only house that prepared books specifically intended to fit into a new history and social studies "framework," or curriculum, that California had adopted.

The framework called for pupils to study history much earlier and more extensively than in the past. Recognizing that the majority of California's 3.7 million elementary and junior high pupils are now young people of color, the framework also required that textbooks "accurately portray the cultural and racial diversity of our society." (Nevertheless, the framework, written by conservative historian Diane Ravitch, by no means advocated equality between peoples.) The main author of the Houghton Mifflin series is Gary Nash, a UCLA professor with a reputation for advocating multiculturalism.

California's Board of Education adopted the Houghton Mifflin series and an additional eighth-grade history from Holt, Rinehart & Winston despite protests from thousands of people in virtually every racial and ethnic sector (including Muslims, who had been the first to object) as well as gays, lesbians, and the disabled. Since local school districts are not legally obliged to buy the state-approved books in California, the struggle continued.

Eventually most local school boards adopted the approved texts, sometimes with supplemental readings. In Oakland, where students are almost 92 percent of color, both the Houghton Mifflin series and the Holt, Rinehart & Winston title were rejected. (The task of finding satisfactory substitutes has yet to be resolved.) In San Francisco, where 83 percent of the student population is of color, the new books were finally adopted on the condition that supplemental readings be used. However, the school district placed just one copy of each supplemental title in each school.

Behind all the highly publicized debate, one can assume some heavy-duty politicking. Houghton Mifflin calculated that the California market alone could yield $52.9 million in sales of the textbook series. With so much at stake, Houghton Mifflin hired a public relations firm for the first time in its history to help win state approval.

Those defending the Houghton Mifflin titles claimed that they were a vast improvement over the past, with much more information about people of color and their perspectives. "We have 80 pages on African history for 12-year-olds," Gary Nash pointed out. But a numerical increase in textual references or images doesn't promote multiculturalism if the content leaves a fundamentally Eurocentric worldview in place. The occasional inclusion of dissenting views from people of color may give some balance to isolated passages; it does not alter the dominant perspective.

The worldview put forth in these texts rests on defining the United States as "a nation of immigrants." This view sees Native Americans as the first "immigrants," based on their having come across the Bering Strait from Asia (but this theory is rejected by many Indians, a disagreement not mentioned in the series). After Indians come Africans (but weren't they brought here in chains?) and then Mexicans (but wasn't their homeland seized by Anglo force?). Europeans and Asians round out the list of so-called immigrants.

The immigrant model has usually included the "melting pot" metaphor; the Houghton Mifflin series rejects that now tarnished image in favor of the "salad bowl," which allows different peoples to retain their ethnic identity and culture inside one big unified society. But how different is the bowl from the pot?

Both ignore issues of power and domination, such as which groups in society have power and which don't or which groups dominate and which are dominated. Both are molded by a national identity firmly rooted in an Anglo-American culture and perspective. As critics of the textbooks pointed out, the norm to which so-called immigrants are supposed to relate is white, Anglo-Saxon, and usually Protestant – in short, WASP – and the Mexican-American, for example, is not a "real" American. The Houghton Mifflin texts hammer home the power and authority of this norm with an extraordinary quantity of U.S. flags (in the K–5 book alone, twenty-nine depictions compared to zero flags from other nations).

The Eurocentric viewpoint of the series can be found in its treatment of all U.S. peoples of color, exemplified by one sentence in a literature selection in the Grade 5 textbook: "She had blue eyes and white skin, like an angel" (which reduces us darkies to being devils, I assume). Scores of inaccuracies, distortions, sanitizations, omissions, and outright racist accounts pepper these books. Here we'll take a look at how the Houghton Mifflin books depict Mexican-Americans and other Latinos in the United States. (Having limited space, we'll defer a review of how Mexico and other parts of Latin America are portrayed, although this certainly affects the image and self-image of Latinos living in the United States. Also, not every error will be noted.)

Five major problems appear, then, ranging from general perspective to the handling of key events involving people of Mexican origin. The first general question is, Do we even exist?

Invisibilization

Increasing the quantity of references to a people doesn't multiculturalize a textbook, as we said; at the same time, invisibility definitely hurts. The Houghton Mifflin series gives very shabby treatment to Latinos in this respect.

By the third grade it would seem reasonable to expect real awareness of Mexicans in the United States, especially when the textbook *From Sea to Shining Sea* has a sixty-page unit called "Settling the Land." But no. In the whole book, Mexican-Americans appear only as farmworkers, and even then their historic role in producing vast agricultural wealth is not recognized (nor is that of Filipinos). A single photo shows an orchard with a rain of almonds being shaken out of some trees – by machine, not people. Nowhere does the text say that agriculture was made possible in the Southwest by an art that Mexicans and Indians taught to Anglos: irrigation.

The fourth-grade book *Oh California* offers many Latinos, but they are almost all "explorers" and "settlers," missionaries, or upper-class ranchers. Nowhere can we find the lower-class Mexicans, nowhere the many Mexicans who were violently repressed and driven off the land – often even lynched – from the Gold Rush days to the 1930s, nowhere the massive strikes by Mexican workers in the 1930s or the deportation of thousands who were actually citizens. Chicanos and Mexicans vanish totally from California in pages 157–259. Then we find a paragraph on East Los Angeles that includes Mexicans in a listing of all immigrant groups; it doesn't say that they formed the original population of Los Angeles and have continued to be a strong presence for more than 200 years.

Oh California briefly describes the United Farm Workers led by César Chávez, in the series' only account of Chicano/Mexicano struggle for U.S. social change. We find nothing about how the courageous farm workers stood up to mass arrests, beatings, and harassment by the growers and their goons. Nothing about Dolores Huerta – one of the best-known women activists for social change in the United States today – who headed the union along with Chávez until his death in 1993. Nothing about the ongoing struggle against pesticides. And nothing about other movements of California Chicanos such as the walkouts by thousands of high school students in 1968 and the anti-Vietnam War march of some 20,000 people on that day in 1970 when police tear-gassed hundreds at a peaceful rally, including this writer, and caused three Chicanos to die. A picture of one "Chicano Power" mural is apparently supposed to suffice for all those years of mass activism.

In *America Will Be,* a basic fifth-grade U.S. history book, Latinos as a people do not exist beyond immigration statistics and other lists, with the exception of a single immigrant family presented totally out of context. Even Latinos as governmental representatives vanish after three pages on Juan de Oñate, who invaded New Mexico for Spain in 1598. From page 128 to page 370, no references at all.

If it is hard to find Mexicans in this series; other Latinos are even less visible. After profiling the great baseball player and humanitarian Roberto Clemente in the Grade 2 text, the series abandons Puerto Ricans. For the millions of Central Americans resident in the United States, Houghton Mifflin includes a single nameless young woman who came from Guatemala for unspecified reasons and lives an undescribed life here (Grade 3 text). In Grades 4 and 5 we get one and two sentences, respectively, referring to refugees from Cuba and Central America – with no explanation of why they had fled.

That Old White Magic: Eurocentrism and Its Values

The books for kindergarten, *The World I See,* and Grade 1, *I Know a Place,* lay the foundation for Eurocentrism. Both include a thematic photo with several pupils of color, including a probable Latino, and the K volume has one story about Mexico. But the drawings in the "Long Ago" pages of the K book are overwhelmingly populated by whites; one image shows thirty-one people out of thirty-five as white, another makes all twenty people white, and so forth. In the Grade 1 book also, everyone from the past is white (e.g., a unit called "Grandma's Album" and another called "I Go with My Family to Grandma's"). The message comes across loud and clear: the foundations of our country are Euro-American (or perhaps people of color don't have grannies). Yet Mexican people settled in what is now the United States from 1598 on.

Some People I Know (Grade 2) introduces Teresa Sánchez of East Los Angeles. The text puts a healthy stress on the merits of being bilingual and bicultural like Teresa, but why did they make her a totally Anglo-looking girl? Any Latina — like this writer — who has grown up longing for blond hair and light-colored eyes will know what a bad message this conveys, especially when everyone else in Teresa's family is dark. (Perhaps she can be one of those angels?)

A special form of the Eurocentric perspective, Hispanicism, flows through the Houghton Mifflin series. Again and again the "customs" and "culture" and "traditions" of the Mexican people in the United States are described as originating in Spain — a European country. Indian or mestizo roots go unnoticed. This would be laughable (how many people in Madrid eat tortillas and beans?) if it were not so racist.

The Houghton Mifflin authors actually discuss Eurocentrism (Grade 8), defining it as "the notion that Europe is the center of the world." They then, however, affirm that point of view by stating, "And for a long period of time it seemed to be. From the 1500s to the 1900s, European countries controlled a large part of the world." End of explanation, leaving readers with a very Eurocentric view of Eurocentrism. The same book tells us that "U.S. citizens...tended to look on Mexico as a backward nation, an attitude that has continued to this day." No comment; no criticism or alternatives to this view are suggested.

If one of the goals of Eurocentrism is to make U.S. history a more comfortable abode for white people, the fifth-grade textbook shows how. The teacher's edition suggests an exercise in which students are asked to think about what it is like to move into a new neighborhood or even a new country: What are the neighbors like? Is it scary? It then says, "Lead them to understand that the colonists in America shared many of the same experiences and feelings." What a novel way to imagine taking over someone's land! Other examples of sanitized treatment abound. For example, the often deadly racism practiced against Mexicans in the Southwest is described as "considerable discrimination" (Grade 4) and "prejudice" (Grade 5).

The series is riddled with a Eurocentric vocabulary: "discoveries," "the New World," "the Age of Exploration," and "Moving West." It also manipulates the reader with self-justifying types of word usage. Again and again Anglo-Americans' "belief" in the rightness of their actions is used to justify how Mexican people and Native Americans have been treated historically. One text (Grade 4) even describes as "idealistic" the U.S. belief that westward expansion would help "bring freedom" to the "less fortunate" Indians and Mexicans.

The use of "dreams" serves a similar purpose, as in statements like, "The forty-niners had *dreams* of becoming very wealthy" (Grade 4, teacher's edition, my italics). Such descriptions tend to make young readers identify with men who in fact often robbed, raped, and murdered people of color. The text goes on to say of the forty-niners that "they did not feel they had to share those dreams with Indians," a remarkably mild way of describing their actual deeds.

Eurocentric usage of "beliefs" and "idealism" and "dreams" – all concepts that many youth embrace – can work wonders. We see this in the series' treatment of three historical periods: westward expansion and the takeover of Texas, the U.S. war on Mexico, and the Gold Rush and Mexican resistance to the U.S. takeover.

Westward Expansion and Taking Texas

"United States expansion in the West was inevitable," says the fourth-grade text. One section, "Texas and the Struggle with Mexico" (Grade 5) describes how Anglos obtained land and settled in Texas with Mexico's permission on certain conditions, including no slaves and being Catholic. When they broke their promises and Mexico tried to tighten its control, the Americans in Texas "were upset...Mexican rule...had become too strict." Being "upset" – a variation on "belief" – apparently legitimizes the Anglo move to take Texas.

The Battle of the Alamo at San Antonio, Texas, in 1836 is the one event involving Mexicans that appeared in every publisher's textbooks submitted for consideration in California. This Mexican military victory, in which all Anglo fighters died defending the fort – or, some scholars say, were executed – sparked a legendary desire for revenge. The Grade 5 teacher's edition emphasizes that students should see the Battle of the Alamo as "an important symbol of freedom and liberty" where "heroes" fought for Texas independence. From a different perspective, it was a symbol of U.S. land grabbing in which the "heroes" featured an escaped murderer (William Travis), a slave runner (James Bowie), and a gunfighting adventurer (Davy Crockett). But that perspective doesn't appear. Since March 1994, however, debate has been raging in San Antonio, site of the Alamo, as a new generation of scholars and politicians reject the heroic view of events. We can hope their efforts are reflected in the next round of textbooks.

Meanwhile, in a unique account of the Texas takeover, Holt, Rinehart & Winston's eighth-grade book, which was adopted with the Houghton Mifflin series, tells how the United States surprise-attacked Mexico at San Jacinto after the Alamo battle. Confronted by the revenge-hungry Anglos, the Mexican troops "fearfully" called out: "Me no Alamo!" supposedly in hopes of being spared. "...in fact," the books says, "these were the very same men who had slaughtered the defenders of the mission." Thus Holt encourages the stereotypes of Mexicans as cowardly, murderous, sneaky, lying buffoons who cannot, of course, outwit the righteous Anglo.

The 1846–48 U.S. War on Mexico and the Treaty of Guadalupe Hidalgo

These two events must rank among the most inaccurately depicted history in U.S. schoolbooks. "Belief" strikes again in the Grade 4 text from Houghton Mifflin, which bluntly states: "In the 1840s many [U.S.] people believed that their nation should rule all the land between the East and West coasts. Mexico owned much of this land. So the United States decided to go to war with Mexico to try to win this land."

More detail comes in the next grade: "Mexican officials refused to talk" (that word "talk" – which sounds like little enough to ask – actually meant negotiating with the United States over its demands for more Mexican land.) So, "President Polk ordered American forces to move down to the Rio Grande. They were now in territory that the Mexican government said was theirs. In April 1846 Mexican troops fought with an American scouting party, leaving 16 dead or wounded. The United States and Mexico were now at war." A teacher's edition section on critical thinking says: "No one really wanted the Mexican War. How could it have been avoided?"

This is a disingenuous, indeed deceptive, version of what even Anglo historians have identified as Polk's deliberate provocation of war with a view to seize half of Mexico. Polk declared his intent in his own diary, but the text remains silent on that. We also find not a word about the atrocities committed by U.S. invading forces during the war or the fact that General Ulysses S. Grant and other Americans denounced the war. In some apparent gesture to objectivity, the Grade 4 text says about the war in California: "In these battles [Mexican] soldiers fought brilliantly. Stephen W. Kearney, a general in the United States Army, admired their horseback riding." Given the failure to identify the invasion of Mexico as naked expansionism, such compliments are patronizing trivia.

The war officially ended with the Treaty of Guadalupe Hidalgo, which, the text states, provided that "as citizens, the Californios would have the same rights as other United States citizens." There's no mention that this treaty was grossly violated. The civil and property rights of Mexicans were not respected as promised by the United States. The land-holding rights guaranteed in a Statement of Protocol accompanying the treaty at the Mexican government's insistence were ignored.

By Grade 8 the textbook does say that Polk deliberately "provoked" the war, and that the treaty was "often not enforced." But at this late date a few facts about what the United States actually did are unlikely to reverse years of conditioning to identify with this nation's policies, no matter how unsavory.

The Gold Rush and the U.S. Occupation

The Houghton Mifflin series sanitizes some of these events and demonizes others. Its treatment of the Gold Rush is wondrous: "Besides the gold they found, what did the forty-niners contribute to California?" The teacher's edition answer: "They contributed the skills, energy, and population increase that would help California grow." One wants to add: not to mention driving out or killing Mexicans and Indians so that California had a white instead of a Mexican majority and could become a state. And what about the crucial skills, beginning with mining technology, that were taken over from the indigenous populations?

Resistance to the U.S. occupation is transformed into sheer criminality: "'Joaquin!' they gasped. No one felt safe.... Who was this Mexican bandit?" Actually, Anglo miners drove Murieta (like other Latino miners) out of the goldfields after reportedly raping his wife; as a result, he began a guerrilla-like movement that enjoyed widespread support. Many Mexican people saw him as a resistance hero. The Holt, Rinehart & Winston book also calls the resistance heroes "bandits."

Confronted by textbooks like these, some California teachers are making special efforts to present the Mexican-American or Latino perspective with other materials. One San Francisco teacher in a largely Latino neighborhood has created a special curriculum around the theme of Manifest Destiny, and another makes minimal use of the adopted textbook at her school. Let's hope many more can make such corrective efforts.

But what is the larger, long-range solution? During the textbook battle, Dr. Sylvia Wynter, a Stanford University professor of African and Afro-American Studies as well as of Spanish and Portuguese, circulated a lengthy, forceful paper. The textbooks present a dual problem, Wynter observed. First, they are dominated by a Eurocentric perspective. Second, this perspective is not acknowledged but is camouflaged by a "multiculturalist alternative." Yet this alternative remains entrapped by its assumption that the United States is integrated as a nation on the basis of a single, Euro-American culture. Thus, this "multiculturalist alternative" seeks to "save" the Euro-American nation model by multiculturalizing it. The real solution, however, is to de-imagine the United States as a nation and then re-imagine it as a "world": a community of communities relating on the basis of mutual respect and integrity.

It goes without saying that achieving such a goal would require a massive shift in power relations throughout U.S. society. Still, defining one's goals – no matter how distant they may seem – matters. Mutual respect and integrity would also lead us to textbooks that make real sense out of American history.

The Lorax: Dr. Seuss Revisited and Revised

BILL BIGELOW

What is a good society, and how can we bring it about? Tackling these not-so-simple questions was the goal of "Literature and Social Change," a class I taught for several years at Jefferson High School in Portland, Oregon.

One of our texts was *The Lorax,* by Dr. Seuss. On first reading, *The Lorax* appears to be a straightforward tale about the horrors of pollution and the necessity to become aware of nature's interconnectedness. Although the book chronicles an environmental holocaust, the story ends on a hopeful note, with a redemptive speech from the formerly evil Once-ler. The earth and its creatures are given another chance to live a sane and ecological life. With luck, we may live happily ever after.

Indeed, *The Lorax* offers wonderful potential to provoke students to think about environmental degradation — from the rape of the ancient forests to the Exxon Valdez oil spill. As many educators have noted, discussing *The Lorax* can encourage students to see themselves as environmental activists in their own communities — even as six-year-olds.

In class we read *The Lorax* as serious political literature, just as we approached Steinbeck's *In Dubious Battle,* Edward Bellamy's *Looking Backward,* and Marge Piercy's *Woman on the Edge of Time.* On this level, *The Lorax* is flawed, offering a severely misleading analysis of environmental ruin and a wrongheaded — albeit implicit — strategy for social change.

I know what you're thinking: What's this guy's problem, picking on Dr. Seuss? The answer is twofold: First, it's the very simplicity of Dr. Seuss's story that offers students such a fine opportunity to hone their skills of social analysis. And second, just because literature is simple does not make it any less influential. Books like *The Lorax* are read to children over and over; even if kids don't grasp every nuance, the books play a major role in explaining a larger world and shaping how children respond to it.

Together, students and I read and critiqued *The Lorax*. The students' assignment was to rewrite Dr. Seuss's book incorporating a more accurate analysis of the causes of environmental degradation and a vision of how change might occur.

The Environment According to Seuss

For Dr. Seuss, the root of ecological destruction is greed. The Once-ler comes to the land of Swomee-Swans and Grickle-grass, cuts down a Truffula Tree, knits his first Thneed, which "some poor stupid guy" buys, builds a Thneed factory, and he's off on his first million. There is no competition and there are no other Thneed factories, just one greedy Once-ler. And as thneed sales feed his lust for wealth, technology must keep pace. He invents a Super-Axe-Hacker to chop down four Truffula trees at a time.

In their rewrite of Seuss, three of my students, Holly Allen, David Berkson, and Rebecca Willner, tried to portray the Truffula Tree Genocide more systemically. They wanted to show that the massive whacking of tress wasn't caused simply by the Once-ler's greed, but derived from the way the system was constructed:

> He'd come in and built up
> A system of power
> That made everything nasty
> and yucky and sour.
> This system, this network,
> was based upon gain,
> Where few reaped the profits
> While most suffered pain.

In class we had discussed how blaming personal greed may appear to be a convenient shorthand way of explaining environmental ruin, but it's misleading. For example, clear cutting – chopping down whole forests at a time – in the Pacific Northwest, results in major ecological damage. However, at the root is neither personal nor corporate greed. If the Weyerhaeuser Once-ler decided to abandon clear cutting in favor of selective cutting, the Louisiana-Pacific Once-ler would surely undersell Weyerhaeuser and force it out of business or back to clear cutting. Also, according to one estimate, lumber companies' exports of whole logs yield a profit of over 60 percent, compared to 10 percent producing lumber for the domestic market. What wood-products corporation could unilaterally forgo log exports and hope to compete? Massive deforestation in the

Northwest is best explained as a result of the functioning of the capitalist system itself, not of individual greed.

My students felt their way toward a more structural analysis, but had trouble shaking Dr. Seuss's narrow focus on the Once-ler's selfish motives. They ended up asserting, rather than showing, the systemic pressures making "everything nasty and yucky and sour."

The Once-ler and the Workers

But when it came to portraying the process of producing Thneeds, Holly, Becky, and David broke decisively with Dr. Seuss. In Seuss's *Lorax,* the Once-ler hires all his brothers, uncles, and aunts to become his work force. This choice allowed Seuss to ignore the hazards and divisions in the workplace. Seuss's workers are all co-owners and co-exploiters along with the Once-ler.

My students decided instead to have their Once-ler draw his workers from the community:

> And who sewed these damn useless
> New Thneeds or whatever,
> Did the rich Once-ler sew them?
> Oh heavens no, never.
> The Once-ler had gotten
> The Creatures of Lorne
> To make all these Thneeds
> To wear and adorn...
> The Once-ler thought Lorne Creatures were all merely slobs,
> So he divvied them up, gave them all different jobs.
> This was a smart thing for the Once-ler to do,
> It made competition – it caused them to stew
> The Bar-ba-loots, Swami-Swans and also the fish,
> Had management jobs for which they could wish.
> They had different jobs – some of them better
> Some of them worse, and so the go-getter
> Who looked out for himself, could get the good job,
> Or so it was thought – it made them all snobs.
> The Barbaloots, they got the best job of all
> Upon you, said Once-ler, the profits will fall.
> They got nicer uniforms and better pays,
> They had longer lunch hours, and shorter days.
> The Swans got jobs that weren't quite as good,
> But still they'd be paid more than the fish would.
> The poor little Humming-fish got least of all,
> They were the Nut and Bolt guys – their prestige was small.

> And so it happened that all of these creatures
> Forgot that the others had many nice features.
> They started to think in the very same way
> That the Once-ler had planned – they honored his say.

My students wanted to portray the work force realistically, as divided and exploited, rather than as one big happy family. Their creatures of Lorne suffered both as workers and as residents of an increasingly polluted and deforested environment. In this way, Holly, David, and Becky wanted to suggest the possibility of alliances between workers and the larger community.

Dr. Seuss doesn't even hint that readers might think in these terms. Instead, he muddies the analytical waters by collapsing workers and owners into one class of environmental spoilers. Thus, workers are portrayed unambiguously as part of the problem – along with the Once-ler as *the* problem. Perhaps unconsciously, Dr. Seuss adopts the stance of too many environmentalists who see workers as enemies rather than as potential allies in a struggle for ecological sanity.

Organizing for Change

In Dr. Seuss's story, the Lorax represents the only opposition the Once-ler faces. But instead of organizing groups like the Swomee-Swans and Bar-ba-loots to fight for themselves and their environment, the Lorax becomes their advocate. He complains angrily to the Once-ler that because of his hacking down all the trees there is no longer enough Truffula Fruit. Although the Lorax models for children a stance of defiance in the face of injustice, he's a dictator, albeit a benevolent one. As the environment deteriorates, he orders "his" Bar-ba-loots to leave. Later, he sends off "his" Swomee-Swans and then, because of all the Schloppity-Schlopp in the lake, sends off the Humming Fish. There is no suggestion that the Lorax might organize these creatures to stand together against the Once-ler. Instead, the creatures are portrayed as pathetic and powerless victims. Because there is no hint that the Lorax and friends could have chosen any other course, the message of Dr. Seuss is a cynical one. Failure was inevitable.

Holly, David, and Becky also introduced a Lorax-like character, named Keith, but patterned him after the manipulative union organizer, Mac, in Steinbeck's In Dubious Battle.

> With his deep-throated yell and his piercing blue eyes

He rallied the creatures and shouted "arise."
He waved his big hands and stomped his big feet
And incited them all to stampede in the street...
Having little experience with self-governed thought,
The gullible creatures, protest they did not.
They followed him blindly, with fever and love,
Thus the Bar-ba-loots, Swami-Swans, and of course the poor fish,
Looked up to this guy to fulfill their new wish.
They followed example, undertook the demand,
Of this weird guy named Keith, who came to command.

Although Keith and followers were able to topple the Once-ler's rule, Keith quickly established a new hierarchy. In theory, the Creatures of Lorne now owned the productive resources of the society, but nothing had really changed:

> The Truffula Trees continued to fall,
> And the water – oh the water – got blackest of all.
> And the fish developed really terrible diseases:
> Ruskus and Fluskus and even the Fleasez.

Slowly, my students' creatures begin to talk to one another about their conditions. They start to criticize their new leader. "The thing that makes him such a terrible bore is he's just like that evil old Once-ler before."

Unlike the creatures in *The Lorax,* my students' creatures do not remain hapless victims. Nor do they arrive at some neat "solution." Their story ends with the Swans and the fish and the Bar-ba-loots confronting their mutual prejudices. They come to agree that reversing the degradation in their working conditions and in the environment depends on their thinking and acting together – without relying on self-appointed leaders:

> If you want me to tell you
> That on that bright day
> That those guys found the answer,
> I'd be lying: No Way!
> We're leaving this story unfinished
> My friends,
> Consider it more of a means
> To an end.
> For the thing that's important
> Is what that tiny fish said,
> If you want to be free,
> You can never be led.

In the students' enthusiasm to distance themselves from the mix of paternalism and elitism embodied in Steinbeck's Mac, or in a somewhat different form, in Dr. Seuss's *Lorax,* they might be accused of advocating a kind of "ultrademocracy." Obviously, there needs to be some kind of leadership in any struggle for justice. In discussion, students recognized the tension between democracy and leadership but insisted that ultimately their message was correct: "If you want to be free, you can never be led" — at least not in the way that Keith or the Lorax "led."

In contrast, Dr. Seuss concludes his tale with a speech by the Once-ler reminiscent in feeling of Scrooge's conversion in Dickens's *A Christmas Carol.* In both instances, greedy owners come to see the error of their ways and, at least implicitly, renounce their earlier rapacious behavior and vow repentance. On the final page of *The Lorax,* the Once-ler is pictured throwing the last Truffula Seed to a little boy, and urging him to plant a new Truffula. The Once-ler implores the boy to care for the seed, to water it, and provide fresh air. The boy must protect the Truffula "from axes that hack."

More than one message can be drawn from this ending. On the one hand, it's a conclusion that calls on readers to be environmentally responsible: saving our rivers and forests is up to all of us. Urging people to protect the forests "from axes that hack" can even be read as a demand to confront the "hackers." However, the deliverer of this enlightenment is none other than the individual who was the original plunderer. And although the Once-ler's conversion may seem hopeful, the misdirected political strategy that might logically flow from this presentation is that concerned citizens should appeal to the latent humanity and generosity of the environmental destroyers. If the Once-ler can change, why not all of them, the story appears to suggest; there probably is an environmentalist lurking in the heart of every lumber company executive.

I prefer the democratic and grassroots approach proposed by Holly, David, and Becky: lasting change can only come from those victimized by an unjust system, not from those who benefit.

In many respects, I still think *The Lorax* is a delightful story and I wouldn't discourage teachers from using the book with students. But what is important is *how* we read with our students. As early as possible, we need to give students the tools to become social detectives, to develop a critical literacy that allows them to read deep between the lines. From kindergarten through college, *The Lorax* may be as good a place to start as any.

Whole Language:
What's the Fuss? An Interview
with Harvey Daniels

The following is condensed from an interview with Harvey Daniels. Daniels teaches at National-Louis University in Evanston, Illinois, where he directs the Center for City Schools. He is the author and co-author of a number of books, the latest of which is *Best Practice: New Standards for Teaching and Learning in America's Schools.* The interview was conducted in the winter 1993 by Barbara Miner of *Rethinking Schools.*

What is whole language?

First of all, I think the term *whole language* is in grave political trouble and I don't think we'll hear it much ten years from now. It's become so compromised and so abused, so unclear and so provocative, that even many whole language people don't want to use it anymore. The philosophy of whole language will certainly last, but the name may fade from use.

That being said, let me give you a definition of whole language. I would say a whole language classroom is a place where teaching and learning is child-centered, experiential, reflective, authentic, holistic, social, collaborative, democratic, cognitive, developmental, constructivist, and challenging.

That's a bit of a mouthful. What would that mean in terms of classroom practice?

Let me begin by outlining what you would see less of. A whole language classroom has less teacher-directed and controlled instruction, like lecturing and talking at children. It has less student passivity and less rewarding of sitting and silence. It has less time given to worksheets, dittos, and workbooks. It has less time spent reading textbooks and basal readers. It has fewer attempts by teachers to cover huge amounts of content area in every subject. It has less rote memorization and less stress on competition and grading. It has less tracking and leveling of students into alleged ability groups, less use of pull-out programs, and less reliance on standardized tests.

What do you see more of? You see more hands-on, inductive, active, experiential learning, which means more noise, more movement, more activity among the children. There is more emphasis on higher-order thinking and a deeper study of fewer topics. There is more time devoted to whole, original, real books, as opposed to short little basal stories that are disconnected from each other.

There is also more acting on the principles of democracy. Thus, a whole language classroom has more cooperative and collaborative activity, more heterogeneous grouping, and the classroom is an interdependent community. There's also more trust in the classroom teacher's observation and judgment about a child's growth.

Another key area is more attention to the affective needs and the learning styles of individual children. It's clear that we need to make a place in the classroom for kids who learn through different channels: visual, auditory, kinesthetic. Attention deficit disorder, for instance, is a perfect example of a curriculum-induced disorder. If you define a learning situation as silent and motionless, then someone who cannot be silent and motionless has a disease.

Most of all — and my feeling is that this is the single most important element — in a whole language classroom, kids have more choices. This means that much of the time they pick their own books to read, their own subjects to write about, their own partners to work with, their own projects to research, and their own topics to investigate.

Choice for kids also means more responsibility, however. Students in a whole language classroom have more responsibility for their work, for setting goals, for monitoring their work, for finding and reading books, for selecting topics, for keeping their own records, and for evaluating themselves.

What you're describing is much broader than whole language as a way to teach reading and writing.

Exactly. I think the whole language movement is the present recurrence of an old set of interlocked and progressive ideas about teaching and learning that have ebbed and flowed throughout American history, whether through the work of John Dewey or some of the movements of the 1960s. Whole language is not just about reading and writing. It's about what learning is, what teaching is, what the classroom should be like, what education should be about.

I read a survey today in which 82 percent of fourth-grade teachers claimed they were whole language teachers. That's ridiculous. Maybe 5 percent of the teachers in America are doing something that I would call whole language.

This takes us back to the name issue. Whole language now means whatever you want it to mean. An incredible number of teachers identify themselves as whole language teachers even as they violate every single precept of whole language.

How did it happen that people are using the name whole language but not the content?

One thing was that the commercial publishers rushed in and appropriated the movement's language and terminology. And suddenly we had things like whole language worksheets and whole language basals and whole language blackline masters and dittos.

One of my favorites is the language arts book that says, "Hey, kids, turn the page, we're going to the writing workshop." And you turn the page and kids are asked to underline the nouns once and the verbs twice.

The producers of commercial materials essentially define whole language as whatever their materials happen to contain. So there's no real change; it's business as usual and everybody's part of it. It's tragic how important terminology gets stolen, but it happens all the time.

This is one of the ways that whole language gets discredited. It gets trivialized and co-opted and translated into something completely tame and marketable. And everyone gets calmed and assured that they're really part of the latest thing, and the movement's momentum is sapped.

The list of assumptions about learning that I just mentioned – the list of things to do more of and things to do less of – is pretty rigorous. It represents a paradigm shift. It's a way of describing a classroom that's radically different from the traditional American public school classroom.

So how many teachers have really changed to create a classroom where they don't rely on worksheets, where they aren't run by standardized tests, where kids aren't yanked out for special help, where there's no ability grouping? Sadly, not very many.

How do you get the whole language movement back on track?

I think that there are basically two competing school reform movements in America right now. One is the sort of governmental, bureaucratic, blue-ribbon commission, business advisory committee, centralized, top-down, Nation at Risk, policing-oriented, rap-their-knuckles reform movement. That's the "official" governmental reform movement, and it's geared toward accountability and testing. But it actually doesn't have any reform in it at all. It doesn't say you should teach this differently, you should add this content. It doesn't say anything about the substance or the process of schooling. It offers no resources. It doesn't offer any professional development for teachers. Instead, it issues threats. It is basically saying that what we're doing is OK, we just need to do it harder, longer, stronger, louder, meaner, and we'll have a better country.

The other school reform movement is not oriented to testing, policing, and punishment. It's rooted in curriculum and instruction. It is a teacher-driven, grass-roots, bottom-up, basically democratic movement that says that what we do in school doesn't work. We've got to change what we teach and the way we teach it.

Up to now, the whole language people have been the most visible part of this grass-roots reform effort. There's a TAWL group (Teachers Applying Whole Language) in every town across the country. Already, there are 32,000 teachers voluntarily organized into "TAWL cells," as one conservative calls them. There's also a more modest movement called Critical Literacy, and a growing movement called Integrated Curriculum. All these efforts are teacher-motivated and rooted in the curriculum.

Why is the whole language movement seen as a threat to the "official" reform movement?

You could argue that the "official" reform movement views the graduates of schools mainly as economic entities and whole language sees them as citizens. Consumers versus citizens is a good way to define the differences.

One of the biggest things we fight over in school reform is kids' choices and responsibilities. And you will never see much student choice and responsibility advocated by [former Education Secretary and Drug Czar] William Bennett or [cultural literacy proponent] E. D. Hirsch or any of the people who are part of the governmental school reform movement. They don't really want citizens who have their own independent judgment about events and culture. They want obedient workers. They have made that very clear. The report that kicked off governmental reform, "A Nation at Risk," talked only about the economic and military significance of schooling.

Now this is not a conspiracy. I don't think the textbook publishers sit in a room with [U.S. Education Secretary] Richard Riley and figure out how to ruin whole language. They're mainly trying to make some money. But it's all too easy to discredit a nascent grassroots, idealistic, progressive movement like this. It has happened many times in American history.

What about those conservatives affiliated with religiously based education groups. Why are they so adamantly opposed to whole language?

There are several nationally organized, right-wing groups that have fixed on two enemies: whole language and outcomes-based education. And these issues have become part of day-to-day partisan politics.

Rush Limbaugh, for example, did a show about a new report card in Houston where instead of giving kids an A, B, C, or D in subjects, they devised a complex rating scale of several levels of achievement in fifty or sixty different criteria. Instead of just getting a C in reading, which told you nothing, parents would get multiple, complex ratings on their child's comprehension, on retellings, on vocabulary, and so forth.

Well, Rush Limbaugh apparently told everybody in TV-land to get on their phones and call their local school district and tell them, "Don't you dare ever change from A, B, C, D report cards." And several school districts we were then working with on alternative assessment strategies received critical phone calls from taxpayers.

The point is, there is organized grass-roots opposition to progressive approaches. In a minute, I'll give you my theory why. But first, I also want to make clear that I am talking here of the organized opposition, not those parents who honestly and sincerely have questions about phonics, spelling, diagramming, and all those related issues.

As far as I know, there are no parent groups that promote whole language, collaborative learning, dialogue journals, detracking, or writing workshops. The only approach to education that some parents get passionate about – enough to go to meetings and print leaflets – is phonics. And it's interesting to me that phonics is the only approach to reading that removes meaning from reading. These people are unconsciously saying that they want their kids to experience reading in a structure and a process in which meaning is taken out. The same people tend to resonate with the idea that writing instruction ought to be composed mostly of grammar rules and diagramming sentences, which is the only approach to writing that takes meaning making out of composition.

So this is really a censorship issue. These are people who are terrified of losing their children, and they are frightened to death of the power of literacy. They know that when their kids really learn to read and really learn to write, they are going to be able to read all kinds of dangerous ideas and they will be able to write all kinds of potentially dangerous, scary, "disloyal to the family" ideas.

I'm not saying that I think these people sit around and think, "How can I keep my kid stupid?" Obviously that is not their motivation. But you find that they are consistent: they want phonics, they want grammar, they want lots of worksheets — and they are the first ones in line to try to censor *Huckleberry Finn* or *Catcher in the Rye* or any controversial content other than Dick and Jane.

It's a package of values and attitudes that speaks to their fear and terror of losing their children to the world of ideas that they, the parents, can't control. So what scares them so much about whole language is that it promotes not skills but thinking. Whole language teachers believe that reading starts not with phonemes but with meaning, and writing starts with things to say. And that can be threatening.

I do sympathize with people's fears. I have two children of my own. What if they go to school and a teacher says, "Let's write in journals." And what if my daughter or son says, "Oh my dad is such a jerk, you know, he forgot to pick me up at school," or, "You know, mom and dad had an argument."

So I can get a twinge of fear about journals too, and feel a little bit vulnerable. But my kids are people with their own voices. They have their life and they have their story to tell. My son publishes a magazine and there's a lot of it that I don't appreciate or understand. But I will defend to the death his right to use writing to make meaning and reach people and create his identity.

If you read some of the right-wing literature, you'll see that they don't want any discussion of any attitudes, values, feelings, or politics; they don't want any journaling, any guided imagery. They essentially want school to be devoid of ideas, thinking, debate, and meaning. But I don't think the public schools of America should have it as a policy to keep children ignorant because of the fears of a few grownups. And if we accede to that reactionary request, how can we call ourselves educators?

Let's address the phonics issue more. One of the key criticisms of whole language is that kids need phonics to learn to read and that whole language doesn't teach phonics.

The phonics approach to reading was popularized only since about 1915. So the first question is, how the hell did everyone learn how to read in the 4,000 years of written language before phonics was invented?

In fact, whole language is a return to the eternal fundamentals of education: kids reading whole, original books, writing whole, original texts of their own in a community of fellow learners with an experienced adult guiding them. That's whole language. That's the ancient way, the "primitive" way, the truly back-to-basics form of education.

This idea of breaking language down into its parts and teaching the individual pieces — diphthongs and gerunds — is a product of twentieth-century behavioristic psychology that's already discredited in most quarters. Twenty or thirty years from now it will be gone. However, we have a problem, which is that a whole generation of parents and taxpayers had lots of phonics instruction and they think they turned out pretty well.

That's how I learned to read.

That's probably not how you learned to read. You probably had extensive and diffuse family and community activities that set the stage, offered models, and taught you a lot about print before you even got to school. Ninety percent of the children in our schools don't need any formal phonics instruction, period. Maybe 10 percent, some people say 20 percent, need some formal phonics instruction in the first two years of school and, at the most, ten or fifteen minutes a day.

For the 10 or 20 percent who need it, I'm all for it. Let's give it to them, amen, hallelujah, wonderful. No whole language teachers worth their salt would ever, ever say that they don't do phonics. But they do it as only a piece, only a part of the day, and they divide the class appropriately.

What about the argument that kids are going to have to take standardized tests, whether you like it or not, and whole language doesn't adequately prepare them for the tests?

Let me tell you an unequivocal, verifiable fact. Every single major educational test given in America — the CTBS, the CAT, the

Iowa Test of Basic Skills — every single test is owned by a company that also publishes basal textbooks. What we're talking about here is cross-marketing. That's all it is. It's like Pepsi owning Fritos. You get thirsty when you eat Fritos, right? So drink a Pepsi. It's the same thing in education. The publishers make tests mainly to create markets for their textbooks, not to help kids learn.

It may be cross-marketing, but kids still have to take those tests.

Even if you want to capitulate to a given test, you don't need to study only the test and distort your entire curriculum eight hours a day, 180 days a year, for twelve years. We've got very interesting studies where teachers do thirty-five or thirty-eight weeks of what they think is best for kids, and then they'll give them three weeks of test cramming just before the test. And the kids do just as well as kids who have forty weeks of test-driven curriculum.

Besides, most of these tests actually do reward a deep and diffuse, long-term, developed capacity with language. Kids who are reading a lot of whole, original books and who are doing a lot of original writing in a wide variety of genres, who are revising and editing their work, who are talking actively about books and their writing — they do fine on standardized tests. You sometimes see some implementation dip, as we call it, where their scores will go down for a couple of years when a new curriculum is introduced, but they come right back. And in other schools, scores go straight up.

Let's talk about the spelling controversy. It's one thing for kids to use invented spelling when first writing, and it's sort of cute when they're in kindergarten and first grade. But by the time children are in fourth grade, shouldn't they be given spelling tests?

Spelling tests are not spelling. I've got a son who's gotten 100 on every spelling test he ever took. But when he is doing an original piece of writing, his spelling isn't nearly as good.

When someone gives you ten words to learn to spell, all your attention is focused on only one thing, which is memorizing them and getting them written down right on Friday. Most anybody can do that. But that same person will turn around on Monday and misspell the same words again in a piece of real, original writing. Because then spelling is just one of a thousand other cognitive demands on your attention.

I don't care whether anybody can spell or not. I care whether they can edit. I care that they know how to find the help they need to turn their misspellings into correct spellings before they release their writing to the public. Kids needs to gradually acquire strategies to correct their spelling. It's unimportant to me to make distinctions between people who are able to do more or less of it in their heads.

Another criticism of whole language is that its practitioners tend to be white, middle-class women who bring certain cultural assumptions to urban classrooms. These assumptions, in particular the lack of structure in a whole language classroom, might be great for white, middle-class kids but disadvantage poor kids, particularly students of color.

One of the canards used to sink a movement is to say there's no structure. There's lots of structure in a whole language classroom; they're just different structures from what people are used to seeing. As Nancy Atwell, who's one of our leaders, says, "I'm still running a very tight ship; it's just a different kind of ship."

Some of these new, different structures include teacher-student conferences, collaborative group investigations, thematic units, partner reading, dialogue journals, portfolios, observational assessment, and dozens more. These are each carefully crafted activities with complex rules, procedures, and norms; they just happen to be different norms from the ones in the traditional classroom.

I don't think that these structures have any racial dimension. They are simply effective patterns of organization that stimulate children's engagement with print and literacy, with books and ideas. Indeed, these structures are based on the psychological concept of scaffolding, the special way in which parents and others instinctively help young children grow. They are the most powerful instructional interactions we currently know how to implement.

However, these classroom activities do have a cultural or economic class dimension, and therefore racial and ethnic politics do enter the picture indirectly. Because many urban children of color are poor, and because poor families often endorse authoritarian discipline styles, the decentralized whole language classroom sometimes seems to clash with family or cultural values. It is often said, especially by educators of color, that minority inner-city kids need more discipline, more authority, more control than middle-class suburban white children.

So this creates a real problem. Should schools recreate for kids the same culture found in their neighborhood, even if that means omitting the best educational models we have and use for other children? Or should schools exclusively operate according to middle-class values, styles, and standards?

I think that, especially for minority children, schooling must be both a mirror and a window. Kids have a right to expect that their school will positively reflect their heritage, their community, their culture. But at the same time, the school must also provide a window for looking at the rest of society, at other ways of being and thinking, and offer youngsters a genuine chance to enlarge their repertoire. Valuable schooling helps kids extend their range, their ability to operate and succeed in a widening arena.

Still, we have to admit that many African-American teachers are wary and skeptical about whole language. It's a real tension and disappointment in the whole language movement.

Might there have been errors, not in the intentions but in the practice of the whole language movement, that might be a cause of that rift?

As with any movement, there's always a kind of messianic spirit, an idealistic, change-the-world, do-gooder mentality. I think that's what sets off some African-American teachers. You get a lot of younger, white teachers saying, "We'll go into this school and this neighborhood and we'll bring the kids the benefits of literacy." And you get teachers of color saying, "Hey wait a minute, those are our kids. We'll take care of it. We know what's best for them."

I think that if white teachers run roughshod over such concerns, yes, they're going to create polarities. But the fact is, in my experience working in Chicago's schools, many black public school teachers are middle-class people who have worked their way up the socioeconomic ladder for the first time to that level. They tend in general to be quite conservative educationally, and pretty cautious. One of the comments you'll sometimes hear from African-American teachers about whole language or other experiments is, "You might be right, but we can't afford to take a chance with our kids." And the question I ask in return is, "Are you arguing that the system of education we have devised for inner-city black kids in America is so effective that we should keep it up because it works so well?"

Everybody knows that, by and large, urban education has been both more oriented to skill and drill approaches and generally less effective than middle-class suburban schools. Whole language people are saying that whole language is not part of the problem of urban education; it's part of the answer. We are offering an option that we think is far, far more promising than the skill-and-drill that has dominated education for seventy-five years.

Let's go back to an issue affecting a whole language classroom, and that is the tension between a child-centered approach — in which you trust children's ability, you give them choices, you give them responsibilities — and the need to provide direction and teach certain skills and facts. How do you deal with that tension?

I advocate that teachers start thinking about doing it fifty-fifty. For about half the day, the teacher guides the learning — planning, organizing, and structuring students' exposure to ideas and topics. Hopefully, this teacher-directed instruction will be embedded in coherent, thematic units and will stress higher-order thinking over rote memorization. But anyway, that's about half the day, composed of what most people would call traditional or "real" teaching.

The other half of the day you create tight, well-regulated structures within which students can make choices and do their own work. We call this "workshop" or "studio" time. In other words, kids pick books to read and write and talk about; kids pick topics to write about, and plan, organize, draft, revise, and publish; kids pick things to investigate individually or in teams, identify the search, plan it, get it done, and prepare reports or ways to share.

I'm the balance guy. If I get run over by a bus tomorrow, I hope people at my funeral will say, "Well, at least he always talked about balance in the curriculum."

How can one build a whole language approach that also has a critical approach toward the society around us and that doesn't fall into the stereotype of a depoliticized, white suburban movement?

I'm not sure I want whole language characterized as a depoliticized, white suburban movement. First of all, whole language is a very political, professional, grassroots, teacher movement, as we've been talking about. Second, whole language is an avowedly progressive, humanistic, democratic innovation.

However, I hear what you are saying and the question is, "How does this kind of classroom address social issues?"

I think it addresses them in the deepest way, and that is by setting up a microcosm community that operates democratically. It creates a classroom where kids are respected and not oppressed, where they take responsibility, make choices, work in groups and teams. It's a socially diverse, productive, and mutually interdependent community of people. That's the first thing.

The other thing is the good literature that is at the core of children's experience. Once you get past these watered-down, pathetic commercial textbooks that suck the marrow out of literature with their abridging and sequencing; once you send kids into real books, now that's political. What are some of the most popular books right now for kids? *Fly Away Home,* about homeless people; *How Many Days to America?,* about refugees; *Encounter,* a native's eye view of Columbus. There's a lot of literature out there that is very political and extremely critical of this society.

In fact, almost all good literature is critical. I don't know any good literature that takes the present state of affairs and spins a tale about how wonderful everything is. Most good literature points toward problems.

Because most parents were taught more traditionally, what can teachers do to help parents understand whole language?

Let me tell you what I do when I work with parent groups, which I find very successful.

If you just walk up to most parents and say, "What do you think you ought to have in a reading program?" they'll say, lots of phonics and a spelling test every Friday, and when they get older they should diagram a bunch of sentences. What parents are doing is dredging up their superficial "received-wisdom" from *USA Today* and Rush Limbaugh. However, if you let parents tell their stories from their heart, from their gut, from what they have lived – and not from the pamphlets they get from Phyllis Schlafly – they give you a completely different set of prescriptions for schooling.

When I'm with a group of parents I say, "Tonight we are going to think back on our own experiences in school, and I am going to throw out some suggestions and ideas and words, and I am going to try to help you remember some of the key moments in your schooling, in your life as a reader and as a writer." I then have people pick out one moment that stands out in their development as a reader or a writer, either positive or negative. I have them draw up some notes on the back of a notecard and then talk to the person next to them and tell their story.

What happens is that you get a whole different set of ideas about what makes good reading or writing instruction. Adults tell horror stories about teachers who put red marks and mean comments all over their papers and tossed them back in their face. Maybe the person will say that after that they gave up on being a writer. Or a parent will talk about what it was like being in the lowest reading group and how it felt to be a "Vulture" when everybody else was a "Bluebird" or a "Chickadee." Some will remember something positive, like the teacher in fourth grade who read every day for fifteen to twenty minutes, and how they fell in love with books.

At some point as the parents are telling all these stories, I hand them a summary of the research on reading and writing. And I say, "Gee, I thought you guys were just a regular bunch of parents. I didn't know you'd been sitting around reading all the educational research. But the stories you have been telling tonight are illustrating everything that I wanted to tell you about what we are trying to do with your kids."

And I tell them, "All those sad stories that you told about being turned off to reading or writing, what we are trying to do is make sure that never happens to your kid. And those few happy stories, about how once in a while you had a teacher who let you write or read great books, we want to have those things happen for your child every single day in this school."

When you tell them that, they say, "Oh yeah? Wow. Where's the punch and cookies?" They don't want to fight. The don't want to argue. They don't want to play phonics. They don't want to have censorship. A lot of these people who at the surface level want to fight whole language, want to fight progressive ideas, if they look into their own heart and their own experience in school, they will strongly support what we are doing.

Now there are always crackpots and lunatics around the fringes. But for 95 percent of just regular good-hearted American parents, whether in cities or suburbs, if they go back and think about what worked and didn't work for them as students, they give us an agenda that whole language teachers are very happy to live by.

Whose Standard?
Teaching Standard English
in Our Schools

LINDA CHRISTENSEN

When I was in the ninth grade, Mrs. Delaney, my English teacher, wanted to demonstrate the correct and incorrect ways to pronounce the English language. She asked Helen Draper, whose father owned several clothing stores in town, to stand and say "lawyer." Then she asked me, whose father owned a bar, to stand and say "lawyer." Everyone burst into laughter at my pronunciation.

What did Mrs. Delaney accomplish? Did she make me pronounce lawyer correctly? No. I say attorney. I never say lawyer. In fact, I've found substitutes for every word my tongue can't get around and for all the rules I can't remember.

For years I've played word cop on myself. I stop what I'm saying to think, "Objective or subjective case? Do I need I or me here? Hmmm. There's a *lay* coming up. What word can I substitute for it? Recline?"

And I've studied this stuff. After all, I've been an English teacher for almost twenty years. I've gone through all of the Warriner's workbook exercises. I even found a *lie/lay* computer program and kept it in my head until I needed it in speech and became confused again.

Thanks to Mrs. Delaney, I learned early on that in our society language classifies me. Generosity, warmth, kindness, intelligence, good humor aren't enough – I need to speak correctly to make it. Mrs. Delaney taught me that the "melting pot" was an illusion. The real version of the melting pot is that people of diverse backgrounds are mixed together and when they come out they're supposed to look like Vanna White and sound like Dan Rather. The only diversity we celebrate is tacos and chop suey at the mall.

Unlearning "Inferiority"
It wasn't until a few years ago that I realized grammar was an indication of class and cultural background in the United States and that

there is a bias against people who do not use language "correctly." Even the terminology "standard" and "nonstandard" reflects that one is less than the other. English teachers are urged to "correct" students who speak or write in their home language. A friend of mine, whose ancestors came over on the Mayflower, never studied any of the grammar tests I keep by my side, but she can spot all of my errors because she grew up in a home where Standard English was spoken.

And I didn't, so I've trained myself to play language cop. The problem is that every time I pause, I stop the momentum of my thinking. I'm no longer pursuing content, no longer engaged in trying to persuade or entertain or clarify. Instead I'm pulling Warriner's or Mrs. Delaney out of my head and trying to figure out how to say something.

"Ah, but this is good," you might say. "You have the rules and Mrs. Delaney to go back to. This is what our students need."

But it doesn't happen that way. I try to remember the rule or the catchy phrase that is supposed to etch the rule in my mind forever, like "people never get laid," but I'm still not sure if I used it correctly. These side trips cost a lot of velocity in my logic.

Over the years my English teachers pointed out all of my errors — the usage errors I inherited from my mother's Bandon, Oregon, dialect, the spelling errors I overlooked, the fancy words I used incorrectly. They did this in good faith, in the same way, years later, I "corrected" my students' "errors" because I wanted them to know the rules. They were keys to a secret and wealthier society and I wanted them to be prepared to enter, just as my teachers wanted to help me.

And we should help kids. It would be misleading to suggest that people in our society will value my thoughts or my students' thoughts as readily in our home languages as in the "cash language" as Jesse Jackson calls it. Students need to know where to find help, and they need to understand what changes might be necessary, but they need to learn in a context that doesn't say, "The way you said this is wrong."

When Fear Interferes

English teachers must know when to correct and how to correct — and I use that word uneasily. Take Fred, for example. Fred entered my freshman class last year unwilling to write. Every day during writing time I'd find Fred doodling pictures of *Playboy* bunnies. When I sat down and asked him why he didn't write, he said he couldn't.

I explained to him that in this class his writing couldn't be wrong because we were just practicing our writing until we found a piece we wanted to polish, in the same way that he practiced football every day after school, but only played games on Fridays. His resistance lasted for a couple of weeks. Around him, other students struggled with their writing, shared it with the class on occasion, and heard positive comments. Certainly the writing of his fellow students was not intimidating.

On October 1, after reading a story by Toni Cade Bambara (1972) about trusting people in our lives, Fred wrote for the first time:

> I remember my next door neighbor trusted me with some money that she owed my grandmother. She owed my grandmother about 25 dollars.

Fred didn't make a lot of errors. In this first piece of writing it looked as if he had basic punctuation figured out. He didn't misspell any words. And he certainly didn't make any usage errors. Based on this sample, he appeared to be a competent writer.

However, the biggest problem with Fred's writing was the fact that he didn't make mistakes. This piece demonstrates his discomfort with writing. He wasn't taking any risks. Just as I avoid *lawyer* and *lay,* he wrote to avoid errors instead of writing to communicate or think on paper.

When more attention is paid to the way something is written or said than to what is said, students' words and thoughts become devalued. Students learn to be silent, to give as few words as possible for teacher criticism.

Valuing What We Know

Students must be taught to hold their own voices sacred, to ignore the teachers who have made them feel that what they've said is wrong or bad or stupid. Students must be taught how to listen to the knowledge they've stored up, but which they are seldom asked to relate.

Too often students feel alienated in schools. Knowledge is foreign. It's about other people in other times (Bigelow 1990). At a conference I attended recently, a young woman whose mother was Puerto Rican and whose father was Haitian said, "I went through school wondering if anyone like me had ever done anything worthwhile or important. We kept reading and hearing about all of these famous people. I remember thinking, 'Don't we have anyone?' I walked out of the school that day feeling tiny, invisible, unimportant."

As teachers, we have daily opportunities to affirm that our students' lives and language are unique and important. We do that in the selections of literature we read, in the history we choose to teach, and we do it by giving legitimacy to our students' lives as a content worthy of study.

One way to encourage the reluctant writers who have been silenced and the not-so-reluctant writers who have found a safe and sterile voice is to encourage them to recount their experiences. I sometimes recruit former students to share their writing and their wisdom as a way of underscoring the importance of the voices and stories of teenagers. Rochelle, a student in my senior writing class, brought in a few of her stories and poems to read to my freshmen. Rochelle, like Zora Neale Hurston, blends her home language with Standard English in most pieces. She read the following piece to open up a discussion about how kids are sometimes treated as servants in their homes, but also to demonstrate the necessity of using the language she hears in her family to develop characters:

> "I'm tired of washing dishes. Seems like every time our family gets together, they just got to eat and bring their millions of kids over to our house. And then we got to wash the dishes."
>
> I listened sympathetically as my little sister mumbled these words.
>
> "And how come we can't have ribs like the grownups? After all, ain't we grown?"
>
> "Lord," I prayed, "seal her lips while the blood is still running warm in her veins."
>
> Her bottom lip protruded farther and farther as she dipped each plate in the soapy water, then rinsed each side with cold water (about a two second process) until she felt the majority of suds were off.
>
> "One minute we lazy women that can't keep the living room half clean. The next minute we just kids and gotta eat some funky chicken while they eat ribs."
>
> ...Suddenly it was quiet. All except my little sister who was still talking. I strained to hear a laugh or joke from the adults in the

living room, a hint that all were well, full and ready to go home. Everyone was still sitting in their same spots, not making a move to leave.

"You ought to be thankful you got a choice."

Uh-oh. Now she got Aunt Macy started...

After reading her work, Rochelle talked about listening to her family and friends tell their stories. She urged the freshmen to relate the tales of their own lives — the times they were caught doing something forbidden, the times they got stuck with the dishes, the funny/sad events that made their freshman year memorable. When Rochelle left, students wrote more easily. Some. Some were afraid of the stories because as Rance said, "It takes heart to tell the truth about your life."

But eventually they write. They write stories. They write poems. They write letters. They write essays. They learn how to switch in and out of the language of the powerful as Rochelle does so effortlessly in her "Tired of Chicken" piece.

Sharing Lessons

After we write, we listen to each other's stories in our read-around circle where everyone has the opportunity to share, to be heard, to learn that knowledge can be gained by examining our lives (see Shor 1987; Shor & Freire 1987). In the circle, we discover that many young women encounter sexual harassment; we learn that store clerks follow black students, especially males, more frequently than they follow white students; we find that many of our parents drink or use drugs; we learn that many of us are kept awake by the crack houses in our neighborhood.

Before we share, students often understand these incidents individually. They feel there's something wrong with them. If they were smarter, prettier, stronger, these things wouldn't have happened to them. When they hear other students' stories, they begin to realize that many of their problems aren't caused by a character defect. For example, a young man shared a passionate story about life with his mother, who is a lesbian. He loved her, but felt embarrassed to bring his friends home. He was afraid his peers would think he was gay or reject him if they knew about his mother. After he read, the class was silent. Some students cried. One young woman told him that her father was gay and she'd experienced similar difficulties, but hadn't had the courage to tell people about it.

She thanked him. Another student confided that his uncle had died from AIDS the year before. What had been a secret shame became an opportunity for students to discuss sexual diversity more openly. Students who were rigidly opposed to the idea of homosexuality gained insights into their own homophobia – especially when presented with the personal revelations from their classmates. Those with homosexual relatives found new allies with whom they could continue their discussion and find support.

Sharing also provides a "collective text" for us to examine the social roots of problems more closely: Where do men/women develop the ideas that women are sexual objects? Where do they learn that it's OK for men to follow women or make suggestive remarks? Where is it written that it's the woman's fault if a man leers at her? How did these roles develop? Who gains from them? Who loses? How could we make it different? Our lives become a window to examine society.

Learning the "Standard" Without Humiliation

But the lessons can't stop there. Fred can write better now. He and his classmates can feel comfortable and safe sharing their lives or discussing literature and the world. They can even understand that they need to ask "Who benefits?" to get a better perspective on a problem. But still, when they leave my class or this school, some people will judge them by how their subjects and verbs line up.

So I teach Fred the rules. It's the language of power in this country, and I would be cheating him if I pretended otherwise (Delpit 1988). I teach him this more effectively than Mrs. Delaney taught me because I don't humiliate him or put down his language. I'm also more effective because I don't rely on textbook drills; I use the text of Fred's writing. But I also teach Fred what Mrs. Delaney left out.

I teach Fred that language, like tracking, functions as part of a gatekeeping system in our country. Who gets managerial jobs, who works at banks and who works at fast food restaurants, who gets into what college and who gets into college at all are decisions linked to the ability to use Standard English. So how do we teach kids to write with honesty and passion about their world and get them to study the rules of the cash language? We go back to our study of society. We ask: Who made the rules that govern how we speak and write? Did Ninh's family and Fred's family and

LaShonda's family all sit down together and decide on these rules? Who already talks like this and writes like this? Who has to learn how to change the way they talk and write? Why?

We make up our own tests that speakers of Standard English would find difficult. We read articles, stories, poems written in Standard English and those written in home language. We listen to videotapes of people speaking. Most kids like the sound of their home language better. They like the energy, the poetry, and the rhythm of the language. We determine when and why people shift. We talk about why it might be necessary to learn Standard English.

Asking my students to memorize the rules without asking who makes the rules, who enforces the rules, who benefits from the rules, who loses from the rules, who uses the rules to keep some in and keep others out, legitimates a social system that devalues my students' knowledge and language. Teaching the rules without reflection also underscores that it's OK for others – "authorities" – to dictate something as fundamental and as personal as the way they speak. Further, the study of Standard English without critique encourages students to believe that if they fail, it is because they are not smart enough or didn't work hard enough. They learn to blame themselves. If they get poor SAT scores, low grades on term papers or essays because of language errors, or fail teacher entrance exams, they will internalize the blame; they will believe they did not succeed because they are inferior instead of questioning the standard of measurement and those making the standards.

We must teach our students how to match subjects and verbs, how to pronounce *lawyer,* because they are the ones without power and, for the moment, have to use the language of the powerful to be heard. But, in addition, we need to equip them to question the educational system that devalues their life and their knowledge. If we don't, we condition them to a pedagogy of consumption where they will consume the knowledge, priorities, and products that have been decided and manufactured without them in mind.

It took me years to undo what Mrs. Delaney did to me. Years to discover that what I said was more important than how I said it. Years to understand that my words, my family's words, weren't wrong, weren't bad – they were just the words of the working class. For too long, I felt inferior when I spoke. I knew the voice of my childhood crept out, and I confused that with ignorance. It wasn't. I just didn't belong to the group that made the rules. I was an outsider, a foreigner in their world. My students won't be.

Resources

BAMBARA, TONI CADE. 1972. *Gorilla, My Love,* New York: Random House.

BIGELOW, WILLIAM. 1990. "Inside the Classroom: Social Vision and Critical Pedagogy." *Teachers College Record.* vol. 91 No. 3: 437–448.

DELPIT, LISA. 1988. "The Silenced Dialogue: Power and Pedagogy in Educating Other People's Children." *Harvard Educational Review* 58 (3): 280–98.

SHOR, IRA. 1987. *Freire for the Classroom,* Portsmouth, NH: Heinemann.

SHOR, IRA, AND PAULO FREIRE. 1987. *A Pedagogy for Liberation,* South Hadley, MA: Bergin & Garvey.

Teachers, Culture, and Power:
An Interview with Lisa Delpit

Following is an interview with Lisa Delpit, an educator who has written several prominent articles on teaching reading and writing to children of color. Her articles have focused, in part, on the controversy between the "process" approach to literacy, which emphasizes immersing children in reading and writing in meaningful contexts, and the "skills" approach, which emphasizes learning the formal rules and patterns of language. Delpit holds the Benjamin E. Mays Chair of Urban Educational Leadership at Georgia State University in Atlanta. She is the author of *Other People's Children: White Teachers, Students of Color, and Other Cultural Conflicts in the Classroom* (The New Press, 1995). She was interviewed in the spring of 1992 by Barbara Miner of *Rethinking Schools*.

Several years ago, you wrote an article challenging the way the process approach to reading and writing affected children of color. Can you summarize your main criticisms?

My concern is that whatever strategy one uses, one has to ensure that all children learn. I don't agree with placing oneself in a political camp, be it process reading and writing, or skills reading and writing. The best strategy depends on what a particular child needs.

Some children may need someone to take them aside and read constantly to them. Others may need someone to point out that letters have a connection to sound and code. The teacher may need to ask, "Why don't you read this with me and after I teach you some sounds you can try to figure out what words come next."

Teachers with many strategies will be less likely to blame the child for not learning, because they can continue to pull something else out and try. There are all kinds of explanations for failure that we internalize: this child comes from a poor family, there's drugs in the neighborhood, this child has an attention deficit disorder. I once made such a list and it was three pages long. While these factors may be true, in essence we are using them to explain our failures as teachers.

There is nothing in the process approach itself that mitigates against students acquiring specific skills. But some advocates give the impression that teaching skills restricts the writing process. Many African-American teachers, on the other hand, see such skills as essential to survival.

In my article, I refer to an African-American teacher who was adamantly opposed to the process approach to writing used by some people in the Bay Area. She especially opposed the idea that African-American children had to learn to be "fluent" in writing before they could be expected to conform to standards of spelling, grammar, and so forth. Our kids are fluent, she pointed out, referring to the amazing capacity of many African-American kids to create elaborate raps and other language forms. What they need are the skills to get them into college. She saw this emphasis on fluency at the expense of skills as just another racist ploy to keep African-American kids behind.

The problem is this tendency to dichotomize — either a skills or a process approach. Why not insist on "skills" in the context of critical and creative thinking? I consider myself a process-oriented teacher. But that doesn't mean I will limit myself to whatever is designated currently as a process approach.

Some people have inferred from your article that you support more of a basal reader approach that emphasizes short, sanitized reading selections and fill-in-the-blank workbooks. Do you?

I believe just the opposite. I believe, first of all, in an approach that seems to work for the child that you are working with. But I also believe that literacy instruction should be in the context of real reading and real writing, and reading and writing for real purposes. This means using literature that children like and that connects with them in their homes and lives. It means writing for purposes the children find useful.

For example, you might start out with letter writing or writing plays, or help the children make written materials for younger children, or produce stories that can be published in a book the children are putting together. In other words, the materials are not just for the teacher's eye.

When I talk about myself as being process oriented, if we're talking about writing, I'm talking about the notion that writing happens over time. It is a process, as opposed to one event. It involves talking, it involves thinking, it involves getting thoughts down and revising.

I don't believe that there is a particular process for all people. For example, some advocates of process-oriented writing believe there is a definite seven-step process that everybody goes through, such as brainstorming, fluency, revising, and editing.

One of the problems that I have seen in process writing – and this isn't just because of process writing but because of the society we live in – is that many times the expectations are less for poor children and children of color.

For instance, let's say in this seven-step approach that the fifth stage is producing fluency and getting one's thoughts out. Because the expectations are lower for many children of color and for poor children, when those children get to that fifth stage, some teachers think, "Isn't it wonderful that this child has gotten to this stage." And they don't push the student any further. And so many children of color never get to the editing stage or the stage of producing a final copy suitable for publication.

Should different strategies be used to teach reading and writing to children of different backgrounds or races? How does a teacher teach students with different backgrounds and levels in the same class?

What I see children needing, first of all, is somebody who responds to their needs. You cannot design your instruction based on the approach, should I teach the Koreans this way, should I teach the Hispanic kids this way, should I teach the African-American kids this way, or the white kids this way. First of all, as a teacher, you can't do it. Second, you'll probably make serious mistakes in ascertaining individual children's needs by assuming generalized ethnic characteristics.

What I would argue for instead is creating an environment that uses reading and writing for real purposes. If there are children who are not being successful – and success cannot be claimed when there is a lower level of performance by poor or nonwhite children – there is something else you need to do. That is when you use your knowledge about culture, as well as about this individual child, to try a different strategy. But I wouldn't suggest that someone design a class based on an abstract knowledge of children's racial or cultural differences.

You refer in your writings to Standard English versus what some call dialect English. What do you mean, and why is the distinction important?

I don't use the term *Standard English*. What I talk about is edited English, which essentially is the English you see in books — English that has been taken through an editing process. Some people's home language is more closely related to edited English than other people's, but nobody speaks exactly edited English.

It's important to make the distinction because edited English is the language of power. If you don't have access to edited English, you don't have the access to the power institutions in this country. If I didn't have access to edited English, I wouldn't be asked to do an interview, I wouldn't be successful in graduate school, I wouldn't be able to work at creating change in the way that I am hoping to do so.

Do some teachers, in trying to value a student's home language that may not be edited English, devalue the importance of teaching edited English?

Absolutely. And they do it for the best of reasons. They will say they want to give their students voice.

I would advocate strongly their doing so. But they also need to understand, as [African-American feminist scholar] bell hooks and Henry Louis Gates Jr. [chair of Afro-American Studies at Harvard University] talk about, that we have the responsibility to speak about justice in as many languages as we can acquire. You certainly need your home language to do that, but you also need edited English.

How do you teach edited English while still preserving a student's home language, if it differs from edited English?

There are all kinds of ways. In writing, you can compare the home language and edited English and directly teach the differences. You can teach the rules of edited English and students can apply that knowledge to their own writing.

In one of my articles, I talk about a wonderful Native Alaskan teacher, Martha Demientieff. Her students, who live in a small rural village, are not aware of the different codes of English. So in one exercise, she takes half a bulletin board with words or phrases from their writings and labels it, "Our Heritage Language." On the other half of the bulletin board she puts an equivalent statement under the label, "Formal English."

She and the students spend a long time on the "Heritage English" section and affirm how good the language feels and how expressive it is. Then she turns to the other side of the board and explains that there are other people who will judge them by the way they talk or write in what is called "Formal English." And she explains how the students will have to learn two ways of talking and writing, but that they will always know that their "Heritage English" is best.

She also does a wonderful exercise where the students prepare a formal dinner for the class, and dress up and use fancy tablecloths and china and so forth. They speak only Formal English at the meal. And then they prepare a picnic where only informal English is allowed. The point is, she is preserving the home language while still teaching the edited English.

How can one teach edited English in a way that forces white middle-class students, whose home language may be more similar to edited English, to value and respect non-Standard English?

That's an important question. A teacher in a group I am working with now noted that her students do not always respect other students in the class, based on the language variety that they use.

The way I would approach the problem, with young children, for example, is to get a collection of children's books written in various Englishes. This way, from early on, children are exposed to different varieties of language. The teacher can help them value the variety by noting, "Isn't this an interesting way that this is put? Doesn't that get the point across nicely?"

Children can also talk about the varieties of English spoken by people that they know, or by people on television shows. I've also seen teachers do translations. They have the children translate certain documents into the language that they use at home. And then they translate in reverse, from nonedited English to edited English. It usually ends up being both a very interesting and exciting venture. It also gives a sense of value to the home language.

I think students can also talk about when you would use different kinds of English, say if you are talking to somebody's grandmother, or to your running buddies. I have said that African Americans should not be allowed to get a doctorate unless they can write their dissertation in a form suitable for *Jet* magazine. I say that because *Jet* is an African-American publication that almost every black person reads. If you can't translate your ideas to other African Americans, then you are not working in the service of African Americans. Certainly, *Jet* uses what you would call edited English, but it's a style issue. All of these questions in terms of language are not just an issue of grammar; they are issues of style and tone as well.

You refer in your writings to the culture of power. How does this culture of power affect the teaching of reading and writing to children of color and poor children?

The culture of power is, essentially, the culture that maintains power – economic power, status power, any of the kinds of power that you can imagine in a society. If students don't have access to aspects of that culture, to the language of that culture, to the style of that culture, then they won't be able to be successful.

For the most part, one is not aware of one's culture. People, having grown up in a particular culture, believe that that's just the way the world is. Many teachers and educators don't realize that, first, they have a particular culture, and second, their culture, generally, is the culture of power.

Teachers have to understand enough about the cultures of the children they are teaching and about the culture of power so that they can make the translation necessary between the two. They have to help children understand and develop their home culture, and understand and acquire the culture of power.

Can you give some examples of how the culture of power affects classroom teaching?

I can talk about an adult learning situation I am familiar with. The teacher was a graduate student steeped in process approaches to writing. The students were African-American veterans hoping to improve their writing so they could continue in school.

The teacher had the students write at home and then come into peer editing groups, share what they had written, and edit each other's papers. But the students wanted the teacher, essentially, to tell them the rules, to tell them explicitly what they needed to do – the grammar, punctuation, style, and so forth. They wanted the teacher to teach them the rules for the language of power that they knew they would be held accountable for.

The students felt they were being shortchanged and became really angry. But the teacher insisted on maintaining her style and felt it was part of her identity. The teacher was asked, why are you doing it this way? She answered that it was important for the students to develop voice.

But it seems the students did have voice, considering the way they were yelling at her about what they wanted to have happen. But she was having a hard time hearing their voice. She didn't realize their need to access the culture of power, or her ability to provide that access. So she and the students were at loggerheads.

By contrast, a teacher whom many of your readers probably know, Mike Rose, who wrote *Lives on the Boundary,* defines himself as a traditional teacher in many ways. What he means is not that he does worksheets, but that he takes a very strong teacher role and makes explicit what the students need to know about academic writing. He also spends a great deal of time going back and forth: giving students clues to the language of power, and then backing away and letting them introduce their own ideas and thinking, which they can transform into academic writing. I should also stress that he and I agree that a *great deal* of student-to-student and student-to-teacher talk is necessary to accomplish this aim.

How do you teach children the rules of the culture of power yet help them struggle against the injustices of that culture?

It's important to speak explicitly in the classroom about power and oppression.

First, you need to make it clear that these particular rules are arbitrary. As [MIT Professor of Linguistics] Noam Chomsky says, what differentiates a language and a dialect is who has the army and the navy. These arbitrary sets of rules were developed because they matched, relatively speaking, the norms of the people in power. In other words, if African Americans had the army and the navy, then edited English would be more in line with how most African Americans speak.

Second, students have to understand that the system is set up to keep certain students from gaining power. One of the barriers is based on knowledge of these rules, or rather the lack of knowledge. One way to cheat the system and turn the sorting system on its head is to learn these rules. That way the system will be unsuccessful – at least in part, because they will always come up with new ways of sorting – in putting you in a particular cubbyhole.

You must also continually focus on the role of power. I was speaking recently to some young white women who are becoming teachers and who are tremendously uncomfortable with acknowledging that they have power or that they should try to use power. I said to them, "Having power is not bad, it's what you do with that power." They must learn to use their power to become advocates for children.

A colleague of mine likened it to a party, where all the African Americans were locked outside. The African Americans became angrier and angrier, and started shouting and banging on the door. The people inside slipped the door open and grabbed two of the loudest, so that they could join the party and help end some of the ruckus. The key then is, what do you do once you are inside? Do you sit down at the table or do you prop the door open? I think we have to help students and teachers understand their role in propping the door open.

You refer in your writings to gatekeeping points that hinder certain students from gaining access to the culture of power. Are you referring to SAT tests, or report cards, or what?

In essence, gatekeeping points refer to structures that are used to screen out people and keep them from moving to the next level of 'achievement, as defined by society's sorting system. Sometimes they are report cards, particularly with regard to moving to the next grade. There are also testing systems that say that if you don't make a certain score, you can't move to the next grade. That is a gate-keeping point. Getting into college is often a gatekeeping point, and SATs have certainly played a role in that.

There are teachers who, knowing the bias of the SATs, might say, "I'm not going to teach to the SAT; I'm going to teach my kids to learn to read, write, and think. I am not going to emphasize test-taking lessons." Are those teachers shortchanging their students or is that a valid way to combat the bias of the SATs?

I think they are shortchanging their students. Herb Kohl [author of 36 Children and other educational books] talks about his high school years in New York and how a group of Jewish teachers would get together with a group of Jewish students and say, "Okay, you've been learning about learning. Now we are going to teach you how to take this test."

It doesn't have to be teaching to the test the whole year. Rather, there appear to be some very specific test-taking strategies that can be taught in a relatively finite period of time. As long as the tests are used to exclude certain groups of people, it's important to give those students access to test-taking strategies.

How can a teacher strike a proper balance between teaching in-depth reading and writing skills, and test-taking skills?

If your classroom has been steeped in the concept of different kinds of languages used in different kinds of settings for different kinds of audiences, then one can approach the test as a particular kind of language. What I am suggesting is that the test be demystified. Students need to understand that the standardized test is not a measure of ability, but is designed to sort people out. So you might have the students say, "Let's figure out how these people think who created this test, how they are thinking about the world." Once you do that, it places it in the context of what you are teaching in the classroom, which is the varieties of English and the varieties of thinking and the varieties of language use.

One of the things that I have done with first graders is have them create tests. They learn the form. It's the same premise that's behind the view that children write in order to learn to read, and they read in order to learn to write. By creating worksheets for each other, which they find great fun, they also are learning a particular format that they are going to be faced with later on. But they are thinking about content and learning a certain kind of thinking strategy.

This process can be used at all grade levels. You give them the rules of how test makers create tests: a couple of conceivable answers, one that is way far out, and one that seems plausible but is a "trick" answer. The tests they create can be about anything, about slang language, or teenage culture, or the content they're studying, or whatever. There are ways to learn about taking tests that can be a lot of fun.

You have written that changing the educational system to ensure more diversity cannot be made from the bottom up, but that "we must push and agitate from the top down." Can you explain this more?

In reality, it has to be both ways. What I was suggesting is that you can't just change what goes on in the earlier grades, and not change what happens when you get to a gatekeeping point. You can't just say, "Okay, the tests are unimportant or unfair, so I'm not going to even consider issues related to the tests." The people who suffer from that decision are the children who then cannot go beyond high school, or into some high schools, because they will then be faced with a test.

It is insufficient to make such changes from the bottom up if you are not also working to change, and have changed, what constitutes being able to move to the next level.

How would this perspective affect teaching strategies?

You have to have a knowledge of what is going to be demanded of kids later on. And then you have to make sure that they have the ability to transcend those barriers. Many times it's just the ability to translate what they actually know into a form that the gatekeeping mechanism demands, like multiple-choice tests.

You may know how to write a coherent essay that is grammatically correct, but may not have thought about it in the context of punctuation rules that may be asked on a test. It's the initial learning that is the hard part, not the translation. After teachers have done all they can to promote learning, the strategy for the teacher comes in helping students make the translation.

Do African-American teachers feel estranged from progressive white educators on issues of learning to read and write? If so, why?

The African-American teachers I am in contact with — I hesitate to say all because nothing is all, but almost all — have talked to me about feeling estranged. It's not only an issue of how the teachers teach literacy. It's more an attitude.

The African-American teachers feel that white progressive teachers seem to believe they know better how to teach African-American children than the African-American teachers. It's often a refusal to include the African-American teachers in the dialogue about what would make sense for the children, particularly for African-American children.

Just this morning I was told of a progressive institution in New York where all the instructors are white and most of the students are not. They understood they needed diversity in their teachers, so they found Latino teachers, and African-American teachers, and Asian teachers, and brought them in as teaching assistants. Then they told them how everything they had done before as teachers was all wrong.

I see this pattern consistently — that many progressive teachers seem so locked into one way of doing things. They believe that in order to maintain their identity as a progressive, they can only teach in a certain way. And they appear to be unwilling to listen to those who may have had more success with the children they are trying to teach using alternative strategies.

Have you felt this condescension?

My experience has been a little different because I had to relearn what African-American teachers know. For example, I had gone to progressive universities and I learned the open classroom style of teaching, discovery learning approach, creating a language-rich environment — all the buzzwords of the time. It wasn't till almost the end of the time I was teaching in the classroom that I realized I was not as successful with the African-American children as I was with the white children.

That led me to try to figure out what I didn't know, or what I needed to know. The African-American teachers — who were viewed by the school at large as being regressive, not as child-centered, essentially not as good teachers — were producing African-American kids who knew a lot more than the kids taught by the progressive teachers.

Was this because of an emphasis on skills? What were they doing differently?

It's not really just so-called skills, it's the explicitness that's important. And this explicitness applies to whatever you're teaching, whether it's a process or an item of information.

For example, one of the African-American teachers told me how to explicitly teach first grade and make use of an open classroom. She told me to have the children *practice* going to a particular center, working there, cleaning up. Otherwise I had kids who were taking the materials and throwing them around the room, particularly the African-American kids, who may not have had the chance to work in those kinds of settings as much as the white middle-class kids did.

There's also explicitness to the point of saying, "Well, yes, there are such things as capital letters and here's when you might see them." Or going back and forth and asking, "Where do you see a capital letter? Oh, you see it there? Let's talk about why it might be there."

Essentially, it is the opposite of assuming that everybody is going to discover everything on their own. I found that the people who appear to be discovering everything on their own have actually received direct instruction at home, although it's not in a way that parents might think of as direct instruction.

As I picked my daughter up from nursery school yesterday, a white father was picking his daughter up at the same time. There was a tree stump in the room and the father was looking at it with the daughter while she was putting on her boots. He said, "Remember what I told you, how you can tell the number of years, how old the tree was. Do you remember? Can you count them?"

That is direct instruction. For myself, I hear myself talking to my daughter. Her name is Maya, and she's going around saying, "M-M-

M-M-M-Maya, M-M-M-M-M-om." And I say, "Right, M-M-Maya. That sounds the same in the beginning as M-M-Mommy, doesn't it? Listen to that, M-M-aya and M-M-ommy. What else sounds like that?

All day long there is direct instruction that middle-class parents provide for their kids. And then the kids go into a "language-rich environment" and appear to achieve without any kind of explicit instruction. So that leads people to think, "What we need — all we need — are these language-rich environments, or science-rich environments, or math-rich environments, and kids will just excel."

What they fail to realize is that there are other children who haven't come in with the same kinds of explicit instruction or direct instruction from parents. By not providing it for them, *along with* the language-rich environment, what teachers are doing is putting those children at a disadvantage.

Recommended Resources

Rethinking the Curriculum

A People's History of the United States

by Howard Zinn, New York: Harper & Row, 1981. The best single-volume history of the United States.

A Different Mirror

by Ronald Takaki, Boston: Little, Brown, 1993. A multicultural history of the United States.

Who Built America? (2 vols.)

by the American Social History Project, New York: Pantheon, 1992. American history from the perspective of working people.

Rethinking Columbus

edited by Bill Bigelow, Barbara Miner, and Bob Peterson, Milwaukee, WI: Rethinking Schools, 1991. A critical teaching guide on the arrival of Columbus in the Americas, mainly from a native point of view.

A Pedagogy for Liberation: Dialogues on Transforming Education

by Ira Shor and Paulo Freire, South Hadley, MA: Bergin & Garvey, 1987. A discussion about how teachers can involve their students in critiquing and transforming the world.

Open Minds to Equality: A Sourcebook of Learning Activities to Promote Race, Sex, Class, and Age Equity

by Nancy Schniedewind and Ellen Davidson, New York: Prentice Hall, 1983. Also by Schniedewind and Davidson, *Cooperative Learning, Cooperative Lives: A Sourcebook for Learning Activities for Building a Peaceful World,* Dubuque, IA: W. C. Brown, 1987. Two activity-packed guides for Grades 3 through 8 that do an excellent job of addressing controversial topics.

Hope and History: Why We Must Share the Story of the Movement

by Vincent Harding, Maryknoll, NY: Orbis Books, 1990. An eloquent history on the significance of the civil rights movement, suggesting ways teachers may draw on and link past struggles with present movements for equity and justice.

Whole Language: What's the Difference?

by Carole Edelsky, Bess Altwerger, and Barbara Flores, Portsmouth, NH: Heinemann, 1991. A careful and rigorous explanation of the theory behind whole language.

Creating Classrooms for Authors

by Jerome Harste, Kathy Short, and Carolyn Burke, Portsmouth, NH: Heinemann, 1988. A rich source of practical, concrete solutions for a whole language classroom.

Teachers and Writers Collaborative

5 Union Square West, New York, NY 10003-3306; 212-691-6590; fax 212-675-0171. An organization of writers and educators offering creative ways to teach writing. Publishers of *Teachers & Writers* magazine, which comes out five times per year.

Civics for Democracy: A Journey for Teachers and Students

by Katherine Isaac, 1993, Essential Books, P.O. Box 19405, Washington, DC 20036. A how-to civics book that encourages student social action.

Power in Our Hands: A Curriculum on the History of Work and Workers in the U.S.

by William Bigelow and Norman Diamond, New York: Monthly Review Press, 1988. A collection of lessons for bringing labor history to life in the classroom.

Teaching for Change

by the Network of Educators on the Americas, NECA, 1118 22nd St., NW, Washington, DC 20037; 202-429-0137; fax 202-429-9766. A catalogue of curricular resources and a quarterly newsletter by the same name.

Radical Teacher

Boston Women's Teachers' Group, P.O. Box 102, Kendall Square Post Office, Cambridge, MA 02142. Many valuable articles and teaching ideas from a critical standpoint.

National Women's History Project

7738 Bell Rd., Windsor, CA 95492; 707-838-6000. An organization offering material and workshops on teaching the history of women.

Coalition of Essential Schools

Box 1969, Brown University, Providence, RI 02912. A network of schools committed to the nine principles for good common schools set forth by Theodore Sizer.

PART III

Stratification in the Classroom: Testing and Tracking

Since the early twentieth century, policymakers in charge of big city school systems have used testing and tracking to cope with diversity. Most school leaders believed it was essential for schools to train the great mass of young people in disciplined work habits, respect for authority, and vocational skills, which would prepare them to function as efficient workers in the corporate economy. Strongly influenced by racist, sexist, and class-biased notions of human ability, they looked to testing and tracking to find systematic ways of sorting children along ethnic, racial, class, and gender lines.

Despite research that demonstrates how standardized testing and tracking hurt many children, these practices are still widespread. The chapters in this section illustrate the injuries inflicted by standardized testing and tracking, and offer practical alternatives that can be adopted by teachers, schools, and school systems.

Vowing never to teach the sort of "memory Olympics" in social studies classes he endured as a student, Bill Bigelow found ways to bring history alive for his students and create a detracked class that enabled "nonacademic" students to succeed. He emphasizes that detracking schools without developing new approaches to teaching simply reproduces stratification in heterogeneous classrooms. Bigelow describes how teamwork, role plays, simulations, and improvisations can make learning accessible to all. His approach is built on flexible assignments and a curriculum that links history to the lives of his students.

Unfortunately, classrooms such as Bigelow's are still relatively rare. Parents need to be alert to how tracking affects the learning opportunities given their children. In the short guide that follows Bigelow's piece, the National Coalition of Education Activists lists questions that parents should ask about the schools their children attend. If the answers to these questions are troubling, policy changes at the school may be in order.

Although systemwide tracking practices may appear firmly set in place, they are not unalterable. In Milwaukee, school officials and teachers were disturbed by tracking practices in high school mathematics. Low-income students and students of color were often tracked out of ninth-grade algebra, a "gatekeeping" course that needs to be mastered in order for students to have a good chance of going to college. Barbara Miner of *Rethinking Schools* describes how the Milwaukee Public Schools are moving toward requiring algebra for all ninth-grade students. The school system is implementing this change through careful coordination, extensive retraining for teachers and counselors, and intensive academic support for struggling students.

Finally, Terry Meier takes a critical look at standardized testing, a nearly universal practice that often has the effect of narrowing opportunities for students of color and working-class students. Summarizing the vast literature on this kind of testing, she uses vivid examples to demonstrate its class and cultural biases. Meier illustrates how standardized tests serve as poor guides to academic excellence, yet continue to be used as a sorting device that consigns many students of color to an academic second-class citizenship. Her research highlights the necessity of finding more equitable and educationally useful ways to assess student achievement.

Taken as a whole, the articles in this chapter offer a convincing critique of standardized testing and tracking. Equally important, they demonstrate that although detracking is difficult, it can be done. Replacing tracking with more equitable and effective educational practices is a key piece of the school reform puzzle. It will require both changes in teaching and a willingness to transform policies that have created islands of privilege for some white, middle-class students by denying opportunities to others.

Getting Off the Track:
Stories from an
Untracked Classroom

BILL BIGELOW

In school, I hated social studies. My U.S. history class was, in the words of critical educator Ira Shor, a memory Olympics, with students competing to see how many dates, battles, and presidents we could cram into our adolescent heads. My California history class was one long lecture, almost none of which I remember today, save for the names of a few famous men — mostly scoundrels. This marathon fact-packing was interrupted only once, as I recall, by a movie on raisins. *Social* studies — ostensibly a study of human beings — was nothing of the kind. "Poor History," writes Eduardo Galeano, "had stopped breathing: betrayed in academic tests, lied about in classrooms, drowned in dates, they had imprisoned her in museums and buried her, with floral wreaths, beneath statuary bronze and monumental marble."

Today, students who prove unresponsive to similar memory games are often labeled "slow learners" — or worse — and find themselves dumped in a low-track class, called "basic" or "skills," understood by all as "the dumb class." This is classic victim blaming, penalizing kids for their inability to turn human beings into abstractions, for their failure to recall disconnected factoids. And it's unnecessary. Tracking is usually advocated with good intentions; but its only educational justification derives from schools' persistence in teaching in ways that fail to reach so many children, thus necessitating some students' removal to less demanding academic pursuits.

Untracking a school requires untracking instruction. Unfortunately, many of those who argue against tracking offer only the vaguest hints of what an effective untracked class could look like. Hence their critique that tracking delivers inferior instruction to many students, lowers self-esteem, reproduces social hierarchies, and reinforces negative stereotypes, may have ironic consequences. Compelled by these and other arguments, schools that untrack without a thoroughgoing pedagogical transformation can end up simply with a system of tracking internal to each classroom. I've seen this in more than one "untracked" school: students who come to class able to absorb lectures, write traditional research papers, memorize discrete facts – and stay awake – succeed; those who can't, sit in the back of the class and sleep, doodle, or disrupt – and fail. Those of us critical of tracking need to take responsibility for offering a concrete and viable vision of an untracked classroom. Otherwise, the results of untracking will replicate the results of tracking, and many educators will lean back in their chairs and say, "I told you so."

Components of an Untracked Classroom

As a classroom teacher, I've found that an antitracking pedagogy in social studies has several essential, and interlocking, components. And while the examples I'll use are drawn from my high school social studies class, these components remain as valid in other content areas or can be adapted.

- *Show, don't tell.* Through role plays, improvisations, and simulations students need to *experience,* not simply hear about, social dynamics.

- *Assignments need to be flexible enough to adjust to students' interests or abilities.* Teachers can assign projects, poetry, personal writing, critiques, and the like, which allow students to enter and succeed at their own levels of competence and creativity. This is not a suggestion to give easy assignments, but to adopt a flexible academic rigor. And in no way should this detract from students developing traditional scholastic skills they will need to pursue higher education.

- *The curriculum needs to constantly draw on students' lives as a way of delving into broader social themes.* Knowledge needs to be both internal and external; history, government, sociology, literature are always simultaneously about "them" *and* "us."

- *The classroom environment needs to be encouraging, even loving.* All students need to know that their potential is respected, that they are included in a community of learners. A rhetoric of caring is insufficient. Both the form and the content of the class must underscore every child's worth.

- *What we teach has to matter.* Students should understand how the information and analytic tools they're developing make a difference in their lives, that the aim of learning is not just a grade, simple curiosity, or "because you'll need to know it later."

- *An antitracking pedagogy should explicitly critique the premises of tracking.* Students need to examine the history and practice of tracking in order to become aware of and expel doubts about their capacity to think and achieve. We cannot merely untrack our classrooms; we have to engage students in a dialogue about *why* we untrack our classrooms. More than this, the curriculum needs to critique the deeper social inequities and hierarchies that were the original stimulus for tracking and continue today to breed unjust educational practices.

· *Finally, the method of evaluating students in an untracked class should embody the flexibility and caring described above.* We can't advocate creating flexible assignments that adjust to students' interests and abilities and then hold youngsters accountable to rigid performance criteria. Evaluation needs to be guided by principles of equity rather than efficiency.

The power of an antitracking approach lies in the interrelationship of these components, not in merely applying them checklist fashion. Lest my examples sound too self-congratulatory or facile, I should begin by confessing that all this is easier said than done, and my classroom is rarely as tidy as my written descriptions. My students, just like everyone else's, get off task, hold distracting side conversations, and frequently fail to complete their homework. The aim here is not to provide a cookbook of tried and true educational recipes but to contribute to a broader discussion about how we can teach for justice in an unjust society, and to explore how such a commitment can contribute to successful classroom practice.

Bringing the Curriculum to Life

Role plays, simulations, and improvisations allow students to climb into history and social concepts and to explore them from the inside. It's a first-person approach to society that gives each student an equal shot at grasping concepts and gaining knowledge. Students who are advanced in traditional academic terms are not held back with this more experiential approach, but neither are they privileged by their facility with, say, Standard English or their stamina in reading and memorizing textbookspeak. Just about every unit I teach includes at least one role play, simulation, or set of improvisations.

For example, in a unit on U.S. labor history, students role-play the 1934 West Coast longshore strike, as described in *The Power in Our Hands.* In five groups – longshoremen, waterfront employers, farmers, unemployed workers, and representatives of the central labor council – students confront the choices that confronted the original strike participants. From each group's respective standpoint, students propose solutions to the strike, decide whether they want the governor to call in the National Guard to protect strikebreakers, and determine how they will respond if the guard is called upon. Not all groups have clear positions on the questions and so students have to use their creativity to design potential resolutions and their persuasive powers to build alliances with members of other groups.

The dynamics of the strike are lived in the classroom, experienced firsthand by students, instead of being buried in the textbook. Longshoremen negotiate with farmers to support the strike, waterfront employers seek to entice the unemployed with offers of work, and more than one group threatens violence if the governor calls in the guard. Students must master lots of information in order to effectively represent their positions, but it's not just a memory Olympics; they have to *use* the information in the heat of deal making and debate.

Most students have a great time, running around the room negotiating and arguing with recalcitrant peers; often, students remain engaged after the bell rings. But the role play is not simply play. As Paulo Freire says, "Conflict is the midwife of consciousness," and the simulated conflict in role plays like this allows students to reflect on much larger issues: When are alliances between different social groups possible? What role does the government play, and should it play, in labor disputes? Is violence or the threat of violence justified in class conflict? Can people be out for themselves, but also support each other? These are big and tough questions, but because they draw on an experience every student watched and helped create, they are concrete rather than abstract. Regardless of past academic achievement, the activities and discussions challenge every student.

These and other questions can also lead us to explore the contemporary relevance of an almost sixty-year-old strike. Often students-as-longshoremen cobble together an alliance including farmers, the unemployed, and the central labor council. "What do you think happened in real life?" I ask. "Sure we can get together," many a student has responded. "But we're just in a role play in a classroom. It's easy to get together in here. I don't think it could happen in real life." Most students are surprised to learn that it *did* happen in real life – working people in 1934 maintained a remarkable degree of solidarity. And from this knowledge we discuss when people can and cannot get together. Students also reflect on their own cynicism about people's capacity to unite for worthy goals.

After the role play, I sometimes ask students to relate our discussion to their lives, and to write about a time when they were able to stick together with a group for a common objective. In our class read-around the next day, I encourage students to take notes on common themes they hear in each other's stories. Here, too, we can continue to pursue theoretical questions about unity, but it's a pursuit rooted in our experience, not one imposed on a class as an abstract academic inquiry. It *is* serious academic work, democratized through students' in-class experience and its connection to their lives.

Improvisation and Equal Access to the Curriculum

Improvisation is another kind of "leveling" role play that seeks to give all students equal access to information and theoretical insight. In a unit on U.S. slavery and resistance to slavery, I provide students with a set of first-person roles for different social groups in the South, which supplements information already gleaned from films, a slide-lecture, poetry, a simulation, readings, and class discussions. They read these roles and in small groups select from a list of improvisation choices. They can also create their own improv topic or combine ones of mine to form something new.

The topics are bare-bones descriptions requiring lots of student initiative to plan and perform. For example:

- A plantation owner tells a mother and father, who are enslaved, that he's going to sell their children. He needs the money.
- An enslaved person encounters a poor white farmer on the road. The farmer accuses the slave of looking him directly in the eye, which is illegal.
- An enslaved person asks an owner if she or he can buy her or his freedom.

There's an obvious danger that students' performances of these and any role plays can drift toward caricature. Caricature may allow students to distance and insulate themselves from the enormity of the subject, but it can also allow them to trivialize one of the most horrendous periods in human history. However, the alternative of students remaining outside, removed from a subject like the enslavement of African people, seems to me a greater danger. So we talk about how we can't possibly know what people experienced, but through our performance, imagination, writing, and discussion we're going to do the best we can. And students have responded with passionate skits that have moved many in the class to tears — that have, in Toni Morrison's words, given "voice to the 'unspeakable.'"

As students perform the improvs, I ask them to take notes on powerful lines or situations, as they'll be writing from the perspective of one or more of the characters. After each skit we discuss the problem posed, and how students handled it. As we progress, I draw on their improvs to teach about laws, different forms of resistance, how certain practices varied from region to region or in different time periods. It's a series of minilectures, but accessible to all students because they are linked to a shared experience.

Afterward I ask students to write an interior monologue — the inner thoughts — from the point of view of one of the characters in an improv. People have the freedom to write from the point of view of a character they represented or one they watched. I encourage students to "find your passion," as my teaching partner, Linda Christensen, likes to say — so they're free to rearrange and massage the assignment to fit their interest. Most students write the assigned interior monologue, but some prefer poems, dialogue poems, or letters. This, too, is a vital part of an antitracking pedagogy: Students need sufficient freedom to enter an assignment at a point of their choosing; they must be able to reconstruct the task according to their interests and abilities.

For example, after one set of improvisations, "Diane," a young woman with a low-track academic history, wrote a dialogue poem about childbirth. The paired perspectives are from the wife of a white plantation owner and an enslaved African-American woman. It reads in part:

> My man is not here to hold my hand.
> *My man is not here to hold my hand.*
>
> He's out in the field.
> *He's out in the field.*
>
> with a whip in his hand.
> *with a whip at his back.*
>
> I lay here on my feather bed.
> *I lay here on the blanketed floor.*
>
> The pain comes. I push.
> *The pain comes. I push.*
>
> Someone, please come and help.
> *Someone, please come and help.*

The midwife comes, the doctor, too.
The midwife comes, no doctor.

Silk sheets in my mouth.
A wood stick in my mouth.

To halt the screams.
To halt the screams.

I push some more.
I push some more.

I sigh relief. The child is born.
I sigh relief. The child is born.

Strong lungs scream.
Silence.

It squirms there, full of life.
It lies there, cold and blue.

It is a boy.
It was a boy.

Another born to be big and strong.
Another one born to be laid in the ground.

A babe suckling at my breast.
This babe lying in my arms.

Tomorrow I will plan a party.
Tomorrow I will go to the field....

None of the improvs had been about childbirth, but this was where Diane found her passion.

There are no wrong answers here. Virtually every interior monologue or poem is plausible, even if students approach the same character's thoughts in very different ways. Chaunetta writes from the point of view of a woman whose children are sold off, Eric from that of a man contemplating escape, Monica from that of a plantation owner reflecting on his dissatisfaction with his overseers. Some of the pieces, like Diane's, are publishable, some not even close. But each student gains an insight with validity, and together their portraits form an emotional and empathic patchwork quilt. And again, the assignment challenges all students, regardless of supposed skill levels.

Untracking the Big Questions

Before students begin the read-around I ask them to take notes on three questions: (1) In what ways were people hurt by slavery? (2)

How did people resist slavery? (3) Explain why you think slavery could or could not have ended without a violent struggle. We circle-up for the read-around. I encourage, but don't require, everyone in class to share his or her writing. As students read their pieces, they compliment each other, offer "aha's," and take notes on the questions. This is not an editing session, so critical remarks aren't allowed; thus, students know they'll hear only positive comments if they choose to share. The read-around, or sharing circle, builds community as youngsters applaud each other's efforts and insights. The medium is in large part the message: we all count here.

Afterward, people look over their notes and write on the questions. Unlike textbook questions, these encourage students to make meaning themselves, not to parrot back the meaning decided by some publishing company. The third question is a difficult one, calling for students to reflect on the obstacles to social change. It's a question that ordinarily might be set aside for the "advanced" class, but because of an antitracking pedagogy it can be approached by everyone: they all watched the improvs, they all participated, they heard my minilectures, they discussed their questions and insights, they climbed inside someone's head to write from his or her point of view, and they listened to the "collective text" created by the entire class. Wrestling with a question like this is simply the next step. Everyone can succeed, and everyone is intellectually challenged. And because theory is grounded in students' in-class experience, the assignment doesn't privilege those students who may be more practiced at abstract thinking.

If we want our classes to be accessible to students regardless of academic background and confidence, we have to discover ways of bringing concepts alive. Simulations are another show-don't-tell strategy. For example, in exploring the history of work in the United States, particularly "scientific management," or "Taylorization" — owners studying and then chopping up the labor process into component parts and assigning workers one repetitive task — a simple lecture would reach some students. But using paper airplanes and students as skilled workers to stimulate changes in the production process provides all students access to a vital piece of history, which can help them reflect on their own work lives. We can tape off the floor and offer pieces of chocolate to simulate land and wealth distribution in different societies; unsharpened and sharpened pencils can represent raw materials and manufactured products to help us show the dynamics of colonialism; and with balls of cotton, shirts, wheat, "guns," and bank notes, we can walk students through pre-Civil War sectional conflicts. An untracked classroom can be both more playful and more rigorous than a traditional read-this/listen-to-this/write-this approach.

We can also allow kids to get out of the classroom and into the community, both as social investigators and change makers. Students can visit a senior citizens' center to interview people about a particular time period. They might tour a factory to learn about working conditions, or travel to a Native American community to meet and talk with activists. Often, I conclude a major unit or a semester by encouraging students to become "truth tellers" — to take their knowledge about an issue beyond the classroom walls. One year, a student of Linda's and mine choreographed and performed for a number of classes a dance on the life of Ben Linder, the Portlander murdered by the Contras in Nicaragua. Numbers of students rewrite children's books from a multicultural standpoint and use them to lead discussions at elementary schools. One group produced a videotape, cablecast citywide, about the erosion of Native American fishing rights on the Columbia River. One year, a student in a global studies class wrote and recorded "The South Africa Rap," questioning why corporations leave communities in the United States and invest in apartheid; it was subsequently played by several community radio stations around the country. A real-world curriculum aims to give students an equal opportunity to understand society — and to change it.

A New Teacher-Student Covenant

An antitracking pedagogy needs to offer alternatives to traditional teaching methods and critique these methods as well. The traditional teacher-student covenant proposes to rehearse students for alienation: I give you an assignment over which you have little or no control. It's not about you; it's about subject x. I think it up — or, more often, a textbook company thinks it up — I design it, you perform it, and I evaluate it. In exchange for successfully carrying out your part of the bargain, I give you a reward: your grade. Neither the work nor the grade has any intrinsic value, but the grade has exchange value that can be banked and spent later for desired ends. Conception and execution are separate, and this dichotomy prepares young people for a life of essential powerlessness over the conditions of their labor and the purposes toward which that labor is used. An antitracking pedagogy needs to offer a new covenant, one that promises students an education rooted in their lives, with much greater initiative and participation.

In Linda Christensen's and my Literature and History course we constantly draw on students' lives as a way of illuminating both history and literature, and in turn draw on the history and literature as a way of illuminating students' lives. In the slavery and slave resistance unit, mentioned above, we read an excerpt from Frederick Douglass's autobiography in which a teenage Douglass defies and physically confronts his overseer. We discuss the conditions in Douglass's life that propelled him into this confrontation, and growing out of the discussion ask students to write about a time in their lives when they stood up for what was right. The assignment gives a framework for students' writing but offers them lots of room to move, and as with the other assignments described, this one adjusts to a student's skill level. Some students may be able to write a personally probing, metaphorical piece, while others may struggle to write a couple of paragraphs, but the assignment offers all students a point of entry.

The read-around celebrates the diversity of students' experience, and, in some cases, their bravery or self-sacrifice: Nate writes about confronting a racist and abusive police officer, Stephanie about attending an antinuclear-power demonstration, Josh about challenging a teacher's unfairness, Zeneda about interrupting an incident of sexual harassment. But the stories also give us the raw material to reflect on when and why people resist, and the relative effectiveness of some forms of resistance over others. And we can test our findings against Frederick Douglass's experiences.

In a unit on the history and sociology of schooling, students write about an encounter with inequality in education, and at a different point, about a positive learning experience. In a lesson on the Cherokee Indian Removal they write about a time their rights were violated. After reading a Studs Terkel interview with C. P. Ellis, who quit his leadership position in the Klan and became a civil rights advocate and union organizer, students write about a significant change they made in their lives.

The personal writing and sharing undercuts a curriculum designed to inure students to alienated work, as the assignment also equalizes students' opportunity for academic success and theoretical insight. Moreover, it is a key part of creating a classroom discourse that in both form and content tells each student, "You matter; your life and learning are important here." That's another aim of breaking from a curriculum that is traditionally male dominated, and extols the lives of elites over working people and people of color. Unless we reorient the content of the curriculum to better reflect the lives of all our students, we implicitly tell young people, "Some of you are better than others; some of you are destined for bigger things."

An Explicit Critique of Tracking

Ultimately, an antitracking pedagogy needs to engage students in an explicit critique of tracking. As Jeannie Oakes and others have shown, one of the by-products of tracking, even one of its aims, is that low-tracked students blame themselves for their subordinate position in the scholastic hierarchy; students come to believe that they are defective and the system is OK. Consequently, the unequal system of education, of which tracking is an important part, needs a critical classroom examination so that students can expose and expel the voices of self-blame and can overcome whatever doubts they have about their capacity for academic achievement.

In our unit on the history and sociology of schooling, students look critically at their own educations. We start with today and work backward in time to understand the origins of the structures that now seem as natural as the seasons. From David Storey's novel, *Radcliffe,* we read a short excerpt that poignantly describes the unequal treatment received by students of different class backgrounds and, as mentioned earlier, ask students to recall an episode of unequal schooling from their own lives. We use the novel excerpt and students' stories to talk about the hidden curricula embedded in school practices – the lessons students absorb about democracy, hierarchy, power, solidarity, race, social class, resistance, and so on. Students make observations on their own educational experiences, both past and present, and informally inventory the building's resources: who gets what kind of equipment, facilities, class sizes and why? Our students' research is subversive in the best sense of the term as they engage in a critical inquiry that subverts the apparent legitimacy of a system of privilege that benefits some at the expense of others.

We read excerpts of Jean Anyon's 1980 *Journal of Education* article, "Social Class and the Hidden Curriculum of Work," which attempts to demonstrate that schools' expectations of students vary depending on the social position of students' parents. For example, through her research Anyon found that schools in working-class communities value rote behavior and following directions; "affluent professional schools" value creativity and student initiative. The article, written for an academic journal, is a real stretch for a lot of students and might stay beyond their reach if we confined our conceptual exploration to reading and discussion. Instead, we test Anyon's theory by traveling to a wealthier, suburban school to make observations on classroom and school dynamics. We return to compare these to the observations of our own Jefferson High, a school in the center of a predominantly African-American, working-class community. Their firsthand experience makes theory student-friendly and allows everyone to participate in the discussion as we evaluate Anyon's argument.

To provide at least a partial historical context for their findings, students participate in a mock 1920s school board deliberation, representing different social groups as a way of examining who promoted and benefited from the introduction of intelligence testing and differentiated curricula. We read excerpts from the second chapter of Jeannie Oakes's *Keeping Track* on the history of tracking, and a chapter on the history of the SAT test, "The Cult of Mental Measurement," from David Owens's *None of the Above.* From Paul Chapman's *Schools as Sorters,* we review a 1920 survey conducted by Stanford University that found high school students had aspirations that were too high for the jobs available: over 60 percent of them wanted professional careers, whereas fewer than 5 percent of jobs were in the professions. Concluded Stanford psychologist William V. Proctor: "For [students'] own best good and the best good of the nation a great many of them should be directed toward the agricultural, mechanical, and industrial fields." Could the "problem" of students' high expectations help explain some social groups' commitment to intelligence testing and tracking? My students react with some anger at this conscious attempt to deflate children's dreams.

Providing new information and ways to question the character of schooling is a vital component of untracking any school or classroom. As I've suggested, tracking is not just a bad idea, but is a practice linked to the legitimation and maintenance of deep social inequality. Undercutting the legitimacy of unfair privilege is thus another necessary piece in an antitracking strategy. As indicated in the classroom examples provided, the curriculum can offer students permission and encouragement to critique social inequities and to think about alternatives. Further, introducing into the classroom a legacy of resistance to injustice helps nurture an ethos of hope and possibility. Learning from individuals and movements working for democratic social change, both past and present, provides inspiration that not only can societies change for the better, but so can we. Because tracking rests on a premise that people's intellectual capabilities and potential for achievement are fixed, an antitracking curriculum needs to demonstrate a more hopeful – and realistic – view of human possibility.

Grades and Equity

At the end of the first quarter Linda Christensen and I taught together, Alphonso came to complain about his grade. "I don't think I deserve a C," he argued. "Maybe I can't write as well as Katy. But she came in writing like that, and I've worked really hard. Compare what I'm doing now to what I wrote when the year began. I think I deserve at least a B." Alphonso's complaint illustrates a dilemma of evaluating or, more precisely, grading students in an untracked class. Alphonso was right: Katy knew more history, wrote with more detail and clarity, and had a firmer grasp of course concepts. But Alphonso had worked hard, made important strides in his writing and comprehension, and regularly shared his insights with the class. Still, were we to grade on a curve or based on some fixed standard of achievement, a C would have been fair, even generous. However, we had told the class we wouldn't grade this way, that their grades would be based on effort, openness, growth, consistency of written and oral participation, respect for one another, as well as clarity of analysis. Thus we gladly changed Alphonso's grade and confessed our mistake.

"Fair grading" is an oxymoron and I'd prefer not to give letter grades at all. I attended an ungraded college, Antioch, where professors wrote students end-of-term letters indicating academic strengths and areas needing work. Students responded with self-evaluations that commented on teachers' assessments. It all seemed to make more sense. Of course, Antioch professors didn't see 150 students a day. Nor were they ordered by school or state authorities to sum up a student's performance with a single letter grade.

An antitracking pedagogy needs a system of student evaluation that does not reward students based primarily on the skills and knowledge with which they begin a class. A system of fixed criteria from the outset benefits some and penalizes others largely on the basis of class, race, gender, or nationality. An untracked class needs an egalitarian evaluation system that lets all students know they can succeed based on what they do in class, not on what they have or have not accomplished in the past.

Linda and I do not assign letter grades on individual assignments during the term. Instead, we write comments on students' papers indicating our evaluation and keep track of in-class participation and completion of written work. Students maintain folders of their work and at the end of each term write extensive self-evaluations analyzing all aspects of their achievement in class and present a case for a particular letter grade. Linda and I read their evaluations, review their folders, discuss their overall progress, and conference with students. Only then do we assign letter grades.

As in Alphonso's case, sometimes we blow it. But students are always free to challenge us, call our criteria into question, and draw our attention to factors we may have overlooked. Every year we tell students about Alphonso to underscore our fallibility and to encourage their vigilance.

Ours is obviously not the only way to grade. But whatever system teachers adopt should derive from a broader antitracking philosophy and strategy. In evaluation, as with everything else, we must be bound by considerations of equity, not tradition or efficiency.

An antitracking pedagogy is more than just a collection of good teaching ideas strung together in a classroom with kids of different social backgrounds and educational histories. That may be a step in the right direction, but we still need to ask: toward what? Is it enough to offer quality education in a heterogeneous setting, as some untracking proponents suggest? I don't think so. Once out of school, our students will still be "tracked" by jobs that require little decision making and initiative, by high unemployment, by racism and sexism. We can't truly untrack schools without untracking society. Thus, an antitracking pedagogy should equip educators and students to recognize and combat all inequity. Its organizing principle should be justice – in the classroom, in school, and in society at large.

Some of the anti-tracking lessons mentioned here, and others, are described in greater detail in the author's curricula Strangers in Their Own Country *(South Africa),* The Power in Our Hands *(U.S. labor history), and* Inside the Volcano *(U.S. foreign policy in Central America), available from NECA, 1118 22nd St., NW, Washington, D.C. 20037.*

Is Your Child Being Tracked?

NATIONAL COALITION OF EDUCATION ACTIVISTS

You may not immediately recognize tracking in your school, or your school system may claim that it does not use tracking. However, if you answer *no* to any of the questions below, you may want to talk with other parents or teachers about your concerns and investigate further.

1. Do most classes have a racial and ethnic mix similar to the school as a whole? For instance, if the school is two-thirds black and one-third white, are most of the classes the same or are some 90 percent black and others 90 percent white?

2. Do most classes have roughly equal numbers of boys and girls?

3. Do students in most classes have backgrounds similar to those found in the school as a whole? For example, do there seem to be classes where most students' parents are professionals and others where most students come from poor or working-class families?

4. Can you see that your children are progressing? Grades may not be the best indicator; notice whether children are reading and writing more or better, moving beyond basic math skills, expressing more complicated ideas, taking on more responsibility, developing skills or talents, and so on.

5. Do your children's teachers seem to know your children's weaknesses and strengths and have a plan for addressing them?

6. When you attend school programs or extracurricular activities, do the participating students seem to reflect the racial, ethnic, and class mix found in the school as a whole?

7. If your school or school system has special programs or schools, do the students who are part of them seem to reflect the mix found in the school or system as a whole?

Adapted from an article that appeared in NCEA's information packet, "Maintaining Inequality."

8. Do your children receive meaningful homework assignments? Ask questions if they:

   · have no homework;

   · get many worksheet drills;

   · are reading and answering questions on paragraphs instead of whole stories and books;

   · have lots of multiple choice questions rather than thoughtful writing assignments.

9. Is your child enrolled in algebra by the ninth grade? This is an important "gateway" course. Students who do not have access to algebra by Grade 9 will have trouble fitting in math courses they need for college, trades, and many jobs.

10. Do your child's classes focus on regular coursework in English, mathematics, reading, et cetera? Or do they focus primarily on basic skills to pass a "competency test" or similar test?

Algebra for All:
An Equation for Equity

BARBARA MINER

It's computer lab day for Angel, and she's having some difficulty with the assignment. As part of a freshman algebra class at Washington High School in Milwaukee, Angel is working on a program that tests students' knowledge of how to apply mathematical concepts to replicate an industrial design. She is initially asked to replicate a design with two punched-out circles and a thick median strip, using a square as the base.

She tries, unsuccessfully. "Oh I forgot to rotate it 135 degrees," she mumbles to herself. She tries again, and suddenly a look of pride washes over her face.

"Hey, look, Mr. Taborn, I got it!"

Angel moves on to the next formula, and before long is expected to use six different functions in a specific order to replicate a design. What began as a seemingly simple exercise has quickly turned quite complex. And Angel, along with other freshmen at Washington, is expected to do it.

A young African-American woman, Angel is part of a citywide effort to "detrack" math and make algebra mandatory for all freshmen. It's a far cry from the day when many freshmen found themselves stuck in remedial classes doing the same frustrating fraction exercises they had been doing since fourth grade.

The algebra initiative began in the fall of 1993. Roughly 5,300 of the 6,000 ninth graders in Milwaukee Public Schools were placed in algebra, and an additional 300 ninth graders took other advanced math courses such as geometry. The rest were primarily in exceptional education, according to Vince O'Connor, mathematics curriculum specialist at MPS Central Office. About 90 percent of the algebra students were in heterogeneous classes, with the remainder in an honors course or program for the "academically talented," O'Connor said. The year before, only a third of MPS freshmen were enrolled in algebra; about a third were taking pre-algebra, which was essentially a remedial course; and a third were in an even lower class known as applied math.

"Algebra for all," as the reform is sometimes called, has several goals. But its fundamental purpose is to ensure that those students previously tracked out of algebra, who tended to be low-income students and students of color, are given a chance to succeed educationally. Ultimately, the goal is to have all ninth and tenth graders in college prep math courses, O'Connor said.

"There are an awful lot of kids who get to tenth and eleventh grade and doors have already been closed for them," O'Connor noted, particularly for those who might want to go to college and find they lack the necessary algebra and geometry for admission. "Math has been a critical filter, and we are committed to changing that." Nationally, high school students who take one year or more of algebra are two to three-and-a-half times more likely to attend college as students who did not take algebra.

Milwaukee's algebra project is part of a six-year national experiment known as Equity 2000. While focusing on math, Equity 2000 has a broader vision that calls for an end to tracking; implementation of a college preparatory curriculum for all students, with the specific goal of increasing college preparation for students of color; and increased expectation by teachers and guidance counselors for low-income students and students of color.

The most ephemeral of those goals, that of expectations, is perhaps the most important, according to Vinnetta Jones, national director of Equity 2000. "If I were to pick one variable that is most important [to academic success], it would be expectations and, more specifically, teacher expectations," Jones told *Rethinking Schools*. "Expectations become self-fulfilling prophecies."

Equity 2000 involves a total of about 450,000 students in six cities: Milwaukee, Wisconsin; Nashville, Tennessee; Fort Worth, Texas; Prince George's County, Maryland; Providence, Rhode Island; and San Jose, California. It is a project of the College Board, a nonprofit membership organization that includes most of the country's universities and colleges and is funded by major foundations such as the Aetna Foundation, the Dewitt Wallace-Reader's Digest Fund, and the Rockefeller Foundation.

Equity 2000 hopes to use detracked math to eliminate tracking in all subjects. Jones said that this is possible because of the project's attempt to change teacher expectations in all areas, using math as an example. Further, many students are tracked in their English, science, and social studies classes based on what math class they are in, Jones said. According to national studies, students in algebra and geometry are nearly always placed in college prep classes across all disciplines.

The Complexities of Detracking

Detracking is one of the most complicated educational reforms, daunting at even a school level. What makes Milwaukee's algebra project and Equity 2000 particularly interesting is the attempt to institute systemwide reform. Part of Equity 2000's philosophy is to get all the necessary players together and to avoid the mistake of top-down reform that is not grounded in day-to-day classroom realities.

"The discussion of whether reform is top down or bottom up misses the point, in my mind," Jones said. "What we need to change school systems is leadership and support from the top, and planning and carrying it out at all phases."

Al Taborn, a math teacher at Washington High School who worked in the central office for several years, echoed that view. "The classroom teacher needs and wants to have leadership from the top, I'm convinced of that," he said. "At the same time, the leadership has to be in touch with the classroom teacher, who is the one who really knows what's going on."

In Milwaukee, the algebra project has involved a high level of coordination and support at all levels — from the superintendent and school board, to the principals and guidance counselors, to the classroom teachers. It has also involved extensive preparation. The project was initiated in the 1990–91 school year during the administration of former superintendent Robert Peterkin. The current superintendent, Howard Fuller, embraced the reform, as did the school board.

To prepare staff and administrators at the schools, workshops, summer institutes, and mini-institutes were held during the preceding three years with hundreds of middle and high school math teachers, guidance counselors, and principals. Each summer teacher institute, for example, involved 100 teachers meeting for two weeks; the teachers then had forty hours of follow-up workshops during the year. Because guidance counselors and principals were also considered key to the project's success, special institutes and workshops were set up to solicit their input and support.

Special math summer classes were set up for 360 incoming freshmen, two hours a day, four days a week for six weeks. In addition, approximately 700 students took part in special Saturday academies (four hours a week for six weeks).

Each school is also expected to develop its own safety net for students who may have difficulty making the adjustment to algebra, O'Connor said. At Washington, algebra teacher Janice Udovich is in charge of developing that safety net as part of her responsibility as coordinator for the school's algebra program.

The Washington teachers decided that one important change would be to develop a uniform algebra curriculum for the first three weeks so that students would know what to expect during the first few weeks when schedule changes and transferring of classes is common. Further, the initial curriculum was designed to help give them confidence. "We know we are getting kids of all different abilities," Udovich noted, "some that like math and some that say, 'Algebra, no way.' And we want them to know that yes, they can do this stuff."

The school also set up a coordination with the Chapter 1 program, and Chapter 1 students have a special algebra support class that meets two-and-a-half times a week. "These are kids who probably would otherwise be in an applied math or a pre-algebra class and may not feel very confident about their math skills. So we wanted to offer then some extra support," she said.

Udovich admitted that some algebra teachers were initially resistant to the change, including herself. "Last fall, many of us felt, 'There's no way, it's not going to work.' But many of us have had to accept the fact that this is going to happen and then the question is, how are we going to deal with it?"

A teacher for ten years, Udovich says the algebra for ninth graders is a fundamental reform whose significance may be lost on some teachers, parents, students, and community members. At issue is not just the opportunity to go to college, but the issue of challenging students, increasing their self-confidence, and broadening their mathematical abilities.

For too many kids, Taborn noted, all they knew of math was addition, subtraction, multiplication, and division. When they failed, they were just given the same tasks over and over, regurgitated in new ways every year until both teachers and students were bored out of their minds. Remedial classes became a self-fulfilling prophecy consuming more and more students.

"If you have classes that are continually geared toward lower and lower expectations," Taborn said, "you are going to fill them up."

Standardized Tests:
A Clear and Present Danger

TERRY MEIER

No phenomenon poses a greater threat to educational equity, and ultimately to the quality of education in this country, than the escalating use of standardized achievement tests.

Fueled by public concern that schools are less rigorous than they used to be, standardized tests are increasingly prescribed as the "get tough" medicine needed to return excellence to our classrooms. Across the country, standardized tests are now routinely used to determine how and when students advance, from first grade through graduate school.

Standardized tests, which are notorious for their discriminatory effect on students of color, clearly threaten whatever small measures of educational equity have been won in recent decades. What is less obvious is that standardized tests threaten the educational experience of all children. The threat is so great, in fact, that standardized testing should be abolished.

It is estimated that a student will take more than thirty standardized tests by the time he or she graduates from high school. Because standardized tests are a constant reality in students' lives, it is essential that parents understand the biases and limitations of such tests. Yet, as in so many other educational areas, parents are often excluded from the debate because they are deemed unable to understand the issue's complexity.

Tests are called "standardized" when the same test is given under similar conditions to large groups of students, whether districtwide, statewide, or nationwide. Most standardized tests ask multiple-choice questions and are corrected by a computer that recognizes only one "right" answer.

Decades of research have documented the biases in standardized tests, with students of color bearing the brunt of that discrimination. Across age groups, standardized tests discriminate against low-income students and students of color. While girls tend to do better on standardized tests at an early age, by high school and college their scores are on average below those of males, according to FairTest, a national group based in Cambridge, Massachusetts, that lobbies against the growing use of standardized tests.

Advocates of testing argue that standardized achievement tests do not create inequities within schools, they merely reflect preexisting inequities. According to this argument, children of color and low-income students tend to perform less well on standardized tests because they receive an inferior education.

Two false assumptions support this view. One is that standardized tests are a valid measure of excellence. The second is that standardized tests can be used to improve education, especially for low-income students and students of color.

No Real Connection to Excellence

Standardized achievement tests tend to focus on mechanical, lower-order skills and to reward students' rapid recognition of factual information. For example, standardized reading tests for young children stress phonics and the recognition of individual words. Research on learning to read, however, has shown the importance of integrating oral language, writing, reading, and spelling in a meaningful context that emphasizes children understanding what they read, not merely sounding out words. Similarly, research on teaching math stresses the importance of young children learning concepts through firsthand experience, while achievement tests for young children define math as knowing one's numbers. Thus, teachers face the dilemma of providing instruction that they know fosters a student's understanding, versus drilling students in isolated skills and facts that will help them do well on standardized tests.

It's not that students don't need to work on isolated skills sometimes, especially when they're first learning to read and write. But such work is only a means to the larger end of applying those skills in a meaningful context. Removed from context as they are on standardized tests, such skills are meaningless. Held up as a measure of achievement, they become mistaken for what is most important instead of what is ultimately trivial.

There is little, if any, connection between quality instruction and standardized test performance. Consider, for example, a successful high school English class in which students learn to write thoughtful, original essays in clear, concise language about topics they genuinely care about and that draw on their experiences. Assume that the teacher taught students to edit their work so that grammatical errors were rare.

Yet what does the American College Testing (ACT) Program test? Whether a student knows if the word "pioneered" is preferable to "started up by," or if "prove to be" is preferable to "come to be," or if "reach my destination" is preferable to "get there."

On one recent ACT test – which along with the SAT is a key determinant of who attends college – students were asked whether the italicized selection in "my thoughts were *irresistibly sucked* toward the moment when…" should be replaced by *pulled helplessly, uncontrollably drawn,* or *propelled mercilessly.* (These examples are taken from a study by researcher Mary Hoover.)

How could anyone argue that such questions test effective writing skills or analytical thinking? In fact, one could well argue that a student who preferred "started up by" to "pioneered" might be a better writer than the student who chose the "correct" answer because she chose the clearest, most easily understood words to communicate her ideas. The point is that the choice is stylistic, dependent upon what one is trying to say and to whom. Removed from real life, the choice is meaningless. It reveals nothing about a student's competence in reading and writing.

Consider another example, from a standardized reading achievement test where the child was asked to determine the "right" answer in the following selection:

> Father said: Once there was a land where boys and girls never grew
> up. They were always growing. What was Father telling?
> The truth_____ A lie_____ A story_____

Any of these could be the "right" answer. If the father were speaking metaphorically, referring to mental and not physical growth, he could be telling the truth. It could also be a lie, for in black speech the word "lie" can also mean a joke or a story. And, of course, its initial "once" signals the conventions of fiction/fairy tales.

Standardized tests also ignore the skills and abilities needed to function in a complex, pluralistic society – such as the ability to work collectively in various social and cultural contexts, to adjust to change, to understand the perspectives of others, to persevere, to motivate, to solve problems in a real-life context, to lead, to value moral integrity and social commitment.

It is tragic that at the time when many developmental psychologists stress a broad and complex conception of intelligence and ability, and when one needs multiple talents to function effectively in the world, we have come to define excellence in our schools within the narrow parameters of what can be measured by standardized tests. When we use standardized tests to decide who gets to go to the "best" high school or college, we may actually be discriminating against those students with the greatest potential to contribute to society.

Excluding Diversity

It is naive to assume that we can solve the problems confronting society without embracing the perspectives and diverse skills and abilities represented in our multicultural population. Yet the continued reliance on standardized testing perpetuates a narrow definition of excellence that excludes diversity.

Standardized achievement tests thus potentially sound the death knell of diversity in our schools. They silence a cross-cultural dialogue that has barely begun, not only in the field of education, but in every area of academic, professional, and political life.

The focus here is on the overwhelmingly discriminatory effects of standardized tests on students of color. It is also well documented that tests such as the SAT and the ACT discriminate against women and working-class students.

In every ethnic and racial group. females score much lower on the SAT than males. African-American and Latina women face a double jeopardy due to the test's racial and gender discrimination. On the 1988 SAT, for example, African-American women scored on average 724 points compared to an average 965 for white males, according to FairTest. At the same time, white women score higher on average than male students of color, with the exception of Asian- and Pacific-American students.

Similarly, there is a direct relationship between family income and SAT scores. In 1988, students whose annual family income was more than $70,00 scored an average 992, with figures declining for each income group to an average score of 781 for students with annual family income under $10,000. Further, upper-income students are also more likely to afford the $600 "coaching" courses that can raise students scores by as much as 100 points.

Tests Won't Improve Education

It is inarguably true that students of color are often ill-served in our schools. But given that standardized tests bear little, if any, relationship to substantive learning, it makes no sense to assume that improving the educational experience of students of color will necessarily affect their test scores. What *is* clear is that in many schools, the opposite tends to occur. As teachers have come under increasing pressure to raise test scores, the quality of education the students receive has declined. In too many classrooms, test content dictates curriculum.

In some cases, abilities and skills not measured on achievement tests have been removed from the curriculum altogether. According to FairTest, when Virginia's state minimum competency tests decided to include only the multiplication and division of fractions several years ago, some teachers in the state stopped teaching students how to add and subtract fractions. Similarly, Deborah Meier, a public school principal in Manhattan, reports that when one New York City test eliminated items on synonyms and antonyms, these were also eliminated from the curriculum.

In some states, matching curriculum with the content of standardized achievement tests has become a systemwide mandate. FairTest reports that school systems in at least thirteen states have attempted to "align" their curriculum with standardized tests so that students do not spend hours studying materials upon which they will never be tested, regardless of the value or benefit that could be derived from that effort.

Pressure on teachers and administrators to standardize curriculum in order to raise test scores can be intense. One 1987 report by researcher John Weiss, for instance, found that in 1985 the superintendent of schools in St. Louis fired sixty teachers and principals because their students didn't improve their scores sufficiently on standardized multiple-choice tests.

Tests as a Sorting System

Clearly, standardized tests neither measure excellence nor foster it in our schools. So why the emphasis on such tests? The fundamental reason is that the tests provide a seemingly objective basis upon which to allocate limited educational resources – to decide who gets into the best classes, high schools, or colleges. To that end, test items are deliberately selected so as to maximize differences between high and low scorers. By design, only some people will do well on the tests.

There can be little doubt that if a large percentage of white middle-class students performed poorly on standardized tests, the test results would be viewed as invalid and discriminatory. There is no similar concern for students of color, despite some twenty-five years of extensive documentation of cultural bias in standardized testing.

According to one study, one-third of the items in typical reading achievement tests are prejudiced against those speaking non-Standard English. For example, they require students of color to distinguish between words, removed from context, that are often homonyms (sound alike) in their everyday oral speech patterns, such as had/hat and right/rat for African-American dialect speakers, or this/these and tag/tack for Spanish dominant speakers. Despite considerable research indicating that phonological distinctions like these do not necessarily affect reading comprehension when the words appear in meaningful context, such distinctions are used on standardized tests to help measure minority children's reading level.

Dialect items place African-American and bilingual speakers at a major disadvantage compared to native Standard English speakers, who do not have to waste energy sorting out the differences between two language systems. Even if the stated intent of dialect-prejudiced items were to determine whether students of color had mastered Standard English conventions (which it is not), such items would not provide valid information about how these students use language in a real-life context as opposed to the highly stressful conditions involved in taking a test.

Distinctions that involve dialect or language don't just discriminate against individual students of color, however. They discriminate against excellence. They turn what is a plus in a multicultural society – the ability to speak more than one dialect or language and thus communicate across a variety of social and cultural contexts – into a negative.

Researchers have also criticized the use of questions that assume cultural values and/or experiences that may not be shared by members of minority communities. On the vocabulary subtest of a standardized reading achievement test, for example, students are directed to choose the best synonym for *inequality* from among the following items: absence, foreign, difference, similarity, poor. Hoover and co-researchers note that "of the responses, all except 'absence' and 'similarity' could be 'correct' in cultures in which students are aware that difference, poverty, and foreignness are associated with inequality."

Class and Cultural Biases

Similarly, Weiss found in his study that questions that appear on the SAT necessitated familiarity with such upper-income pursuits as polo, golf, tennis, minuets, pirouettes, property taxes, melodeons, and horseback riding. Again, even leaving aside the issue of cultural bias, what does knowledge of these activities have to do with scholastic aptitude?

Some research indicates that minority children do much better on test items whose content relates to familiar cultural experience. Statistician A. P. Schmidt found, for example, that on a reading comprehension passage about life-style changes in Mexican-American families, Mexican-American students scored significantly higher than they did on reading comprehension passages whose content was less related to their lives. Similarly, researcher Darlene Williams found that the IQ scores of black students rose when test items included pictures of black people and of events related to black culture.

Doubtless many people would strongly object to the proposal that standardized tests be revised so as to include a sizable body of content specifically related to minority cultural experiences on the grounds that this would place middle-class white students at a disadvantage. After all, why should they be expected to know anything about minority experience?

Yet aren't minority students placed at an even greater disadvantage when standardized tests reflect little or nothing about their cultural experience, while for middle-class white students almost everything on the test is familiar cultural terrain? There is some common ground on tests, to be sure. But middle-class white students have to struggle far less often than minority students to make meaning out of tests items that take for granted experiences they've never had and that have absolutely nothing to do with ability.

✳ Is it ability or cultural experience that is being measured, for example, on the following item from the Scholastic Aptitude Test:

RUNNER : MARATHON
(A) envoy: embassy
(B) martyr: massacre

(c) oarsman: regatta

(d) horse: stable

In this example, it is marathons and regattas a student must be familiar with to prove fitness for college. At the other end of the educational ladder, it's piano lessons, airplane trips, zoo excursions, musical recitals, museums, daddies who read story books, farm animals, historical sites, and friendly policemen.

The advantages that middle-class white students have on standardized tests extend beyond the linguistic features and the content of test items, however. There is good reason to believe that the test-taking situation itself is experienced very differently by majority and minority students. Test taking is a skill many middle-class students are very good at because they tend to receive extensive practice in answering "test questions" from the time they first learn to speak.

Numerous studies of language socialization in white middle-class communities indicate that the largest percentage of questions addressed to preschoolers by mothers and other primary caregivers consists of simply structured questions to which the questioner already has the answer (e.g., "How many eyes do you have?"; "What color is this dolly's dress?"; "How many fingers is mommy holding up?"). The purpose of such questions is not for the questioner to gain information, but for the child to *display* information, for which she is typically rewarded with extensive verbal and non-verbal praise.

When reading stories to preschool children, many middle-class parents often intersperse their reading with questions that focus the child's attention on noting and recalling specific details of the text (e.g., "*Now,* how many balls is the little boy holding?"; "What is the bird doing?"). Perhaps the most important "lesson" preschoolers learn as a result of such interactions is how one is expected to communicate about, and respond to, text.

Research indicates that many working-class and minority children come to school with very different values and assumptions about what constitutes meaningful communication. In a 1983 study, Shirley Brice Heath found that in the working-class black community where she spent eleven years studying language socialization, children were almost never asked questions to which the adult or older child already knew the answer. According to Heath's data, the most prevalent type of question addressed to preschoolers in this community was the "analogy question," calling for an open-ended response drawn from the child's experience (e.g., "What do you

think you are?" to a child crawling under the furniture). Other frequently asked questions were "story starters" (e.g., "Did you see
Maggie's dog yesterday?") and accusations (e.g., "What's that all
over your face?"). Children were also asked questions to which only
they knew the answer (e.g., "What do you want?"). But very seldom were they asked test-type questions, the assumption being,
why would you ask someone something you already know the
answer to?

Reading was also often perceived differently, according to Heath.
It tended to be a social event in which listeners, young and old,
were free to throw in comments or to elaborate on some connection with their personal experience, rather than a context for testing
children's reading comprehension or teaching appropriate school
behaviors. People in this community were admired for their ability
to tell a good story, draw insightful analogies, or present an interesting and unique point of view, rather than for their ability to display information or show off knowledge for its own sake.

Research in other communities corroborate Heath's findings.
Many working-class and minority children grow up in communities
where little value is placed on asking children to display information
for its own sake and where "stating the obvious" or "saying what
everyone knows" is not encouraged because it is perceived as having
no meaningful communicative purpose. Thus, for many working-
class and minority students, the testing situation violates deeply held
assumptions and values about the nature and purpose of communication.

Communicative style – including how one interprets the meaning
of what another says, how one frames questions and structures
answers, notions about what is worth talking about – is learned
early in life and is deeply tied to one's personal and cultural identity. To suggest that members of minority communities change the
way in which they interact with their children so that they will be
better prepared to take tests in school is really to ask that they surrender part of their cultural identity.

Those who argue that it is possible to make standardized tests less
discriminatory by removing their cultural bias seriously underesti-
mate the enormity of their task. What is a "culture-fair" test in a
multicultural society? And who could design such a test? The truth
is that any knowledge worth having is inextricably linked to culture
and to context – and thus can't be reduced to measurement on a
standardized test.

In the final analysis, the most fundamental question to be answered about standardized testing is not why students of color tend to perform less well than white students, or even what can be done about it. Rather, the fundamental question is, What is wrong with a society that allocates its educational resources on the basis of tests that not only fail to measure excellence but also discriminate against the vast majority of its minority population?

Resources

DELPIT, LISA. (1988). "The Silenced Dialogue: Power and Pedagogy." *Harvard Educational Review,* Vol.58, No.3.

HEATH, SHIRLEY BRICE. (1983). *Ways With Words: Language, Life, and Work in Communities and Classrooms.* New York: Cambridge University Press.

HOOVER, MARY R. (1981). "Bias in Composition Tests with Suggestions for a Culturally Appropriate Assessment Technique." In M.F. Whiteman (Ed.), *Writing: The Nature, Development, and Teaching of Written Communication.* Hillsdale, NJ: Lawrence Erlbaum.

HOOVER, MARY R., ROBERT L. POLITZER, & ORLANDO TAYLOR. (1987). "Bias in Reading Tests for Black Language Speakers: A Socio-linguistic Perspective." *Negro Educational Review,* Vol.38, Nos.2, 3.

SCHMIDT, A. P. (1986). "Unexpected Differential Item Performance of Hispanic Examinees on the SAT-Verbal, Forms 3FSAOS and 3GSAOS." Unpublished statistical report of the Educational Testing Service.

SCOLLON, RON, & SUZANNE B. K. SCOLLON. (1981). *Narrative, Literacy and Face in Interethnic Communication.* Norwood, NJ: Ablex Publishing.

SMITH, G. PRITCHY. (1986). "Unresolved Issues and New Developments in Teacher Competency Testing." *Urban Educator,* Fall 1986.

WEISS, JOHN G. (1987). "It's Time to Examine the Examiners." *Negro Educational Review,* Vol.38, Nos.2, 3.

WILLIAMS, DARLENE. (1979). "Black English and the Stanford-Binet of Intelligence." Ph.D. dissertation. Stanford University School of Education, 1979.

Recommended Resources

Stratification in the Classroom: Testing and Tracking

National Center for Fair and Open Testing (FairTest)

342 Broadway, Cambridge, MA 02139; 617-864-4810. Critical resources on student and teacher assessment. See especially *FairTest Examiner,* a quarterly newsletter on testing issues.

None of the Above: Behind the Myth of Scholastic Aptitude

by David Owen, Boston: Houghton Mifflin, 1985. A highly recommended exposé of the Scholastic Aptitude Test (SAT).

Crossing the Tracks: How "Untracking" Can Save America's Schools

by Anne Wheelock, New York: New Press, 1993. A critique of tracking with an emphasis on groups across America that are successfully detracking their local schools.

Keeping Track: How Schools Structure Inequality

by Jeannie Oakes, New Haven: Yale University Press, 1985. A classic work revealing how tracking hurts all students, not just the ones in lower tracks.

Maintaining Inequality: A Background Packet on Tracking and Ability Grouping

by the National Coalition of Education Activists (NCEA), P.O. Box 697, Rhinebeck, NY 12572-0679; 914-658-8115. A collection of basic information on what tracking is and how it affects children.

PART IV

Beyond the Classroom: National Policy Concerns

During the last twenty years, urban education has suffered because of growing economic inequality, which has had a devastating impact on many cities. Corporate flight to low-wage regions in the United States or foreign countries, and white flight to the suburbs have deprived cities of jobs and the property tax base needed to support good schools. Tax law changes have reduced the amount of state aid going to urban centers. These blows have made city school systems especially vulnerable to ill-considered national initiatives. Some policymakers are keen to subordinate schools to the training needs of large corporations. Others want to privatize education through vouchers, a potentially effective means of dissolving public commitment to provide decent schools for every child. Taken as a whole, these threats put the democratic promise of equal education for all in jeopardy. The authors in this section tackle strong trends that in different ways all sap the vitality of public schools. They argue that sustaining and transforming, rather than abandoning, public education is the only way to reach educational equality.

Exploiting an understandable despair over the failure of many inner-city schools, conservative policymakers are advancing school choice as a path to educational equity. As Robert Lowe explains, Milwaukee's limited choice plan, which may provide some educational gain to a small group of "minority" students, is being used as an ideological wedge to launch a full-blown privatization of K–12 schooling. Overblown claims of public school failure, unsubstantiated belief in the efficacy of private schools, and unrealistic faith in the reforming power of markets mar the analysis of voucher advocates. Lowe argues that school privatization offers the privileged a means to ensure quality schooling for their own children while abandoning responsibility for increasingly imperiled public schools.

Although choice plans for public schools avoid the most grave defects of private choice plans, Ann Bastian contends that they should not be endorsed without careful examination. Unless every school in a district is a choice school, she warns that public school choice plans can create elite enclaves while most students languish in second-class schools. Poorly designed plans can also weaken community involvement in schools and promote test-driven instruction. Bastian explains that choice strategies are only likely to succeed if they are part of a comprehensive reform program.

Reflecting on school violence, Pedro Noguera is critical of technological solutions such as metal detectors and elaborate security systems, which don't address the underlying human failures that bring violence into schools. Hearkening back to the pressures he felt growing up in a tough neighborhood in New York, Noguera cautions against dehumanizing labels that obscure the social roots of destructive behavior and trap young people in self-fulfilling prophecies. He contends that school violence will only subside when youth are offered effective schools and guidance from adults they respect.

Many public officials and corporate leaders believe that both school problems and economic woes can be addressed through new vocational programs that orient schools around the needs of the corporate economy. In "The Hollow Promise of Youth Apprenticeships," Harvey Kantor critiques the current incarnation of this approach in the Clinton administration's School-to-Work Transition Act. Kantor notes the historical failure of vocational education to enhance student opportunity and explains why hopes for the new vocationalism are not supported by actual employment trends. Rather than solving economic problems, he argues, such initiatives as youth apprenticeships may actually deepen divisions between college bound and non-college bound youth. Real employment opportunity, Kantor believes, will only come through providing a good academic education for all, lessening racial discrimination in the job market, and implementing full-employment policies.

The developments analyzed by these writers testify to the powerfully conservative drift of American education. In the long run, they can only be successfully countered if public school advocates find increasingly effective ways to make their voices heard and heeded at the national level. While building good schools is a painstakingly local process, it will only be able to unfold effectively if reformers can organize themselves to influence nationwide educational debates and decisions.

The Perils of
School Vouchers

ROBERT LOWE

For nearly 150 years, public education in the United States has been recognized as a fundamental public good. That recognition is now under attack. Building on a decade of national power that has radically redefined the nature of public responsibility, conservatives, under the aegis of "choice," have proposed the substitution of markets for public schools. Further, they have made their arguments plausible to diverse constituencies. Despite the grave inadequacies of public education today, however, throwing schools open to the marketplace will promote neither excellence nor equality for all. Rather, it will enhance the freedom of the privileged to pursue their advancement unfettered by obligation to community.

Current efforts to promote an educational marketplace through choice trace directly to the work of conservative economist Milton Friedman. Writing in the mid-1950s, Friedman proposed that every family be given a voucher of equal worth for each child attending school. Under this plan, families could choose any school that met rudimentary government oversight (which Friedman likened to the sanitary inspection of a restaurant). Parents could add their own resources to the value of a voucher, and, presumably, schools could set their own tuition level and admission requirements.[1]

At the time, Friedman's proposal failed to attract widespread support. While some people excoriated public schools during the 1950s for curricular laxity that allegedly gave Russians the jump in the space race, optimism prevailed that curriculum innovation and more attention to advanced placement classes would remedy the problem. Further, for the first decade after the 1954 *Brown v. Board of Education* decision, optimism remained high that public schools could create equality of educational opportunity. In fact, it was school desegregation that most underscored the conservative nature of Friedman's stance.

A version of this essay appears in Theresa Perry and James Fraser, eds., *Freedom's Plow: Teaching for a Multicultural Democracy* (New York: 1993)

The First Choice Program

The first choice program provided white students in Virginia public funds to attend private academies in order to avoid attending public schools with Blacks.[2] Friedman addressed this matter in his proposal. Although he expressed his personal desire for integration, he believed that state-imposed desegregation violated parents' freedom to choose. Thus Friedman asserted the primacy of freedom over equality and finessed the lack of freedom the less-than-equal possessed.

During much of the 1960s, confidence prevailed that public education could promote both excellence and equity. But by the 1980s, such confidence had seriously deteriorated in a political climate that identified the state as the perpetrator rather than the ameliorator of social and economic ills.[3] A wave of national reports contributed to this climate by maintaining that the United States was losing its competitive edge because schools were inadequately developing students' skills.[4] At the same time, sustained inequities in educational outcomes between white students and students of color seriously undermined faith in public schools' capacity to provide equal educational opportunity. In such an environment, a new private school choice program that emphasizes opportunities for low-income students of color was linked with a new, more public relations oriented defense of the educational marketplace. This new approach met considerable success in creating the illusion that choice would serve all.

The link was forged publicly in June 1990 when Wisconsin State Representative Annette "Polly" Williams (D-Milwaukee), the African-American sponsor of the highly publicized Milwaukee Parent Choice Program, traveled to Washington, D.C., as a featured participant in the unveiling of *Politics, Markets, and America's Schools* by John Chubb and Terry Moe.[5] Rarely do scholarly works become media events, but this event signified the launching of a vigorous campaign to promote educational choice. It also implied the existence of far broader support for opening schools to the marketplace than the historically conservative constituency for choice would suggest. Although it would be a mistake to conclude that support for "choice" represents a consensus among diverse political forces, it rapidly is becoming the major policy issue affecting schools in the United States today.

Neither Equity nor Excellence

At the cutting edge of this issue are the choice program in Milwaukee and Chubb and Moe's *Politics, Markets, and America's Schools.* The former, a modest program that provides public funds for private education, appears to demonstrate in practice that choice expands equality of opportunity. The latter attempts to theoretically justify the abandonment of all public education on the ground that choice will produce educational excellence.

Taken together, the program and the book suggest that choice will provide both equity and excellence. Yet nothing could be farther from the truth. While the Milwaukee program — a kind of affirmative action effort — may indeed provide greater opportunity for some of its participants, Chubb and Moe's brief for providing all individuals with vouchers to attend private schools fails to sustain its thesis and has dire implications for equality of educational opportunity.

The Milwaukee Parent Choice Program has received attention far out of proportion to its immediate impact. In a district that enrolls nearly 100,000 students, the program was originally intended to provide 1,000 low-income students with approximately $2,500 each so that they might attend a nonsectarian private school. Only 558 students applied for the 1990–91 school year, and merely 341 ultimately enrolled in the seven schools that agreed to participate.

Despite the program's small scale, nationally prominent conservatives vocally endorsed it. Even before the school term began, it won praise from the Bush administration, the *Wall Street Journal,* Wisconsin's Republican Governor Tommy Thompson, and the head of the powerful Bradley Foundation. And despite the questionable success of the program during its first year, many advocates persist in seeing it as a first step in restoring the nation's educational health. They believe this can only be accomplished by breaking up the public school monopoly.

The program also has spawned vocal opposition. Some antagonists, like former Wisconsin superintendent of public instruction Herbert Grover, view Polly Williams as the unwitting accomplice of right-wing business interests bent on destroying a public good.[6] Ohters oppose the program because they fear that it presages an end to a variety of perceived goods, including desegregation, teachers' unions, a common curriculum, and provisions for children with special needs.

Thus, both proponents and opponents rightly see the Williams initiative as an entering wedge in a national battle over the future shape of education in the United States. It is important, however, to see the Milwaukee Choice Program on its own terms. That many conservatives support the plan does not make Polly Williams their agent. Rather, she has responded to the sustained failure of the Milwaukee Public Schools to provide an acceptable education to low-income children of color.

During 1989–90, for instance, Hispanics maintained an average GPA of 1.47, and African-Americans averaged 1.31. In three of Milwaukee's fifteen high schools, between 36 percent and 40 percent of blacks were suspended. The previous year the annual dropout rate was 17.8 percent for African-Americans and 17.4 percent for Hispanics.[7]

In the face of miserable average grades and appalling suspension and dropout rates, Williams has enabled a small number of students to seek an education elsewhere – partly in community-based schools that have long served African-Americans and Hispanics. Under the circumstances it makes little sense to berate the program for violating the ideal of the common school or the goal of an integrated society. Such unrealized visions are inadequate justifications for denying a few children a potential opportunity to pursue an education of value. As advocates of choice are quick to point out, the Milwaukee program gives some options to low-income families that the well-to-do have long exercised, and virtually no one challenges the right of the privileged to either move to their schools of choice in the suburbs or to attend private schools.

Troubling Questions

Yet the program does raise questions. While the $2,446 each student could bring as tuition to a private school did expand choice during the program's first year, this relatively small voucher meant that parents could not choose, if they desired, elite, overwhelmingly white preparatory schools. Second, those who applied for the program were probably among the most aggressive about pursuing quality education for their children and, consequently, among the most enfranchised. Third, applications exceeded openings in participating private schools. Admission was to be based on a lottery system, but without the Department of Public Instruction monitoring the process, it might have been difficult for participating schools to resist taking the strongest applicants. Even if the program were an outstanding success, it would not constitute a brief for substituting the marketplace for public schools.

The continuing praise of the Bush administration notwithstanding, there were troubling signs during the program's first year. Most important, the Juanita Virgil Academy, the one school essentially created in response to the voucher-bearing clientele, suffered inadequate books and supplies from the outset and soon closed, disrupting the lives of the 63 "choice" students who had enrolled. In addition, some 15 students were dismissed for disciplinary reasons or learning problems, so that only 259 of the 341 enrollees completed the first semester of choice.[8] Finally, nearly 100 nongraduating members of that group elected not to participate in the program during its second year.[9] Problems within the Milwaukee Choice Program, as the following analysis of Chubb and Moe's book will indicate, multiply when "choice" expands to include everyone.

In *Politics, Markets, and America's Schools,* Chubb and Moe offer an elaborated version of Milton Friedman's argument. Like Friedman, they say little about equality of educational opportunity per se, but hold that education will improve for all through opening it to the competition of the marketplace. They go so far as to maintain that public schools generally are incapable of providing effective education because the way they are governed limits their capacity to remedy shortcomings.

Chubb and Moe point out numerous problems that afflict public education today. They observe that principals cannot hire or fire teachers. They note that teachers run a gauntlet of irrelevant certification requirements, possess limited autonomy in the classroom, and are denied colleagues who share a common purpose. And they recognize that parents have little influence over the schools their children must attend. The authors identify such unsatisfactory conditions as key contributors to what they perceive as the degenerate character of education in the United States.

They further contend that many of the educational reforms mandated in the 1980s — such as longer school terms, more homework, and increased academic requirements for high school graduation — were guaranteed to fail because they were imposed bureaucratically. In fact, they see bureaucracy as the central impediment to effective schools. They believe it strangles the capacity of principals and teachers to fashion schools after their own vision and renders them unresponsive to the interests of parents. The solution to poor education, according to Chubb and Moe, is not the futile effort to impose quality through increased bureaucratic controls but to eliminate such controls.

Chubb and Moe hold that public schools are necessarily bureaucratic since in democratically controlled organizations bureaucracy is the means through which competing political interests institutionalize their influence. They argue that private schools, in contrast, tend to be autonomous because accountability does not spring from bureaucratic regulation but from the market mechanism. If a private school fails to do an effective job, according to their reasoning, clients will leave it for another. Chubb and Moe consequently look to the marketplace to create excellence in education.

Problems with Formulations

To summarize their argument, Chubb and Moe assert that public schools provide inadequate instruction because they lack the autonomy necessary to create effective education; they lack autonomy because they are bureaucratic; and they are bureaucratic because politics shapes them. Thus, they claim the way to create effective schools is to substitute the market for politics. The clarity of their argument and the simplicity of their solution, apparently buttressed by the analysis of massive data bases, may seem persuasive. But problems with their formulations abound.

First of all, Chubb and Moe assume that *A Nation at Risk,* along with less influential reports of the 1980s, provides such telling evidence of educational malfeasance that drastic measures are justified.[10] Serious questions might be raised about the test results marshaled to document this state of affairs. It is questionable whether standardized test scores can accurately gauge the nation's educational health, a point Chubb and Moe themselves make in another context.

Even assuming such scores have value, the strategy of *A Nation at Risk* to document both declining scores within the United States and unfavorable comparisons of scores with other countries hardly withstands close scrutiny. Its authors fail to note that their data suggest only a modest decline in scores since the 1960s. They do not acknowledge the upward trajectory of scores on several tests in the 1970s and 1980s, and they ignore tests that showed no decline.[11] Further, the report inappropriately contrasts the achievement of twelfth graders in the United States with those of other countries, since the groups are not comparable. Most students in the United States reach the twelfth grade, and a high percentage progress beyond. In many other countries, only an elite group completes high school, so international comparisons below the collegiate level have limited utility.[12]

Lack of evidence indicating "a rising tide of mediocrity," to use the unfortunate phrasing of *A Nation at Risk,* in no way suggests that children of color are receiving an adequate education. But it undercuts the justification of a market-based educational system for all based on the assumption that nothing could be lost by dismantling public schools. More important, Chubb and Moe fail to prove that private schools do a better job than public ones. Scholars have raised a number of questions about the data Chubb and Moe relied upon, including whether a brief multiple-choice test adequately documented student performance and whether the private school sample overrepresented elite preparatory schools.[13] Although many black and Latino families have avoided the degradations of miserable public schools by enrolling their children in Catholic institutions, the mere fact of private status obviously does not confer excellence on schools. Thus it is hardly surprising that recent data on achievement in Milwaukee's Catholic schools point out a vast chasm in student achievement between those serving high-income and low-income neighborhoods, and they suggest racial differences in performance that closely parallel those of the Milwaukee Public Schools.[14]

Even setting aside problems with their data, Chubb and Moe's claims far outstrip their findings. Despite their argument that the autonomy they associate with private schools profoundly affects student performance, in their model autonomy accounts for a tiny percentage of variance in achievement. Thus, as scholars Gene Glass and DeWayne Matthews note, "A school that moves from the 5th percentile to the 95th percentile on autonomous organization would be expected...to climb a month or so in grade equivalent units on a standardized achievement test."[15] Further, Chubb and Moe cannot even truly determine whether greater autonomy creates better students or whether better students permit more autonomous schools.[16] In addition, they cannot demonstrate that higher achievement in private schools stems from the way they are organized or from the select group of students who attend them.[17] Finally, they fail to confront the hypothesis that the real issue is not autonomy but wider reliance on an academic curriculum in private schools — something that can be replicated in public institutions.[18]

Overstating Private School Advantages

Chubb and Moe also overstate the advantages of private schools in supporting teacher professionalism. Principals tend to have greater power in private schools, but it scarcely follows that teachers are more able to act as professionals. Unprotected by unions, the jobs of private school teachers are precarious. This vulnerability can exert greater constraints on teachers' autonomy than the bureaucratic regulations common to public schools. In addition, there is nothing professional about most private school teachers' salaries. Compensation typically too meager to support a family has meant that private school positions have been most acceptable to the independently wealthy, to members of religious orders, and to families with more than one wage earner.[19]

Overblown bureaucracies, of course, do limit institutional change and absorb huge financial resources for little direct educational service. Chubb and Moe correctly argue that many private schools are relatively free of bureaucracy, yet Catholic schools, which enroll a high percentage of nonpublic students in the United States, are certainly bureaucratic institutions. More broadly, the organization of the private sector as a whole fails to confirm Chubb and Moe's notion that bureaucracy characterizes public rather than private institutions. Intricately bureaucratized corporations produce a high percentage of the nation's wealth. Business influence, in fact, had much to do with the development of bureaucratic, centralized systems of public education.[20] Recent developments, however, hold out the possibility that public schools, like innovative corporations, can balance bureaucracy with autonomy.[21] Chubb and Moe offer scant attention to reform efforts in many communities that have moved toward various forms of school-based management.[22]

Furthermore, Chubb and Moe exaggerate when they suggest that public schools are rendered incoherent by the variety of political influences that shape them. Their pluralistic notion of educational politics fails to recognize that through most of the twentieth century schools were elite-dominated. Bureaucratic structures, in part, were designed by elites at the turn of the century to remove schools from popular political control.[23] Yet altered power relations can inspire bureaucratic measures that protect the rights of minorities and the poor. Thus, recent bureaucratic regulations, engendered by the Civil Rights movement of the 1960s, are the real objects of conservative complaint. These have promoted desegregation, bilingual education, and education of the handicapped, institutionalizing a modicum of equity in public schools as a response to the demands of those traditionally denied power. That such regulations cannot adequately secure equality of educational opportunity does not mean that the market can do any better.

Chubb and Moe assume that the market will create quality education for everyone through the mechanism of choice. Yet choice certainly has not accomplished this in the private sector of the economy. If the affluent can choose health spas in the Caribbean and gracious homes, the poor must choose inadequate health care and dilapidated housing. To the extent that those with limited resources have won forms of protection, it has not been guaranteed by the play of the market but by governmental regulation. The conservative agenda of deregulation over the past decade has eroded those protections and greatly increased the disparity between the wealthy and the poor in the United States. A market system of education is merely an extension of deregulation and promises to compound social inequities.

Choosing the Advantaged

In the market system promoted by Friedman, Chubb and Moe, and conservative political and corporate leaders, public taxation would guarantee relatively modest vouchers worth the same amount for every student in each state. Families, acting as consumers, would then choose the schools their children would attend. But unlike the Milwaukee program where a lottery determines admission, schools may choose as well. Chubb and Moe are adamant about this:

> Schools must be able to define their own missions and build their own programs in their own ways, and they cannot do this if their student population is thrust on them by outsiders. They must be free to admit as many or as few students as they want, based on whatever criteria they think relevant – intelligence, interest, motivation, behavior, special needs – and they must be free to exercise their own, informal judgment about individual applicants. [24]

It is in schools' interest to choose those students who are already high achievers, and it is in their interest – especially for smaller schools – to accept those whose families can supplement the amount of the voucher they are given. Friedman's version of the plan would allow individual families the right to add their own cash to a voucher. Chubb and Moe would allow local districts to augment the value of vouchers through increased local taxation. In either case, the wealthy would have greater choice than the poor.

Advocates of an educational marketplace, then, have won a significant ideological victory by successfully labeling their program "choice" rather than the more neutral-sounding "voucher." While no one in their right mind would deny families educational options, choice obscures the reality that those who come from economically empowered families are those most likely to be chosen by good schools. As in the marketplace writ large, what one can purchase depends on how much currency is brought to the transaction.

Choice also obscures how the already advantaged would benefit financially at the expense of the less fortunate. A reduced tax rate would provide the well-to-do with a voucher for part of their tuition for private schools. This contrasts favorably with the current situation, which requires them to pay higher taxes for public schools in addition to relying solely on their own resources if they choose private institutions. Such a tax advantage, obvious in the Friedman plan, would exist in the Chubb and Moe variant as well, since wealthy districts' decisions to raise taxes above the lower limit would be offset by the abolition of federal and state taxation that redistributes resources to poor districts. For the poor, in contrast, the baseline vouchers would be difficult to add on to, creating a situation reminiscent of southern Jim Crow education, where vast differences existed between per-pupil expenditures for black and white schools.

Under Jim Crow it was common for African Americans to supplement meager public funding by constructing schoolhouses with their own donated labor and paying teachers out of their inadequate incomes.[25] But Blacks could not rectify these inequities despite extraordinary sacrifices. As the scholar W. E. B. Du Bois maintained, if some of these starved schools managed to achieve excellence through unusual efforts, greater funding would have made such excellence far more widespread.[26]

A voucher system of education can provide support for long-established community-based education programs that have effectively served children of color on shoestring budgets. But as the failure of the Juanita Virgil Academy suggests, the notion that choice would create a nation of small, effective schools is a construction as mythical as the notion that the market can maintain a nation of shopkeepers. A high level of capitalization and economies of scale would be necessary to construct buildings, to conduct advertising campaigns, to maintain staffing with an unpredictable number of students, and to make do with the unsupplemented vouchers those without wealth would bring. A likely result would be educational versions of fast-food conglomerates, with scripted teacher behaviors similar to the standardized patter of McDonald's order clerks. Like nineteenth century charity schools, such schools would compose the bottom tier of an educational hierarchy based on privilege.

Aside from the inequities associated with a market-based approach to schooling, such a strategy raises fundamental issues of educational purpose. Should taxpayers contribute to financing schools that have no public accountability no matter how objectionable many might find their goals? Should the public subsidize elite prep schools, schools run for profit, schools with racist ideologies, and schools run by corporations to train future workers? Should families be regarded as entrepreneurial units charged with maximizing their children's educational opportunities? This market ethos ignores any sense of responsibility for other children's education, any obligation for community control of education, any commitment to schools as sites of democratic discourse, any need for the new common curriculum some educators are forging out of the cultural works and political struggles of the diverse peoples who have shaped the United States.

Conservatives Exacerbate Differences

It is no small irony that so many conservatives have accused the multiculturalist movement of balkanization when their own policies have profoundly exacerbated the real differences that exist between groups in the United States. Certainly Republicans are not solely responsible for a long history of governmental policies that have developed suburban preserves for middle-class whites at the expense of urban economies inhabited by the poor and people of color.[27] Yet since the early 1980s regressive tax reform, diminished social services, and a benign attitude toward the flight of manufacturing jobs beyond U.S. borders have significantly increased the disparity between the wealthy and the poor. Already by 1983, according to historian Robert Weisbrot, "the cumulative impact of Reagan's policies involved a $25 billion transfer in disposable income from the less well-off to the richest fifth of Americans, and a rise in the number of poor people from 29.3 million in 1980 to 35.3 million."[28]

There are now signs that the strategy of suburbanization is yielding to urban gentrification as professional jobs in the service sector replace blue-collar positions. Historian Kenneth Jackson has indicated that rising fuel, land, and housing costs, along with changes in family organization, make suburban living less desirable.[29] In addition, privatization is a major incentive for the affluent to resettle in cities where inadequate revenues are starving public services. Increasingly in cities, where deindustrialization and reduced federal aid have devastated public spaces, urban professionals are paying only for those services that benefit themselves. These enclaves of privilege support private country clubs, private security guards, private road repair services, and private schools.[30]

Adding to such services, choice is a way of subsidizing urban professionals's taste for private education in environments where even the best public schools do not always accommodate them. Although virtually every city has magnet schools, which disproportionately concentrate school districts' resources on college preparatory programs for middle-class children, they typically practice at least a rudimentary form of equity that requires some degree of racial balance, and they cannot guarantee admission to all white middle-class applicants. As choice invites suburbanites back to the city to enjoy their private pursuits at the expense of reinvigorated public services, they will displace and further marginalize the poor.

In the conservative imagination, the divestment of state redistributive functions does not terminate responsibility for the less fortunate. Rather, such responsibility becomes voluntary, an act of private choice. Much, in fact, is made of the public spiritedness of the affluent, who voluntarily participate in contributing to the common good. Enormous publicity, for instance, has attended the offer of New York businessman Eugene Lange and several others to guarantee college scholarships to low-income school children, as well as to provide various supportive academic and counseling services to see them through high school. Oddly, we hear little about the federally funded TRIO programs that realized such practices worked decades ago. They have a long record of demonstrated success limited only by funding that is inadequate to reach more than a small percentage of the eligible population.[31] Massive federal support of such initiatives, in fact, is paramount because Lange and a few other philanthropists devoted to equity are exceptions. As policy analyst Robert Reich has pointed out, the wealthy contribute a lower percentage of their incomes to charitable purposes than the poor, and what they do give is disproportionately dispensed on elite cultural activities and institutions that serve themselves. Further, Reich notes that the much ballyhooed support of corporations for public schools is less than what they receive in the tax breaks they have successfully won.[32] Choice in giving, like choice in selecting private schools, provides a poor case that private spending will support public goods.

None of this is to say that public schools are beyond reproach. If they adequately served children of color, interest in choice would be limited and efforts to secure multicultural education unnecessary. Typically, students in public schools have suffered curricula that are ethnocentric and unquestioningly nationalistic. They also have experienced wide variation in academic quality based on their race and class. Author Jonathon Kozol, for instance, poignantly describes such grave inequities between public schools, underscoring the obvious unfairness of favoring the already advantaged with disproportionate resources.[33] Thus it might make sense to restrict choice programs to the underserved.[34]

Opposition to Affirmative Action

This clearly is not what the Bush administration had in mind, however, since it steadfastly opposed affirmative action. The Republican administration and conservative groups like the Landmark Legal Center for Civil Rights, which defended the Milwaukee Choice Program in the courts while it opposed the 1990 Civil Rights Act, merely view the Milwaukee program as an opening gambit in an effort to institute vouchers for everyone.[35] This agenda is explicit in a proposal for California initiated by the Excellence through Choice in Education League. The league's successful effort to place a statewide measure on the November 1993 ballot mandating vouchers for all was articulated initially as a measure to serve low-income families only.[36]

If public education has inadequately fulfilled its responsibilities to educate all, market-driven educational enterprise cannot fulfill them. At best, the popularity of choice among those with the least privilege should send a powerful message to public school educators that the common school for many remains a myth. It highlights the need to support a multicultural agenda that widens public discourse on equity issues and transforms public education in ways that enable people of color to exercise co-ownership of society. Yet the very idea of schools that educate people in common – drawing on the richness of diversity – is antithetical to the intent of the conservative leaders and foundations advocating choice.

Early in the twentieth century, corporate elites claimed to take the schools out of politics by creating expert-run centralized and bureaucratic public schools. Their demand for efficiency and impartial expertise masked a politically motivated effort to replace working-class influence over education with their own influence. Today, Chubb and Moe articulate the position of corporate elites who rail against the bureaucratic schools their predecessors were so influential in creating, once more claiming they want to take schools out of politics. Yet their desire to open them to the marketplace is also an inherently political strategy. It will enable the more affluent to free themselves from the yoke of all the legislative and legal safeguards people have won through the freedom struggles of the 1960s. It furthermore will free the rich from all public educational responsibility, striking a major blow against the current multiculturalist effort that seeks a radical expansion of democracy and a reinvigorated vision of community. The implementation of choice would be a victory for narrow class interest over community, accelerating the drastic maldistribution of opportunity that exists today.

Is Public School "Choice" a Viable Alternative?

ANN BASTIAN

Being asked to write an article against school choice is a bit like being asked to burn the American flag at a VFW meeting. You have every right to do it, but do you want to? After all, choice is a bedrock American value. Applied to schools, it sounds great: students and parents get to choose, deserving schools get chosen.

But what if this is not the reality of school choice? In reality, school choice means very different things in different contexts. From the many versions of choice, we can construct three broad categories.

First, there are choice programs within a single public school district. These local, "controlled choice" plans seek to expand educational options.

Second, there are interdistrict and statewide public school plans. These seek to establish a public marketplace of schools through competition for enrollment.

Third, there are voucher plans that include private schools. These seek to create an unrestricted marketplace of competing public, private, and parochial schools.

Much of the debate over school choice has focused on vouchers. It was, after all, the key educational platform of the Bush administration. Vouchers deserve the most critical scrutiny as a threat to public education. But we should also look closely at the problems and potentials of choice programs that are strictly within the public schools.

The most promising examples of choice have occurred in the first category, within single public school districts. The programs most often cited are East Harlem in New York City; Montclair, New Jersey; and Cambridge, Massachusetts. These programs, while not perfect, suggest several important features of a good choice model:

- Choice is just one element in a comprehensive reform strategy.
- Every school in the district has become a school of choice.

- School missions are diverse, but have been developed in complementary rather than competitive ways.
- Teachers are given the time, training, and power to shape the school mission; parents also have a strong voice.
- Transportation costs are covered by the district.
- Parents and students are given enough information to make informed choices.
- Districts have secured significantly higher funding to sustain school improvement.

We should be fully aware, however, that even within a single public school district, controlled choice is no miracle cure for education. Where it works, it is one tool among others, and it only works well when there is a prior and steadfast commitment to equity, adequate funding, and internal school restructuring.

School districts should be particularly cautious about choice programs that improve only a limited number of schools. This is often the case in "magnet" programs where students apply to "specialty" schools that receive extra resources and funding. When there are not enough good schools to go around, choice is more likely to create islands of excellence (or adequacy) than it is to stimulate improvement across the board. We can see the stark result when we look at America's urban high school systems, where flagship academic magnet schools serving middle-class students contrast with desperately deprived neighborhood high schools for the working class and poor.

The same problems are posed by charter schools, which are special, privately run schools under contract with school boards. Like magnets, charter schools are promoted as models for innovations, but in the context of fiscal crisis and polarized resources, they are more likely to end up as isolated refuges for the lucky, the adamant, and by design, the privileged.

Unless our commitment to quality includes all schools, we are building more lifeboats, not better ships. The challenges for school choice are compounded in the second category, which includes interdistrict and statewide public school choice. In this marketplace model, every public school competes for enrollments, on the premise that enrollment dollars are sufficient incentives for school innovation and improvement and that competition will reward the best. Fourteen states and Puerto Rico have implemented varieties of statewide public school choice.

The data thus far are sketchy, except for the fact that nowhere has interdistrict choice ignited a revolution of school restructuring, parent engagement, and educational improvement as its proponents originally claimed. None of the statewide choice plans have included significant new resources for multiplying better schools or helping those at the bottom. The Massachusetts example highlights the potential fiscal nightmare for poor districts as students transfer out. Moreover, few states subsidize transportation costs for interdistrict transfers, ensuring that the class barriers to choice remain high and that outcomes remain skewed.

Overall, it appears that only a small number of parents have opted for the open enrollment program, often fewer than 1 percent. Moreover, data that exist for four states (Minnesota, Massachusetts, Arkansas, and Arizona) indicate that choice participants are disproportionately white and affluent.

If the interdistrict and statewide choice model gains a greater hold, its flaws will have a much graver impact. The dangers include:

- *Widening the gap between education "haves" and "have-nots."* Instead of becoming a tool for reform, this choice model rationalizes and accelerates inequity. It allows already advantaged schools to cream students and resources from other districts, leaving poorer schools and their students further depleted.
- *Weakening the link between schools and local communities.* In a large-scale marketplace model, schools are no longer bound by geographical or political communities. Schools and students would become even more removed from their neighborhoods. Community control of schooling would be further eroded, making it even harder for communities of color and the poor to fight for equity and reform. Taxpayers, voters, relatives, and citizens would feel even less invested in education.
- *Promoting the marketing of schools.* Where schools are competing for premium enrollments, the ability to attract students would depend as much on their ability to advertise as their capacity to educate. The obvious temptation would be for schools to rely even more heavily on standardized test scores and test-driven instruction, the "steroids approach" to performance enhancement.

The debate over school choice will be with us for a long time, even if voucher plans and private school choice options are soundly defeated. In weighing the problems and potentials, we need to keep in mind the most basic and practical question for any choice program: Does it fix what's really wrong?

There is nothing inherent in school choice that deals with key issues such as smaller class and school size, teacher training, multicultural curricula, teacher-parent collaboration, youth services, or equal and adequate funding. Moreover, choice is deflecting attention from such key issues.

The hard reality is that there's no shortcut to building good schools. Like parenting children, educating children is based on human relationships, the quality of which depends very much on the support systems surrounding the family and school. We have public education because we need a community and government support system to sustain this enormous undertaking, to make an unconditional investment in every child, to invest in the future as well as the present, to serve both individuals and communities.

School enrollments are not chips to be brokered in a marketplace, public or private. Even in our postindustrial consumer society, some choices are not about buying and selling.

Coming to Terms
with Violence in Our Schools

PEDRO NOGUERA

Violence in schools is not new. If one looks at the history of education in the United States, particularly of urban public schools, it is clear that problems of violence have been around almost as long as schools have been in existence. What is new, however, is the dramatic increase in school violence and the growing use of guns to resolve disputes.

As a first step in addressing this problem, we must recognize that in many ways our schools are safer than the communities where many children live. Many of the kids that I have worked with tell me they are more worried about violence in their neighborhood than they are about violence in school. At least in schools there are rules against violence and adults present who are supposed to enforce such rules. On the streets, in the playgrounds, and even at home, there is often no such protection.

Too often we unfairly place unreasonable expectations on our schools. We expect schools to be safe places, and of course they should be, but we ignore the fact that our society is increasingly unsafe. It is unrealistic to expect that our schools can escape the violence that pervades our society.

Combating violence is difficult because it is promoted and legitimized by the mass media and by political leaders. While it is difficult to determine to what extent the glorification of violence in movies and on television affects young people, psychological studies suggest that, at the minimum, such exposure has a numbing effect on viewers.

Children receive mixed messages when violence is construed as a legitimate way to achieve political and military objectives. The justification of the killings in Waco, Texas, by FBI agents; Clinton's rationalizing the deaths of Iraqi civilians during the 1993 bombing raids by U.S. war planes as unfortunate "collateral damage"; the U.S. invasions of Panama in 1989 and of Grenada in 1983 – all legitimized the use of deadly force against civilians.

Given the regularity with which violence is used for "legitimate" purposes, it is not surprising that children are confused about the appropriateness of responding violently to conflicts with others.

Problems Within Schools

There are also internal reasons, however, that schools are vulnerable to violence. Many teachers receive no training on how to deal with violence; it is rarely part of the curriculum in teacher training. Further, the individuals responsible for enforcing discipline often have no legitimacy or credibility in the eyes of the students. There is an absence of moral authority — which is different from institutional authority or the authority derived from one's job title. Just being an adult or holding a certain title doesn't mean that kids will automatically accept your right to exercise authority over them.

I can think of several schools where you can find kids shooting dice in the hallways or engaging in some other blatantly inappropriate behavior, and teachers will pretend not to see it because they are afraid to tell them to stop. Yet in the same school there will be certain individuals who can stop them, not through force or intimidation, but because of the relationship they have developed with the students. These are adults who can tell kids, "That's not allowed here. I expect better of you than that," and they respond.

When we don't have adults in schools who understand the experience of the children, who can speak in a language they understand and communicate in ways that are meaningful to them, then it becomes almost impossible to develop a safe and respectful school environment. In urban schools, most teachers do not live in the communities where they work. They have a limited knowledge of their students' lives outside of school. This physical and psychological detachment from the students' lives is often compounded by differences based on race and class. Together, these factors add considerably to the inability of teachers and school personnel to respond effectively to the causes of violence in schools.

In addition, schools typically rely on ineffective methods to deal with violence. The threat of suspension or expulsion — the ultimate punishment and the one that is often relied upon as the *only* way to deal with violence — may not mean much to some children, particularly to those who have already experienced failure in school or who may not attend school regularly.

Currently, the most fashionable response to school violence is the tendency toward making schools more like prisons. Many schools now have metal detectors stationed at the entry points. In the last few years, New York City has spent close to $28 million to install metal detectors. Other districts have hired armed security guards or installed sophisticated security systems, turning schools into lockdown facilities. It is ironic that we are using prisons as our models for safety and security, even though prisons are generally not safe places. Further, these measures are undertaken without sufficient thought to the social and psychological consequences that may result from changing the school environment in this way.

When I look at this problem, I see it not only through the eyes of a researcher and policymaker, but through my own personal experience. As a former teacher of African Studies at a continuation high school, I have worked with many young men who have been incarcerated and who have lived within an environment filled with violence. As a school board member, I have presided over expulsion hearings for students who have committed acts of violence and have had to make decisions that profoundly affect the lives of students and the schools they attend. Finally, as an activist in my community, I also work closely with parents and teachers, trying to develop an effective response to the violence that consumes our youth.

Growing Up in New York

I remember what it was like for me growing up in New York. The threat and possibility of violence permeated my school and community, and most people I knew accepted it as an ugly but unavoidable part of life.

At an early age I learned that bullies often got their way; that the best way to avoid a fight was to show no fear; that you must always be willing and prepared to hurt someone if necessary. I learned that violence was an effective means to get status and respect. I learned that in order to survive, I would have to deal with violence. At fourteen my cousin of the same age was stabbed to death for refusing to give up his leather jacket. The next year a kid I knew in school was arrested for the kidnap and rape of a female student. Only luck and the fear of getting caught, of ruining my future and embarrassing my family, prevented me from falling victim to violence.

Still, my experience has influenced my understanding of how kids view violence. At a gut level, I understand why they fight or why they might react violently toward a teacher. I know why so many see violence as a legitimate way to resolve problems, because I once felt the same way.

Useless Dichotomies

In our society we often categorize individuals who commit violence as deviants and sociopaths. Many counselors and psychologists view violent behavior as a form of conduct disorder based on socially maladaptive tendencies. This type of labeling presumes that there are some individuals who are potentially violent and who should be kept away from the rest of the population, which is ostensibly made up of good, honest, law-abiding people. Labeling children in this way influences how we see them and contributes to self-fulfilling prophecies.

Such dichotomies prevent us from understanding an issue like violence because they set up artificial dividing lines that presume the existence of fundamental differences between people based on morals or social conduct. Moreover, such distinctions keep us from recognizing how difficult it is to predict who is potentially violent, and leave us dumbfounded when a young person with no past record of violent behavior suddenly "goes off" violently on someone else. Although many children do need individual attention, and isolation may at times be the only way to respond, policies aimed at deterring violence should not be directed solely at those considered likely to engage in violence.

As a starting point toward dealing with violence in schools, we must identify some of the factors that contribute to the problem. Some, such as the availability of guns and the promotion of violence in the media, may seem beyond the control of parents and school personnel. While we must devise strategies for addressing these issues, we may want to first focus on how to create a school environment that promotes respect, dignity, and nonviolence.

For too many students, going to school is a violating and demeaning experience. The anonymity of large schools and the irrelevance of much of the subject matter to the experience and aspirations of children cultivates indifference and disrespect toward school and the adults who work there. Feelings of hostility and resentment are exacerbated when adults arbitrarily enforce rules, forgetting that they are working with children. Moreover, some adults are just plain mean when they deal with kids, exercising their authority over children in a pernicious and vindictive manner.

I have found that children consistently respect those teachers that set high standards for behavior and academic performance, and who demonstrate a personal interest in their students. Most schools have at least one teacher that fits this description. But too often that person works in isolation rather than being used as a role model for effective teaching. One way to spread around the knowledge and experience of such teachers is to establish mentoring relationships and to encourage collaboration between teachers.

There are also ways to provide security that do not dehumanize the environment. At one junior high school in Oakland, California, an elderly woman serves as the campus security monitor, rather than an armed guard or large, intimidating man. This woman lives in the neighborhood surrounding the school and understands the kids' reality, culture, and needs. Without the threat of force she is able to break up fights, enforce basic school rules, and keep those who do not belong off the school campus. She can do this because she speaks in terms the children understand and, most of all, because the kids know that she truly cares about them. She has moral authority, derived not from her position but from who she is and what she represents in their community.

In my conversations with students who attend schools with a reputation for violence, I am struck by their total dissatisfaction with the schools. Rather than appreciating the potential opportunities that might result from their education, they see attendance at school primarily as a way to meet and socialize with friends. These children have no respect for their schools or the adults who work there. School, like the park, the neighborhood block, or the hang-out spot, is seen as appropriate a place as any for carrying out reprisals against enemies or sorting our personal conflicts. School is not a special place where violence is often inappropriate. Further, their feelings about school may be so negative that the institution itself becomes the object of their violence through vandalism or harassment of teachers and other adults.

As we look at the problem of violence within schools, we must connect it to the larger issues confronting schools, particularly inner-city schools. School violence is not strictly an urban phenomenon, nor is it limited to low-income communities. Increasingly, middle-class suburban schools, and even schools in affluent areas, have problems with violence. However, the problems of urban schools are particularly acute and are complicated by their connection to the prevalence of poverty, crime, and despair in our cities.

Urban schools must not only address the academic needs of their students, they must also find the resources to provide social and psychological support to students and their families. Yet many schools define their mission too narrowly. Problems like violence, drugs, and teen pregnancy are often seen as beyond the scope of what schools can or should address. Clearly, extra resources in both funding and skilled personnel are needed to expand the services that schools provide. Perhaps even more important, schools need a broadened vision of what they can do to respond more effectively to the needs of children.

Violence in our schools is only a symptom of a much larger problem facing schools and society generally. To treat the problem in isolation only perpetuates a reliance on failed methods. There are no easy answers. But at the minimum we have to find more ways to bring together, on a regular basis, students and those adults with whom they can identify. We must also work toward making our schools more humane and responsive to children's needs. This may not sound like much, especially when compared to the high-tech solutions promoted in most quarters. But in the long run, it may have the greatest impact.

The Hollow Promise
of Youth Apprenticeships

HARVEY KANTOR

President Clinton's recently enacted School-to-Work Opportunities Act proposes over the next five years to create as many as 300,000 youth apprenticeships for those who have been called the "forgotten half" of American youth – the more than 50 percent of high school students who do not go on to college and whose life chances have been diminished by changes in the American economy. Patterned after similar programs in Europe, especially the system in Germany where upwards of one-half of all high school students are apprentices, Clinton's proposal would combine paid work and on-the-job training with related classroom instruction in the last two years of high school and a third year of "professional-technical" education. At the end of that time, according to the Clinton plan, students would receive a certificate of occupational competence in addition to a high school diploma and would have the option of going on to college or entering the workforce in their chosen field.[1]

Support for such a job-based education program has been remarkably widespread. In addition to the Clinton administration, several educational policymakers, foundation heads, blue-ribbon commissions, and state legislatures have endorsed similar ideas. In a 1988 report title *The Forgotten Half: Non-College Youth in America,* the W.T. Grant Foundation Commission on Work, Family, and Citizenship headed by former U.S. commissioner of education Harold Howe III underscored the economic difficulties facing noncollege youth and endorsed a variety of policies, including cooperative education, preemployment internships, and apprenticeship, to help young people bridge the gap between school and work. In its 1990 report, *America's Choice: High Skills or Low Wages!* the Commission on the Skills of the American Workforce also commented on the declining earnings of high school graduates and the lack of career-oriented programs for those not enrolling in college. It proposed a system of national competency standards for various occupations and called on employers to help prepare young people for employment through part-time work and training. Finally, the Pew Memorial Trust, the nation's second largest foundation, recently lent its support to a project to implement youth apprenticeship programs in fifteen sites around the country, and in the last few years, legislatures in Arkansas, Georgia, Maine, Oregon, and Wisconsin have passed legislation to establish youth apprenticeship programs in their states.[2]

Although the sponsors of these proposals and projects acknowledge that implementing an apprenticeship system will be difficult, all of them believe that success in developing such a system will have a number of beneficial economic and social effects. By upgrading the skills of future workers, they contend, apprenticeship will improve the quality of the nation's workforce and thus make the American economy more productive and competitive. In addition, many say, after starting their apprenticeships, noncollege-bound students will see a direct link between what they do in the classroom and their future occupational careers. Consequently, they will work harder in school in order to acquire the skills they need to succeed in the labor market. Finally, some have even argued that by exposing young people to more responsible adults in the workplace, an apprenticeship system would help adolescents mature more quickly and thereby make it less likely they will get involved with drugs, commit crimes, or get pregnant.[3]

Even allowing for the rhetorical oversell that usually accompanies the introduction of new educational programs, much of this sounds persuasive. Since the introduction of vocational education early in the twentieth century, reformers have argued that linking the classroom more closely to the workplace would make school more attractive to disaffected young people and improve the nation's economic competitiveness. But, despite its apparent potential, there are good reasons to question whether apprenticeship can do much more than previous vocational programs to get young people to study more, to improve their job prospects, or to make the economy more productive. In fact, by focusing attention so exclusively on education at the expense of other public policies designed to end racial discrimination, encourage high wages and full employment, and foster the reorganization of work, it may actually do more to dim the prospects for genuine economic reform than to brighten them.

Apprenticeship and the Youth Labor Market

The arguments for apprenticeship are premised on two assumptions about the problems noncollege-bound high school graduates face when they enter the labor market. One is that the difficulties young people experience early in their work careers are damaging to their long-term economic prospects and contribute to a good deal of their antisocial behavior. The other is that many of these problems can be ameliorated by new institutional arrangements that help young people make a smoother transition from school to work. Both of these assumptions are highly problematic, though neither of them is entirely unfounded.

To begin with, although many young people spend their initial few years after high school in unskilled, poorly paid jobs in what economists call the secondary labor market, there is little evidence that these early experiences necessarily lead to serious economic difficulties later on. Rather, as young people get older, many move out of these secondary labor market jobs into better paying, more stable employment in the preferred, or what is often referred to as the primary, sector of the economy. In fact, while those concerned over the transition from school to work have tended to view youth unemployment and job hopping as "pathological," since the 1930s most studies of the youth labor market have concluded that for the majority of young people, this period in their work career is a temporary one and that many eventually "settle down into permanent employment."[4]

It would be wrong to attribute the characteristics of the youth labor market chiefly to youthful instability, however. More important is the structure of the labor market and the nature of the demand for labor. Put simply, many young people work in secondary labor market jobs after high school because most employers are not interested in hiring young workers for jobs with better compensation and opportunities for advancement. For these jobs, employers generally prefer to hire slightly older workers who they believe are more reliable and responsible and thus a better risk for investment in training and promotion. This benefits workers in their mid-twenties by enhancing their opportunities for more financially remunerative and secure employment, but it also means that most students just out of high school are confined to less desirable jobs in the secondary labor market, at least until they grow older.[5]

These structures and practices have proven remarkably stable, despite past efforts to change them. During the 1970s, for example, the Youth Entitlement Demonstration Program tried to get students to stay in high school by guaranteeing them jobs. But the program could not get many employers to participate. In fact, a survey of employers in the demonstration area revealed that less than one-fifth were willing to take part even if the government subsidized the entire wage of those hired. Why these employers were so unenthusiastic about this program is unclear. Most labor market economists have assumed that wage subsidies for young workers would make them more attractive to employers and improve their position in the job queue. But apparently most believed, as Thomas Bailey has recently suggested, that "these young workers would not contribute enough to justify the effort needed to supervise them" even if someone else paid their wages.[6]

At first glance, employers in many European countries seem to be considerably less resistant to hiring young workers. As supporters of apprenticeship point out, German employers are much more willing to accept responsibility for training young workers and for helping them enter the labor market. Yet even in Germany, where there is a widespread national commitment to the apprenticeship system, many employers remain reluctant to hire youth for "career ladder jobs," and only a minority participate in the apprenticeship program. In 1980, only about 12 percent to 13 percent of large industrial and commercial firms trained apprentices. More small artisan firms took on apprentices (about 40 percent). But these smaller firms train many more apprentices than they can hire (in 1980 they employed only 17 percent of the workforce but trained about 40 percent of all apprentices), and many youth are forced to leave these firms within a year of completing their training. More critical observers of the German system contend that these employers participate chiefly because they see the apprenticeship system as a source of low-wage labor, hardly a better prospect than many young workers in this country now face in the youth labor market before they are able to move into more secure and financially rewarding employment.[7]

Given the evidence that American employers do not readily offer adult jobs to teenagers and that dead-end youth work does not inevitably portend future economic problems for many youth, much of the policy focus on smoothing the transition from school to work for high school graduates not only seems "doomed to remain...at the mercy of individual enthusiasts"[8] but also seems somewhat misplaced. The chief focus of public policy should be on generating

enough employment for those youth who are having unusual difficulty making the transition to adult employment in the preferred
sectors of the labor market — especially the disproportionate numbers of minority youth, particularly young African-Americans, who
are experiencing greater and greater difficulty both finding work
and holding any stable, better-paying jobs at all.

Indeed, whatever significance is accorded to the problems white
youth face in the secondary labor market, there is no disputing the
obstacles young African-Americans encounter in finding and holding
work even as they get older. Not only are black unemployment
rates more than double the rates for similarly educated white youth,
but over the last two decades the labor force participation rate for
young African-Americans — especially for young African-American
males — has worsened considerably, both absolutely and relative to
their white peers. Whereas in the 1950s black and white men ages
eighteen to twenty-four not in school participated in the labor market at roughly the same rate (about 90 percent), in 1983, only 72
percent of eighteen to twenty-four-year-old African-American
males not in school were in the labor force, compared to 89 percent
for whites. In short, although many African-American youth also
develop greater attachment to the labor force as they get older,
today they are much more likely than in the past or in comparison
to whites to have stopped looking for work and dropped out of the
labor market altogether. But whether the barriers young African-
Americans face in the labor market can be overcome mainly by
improving the institutional linkages between school and work is
questionable.[9]

Race, Apprenticeship, and the Transition to Work

Although advocates of apprenticeship believe that linking education
more closely to the work place will benefit a variety of students,
one of the chief selling points is that it will be especially beneficial
for low-income, minority youth, particularly black youth living in
inner cities. This is partly because they believe that apprenticeship
will link effort in the classroom with rewards in the workplace and
thereby give minority students greater incentive to study and
achieve in school. In addition, they argue that job-based education
programs like apprenticeship will help minority youth improve their
prospects in the labor market not only by equipping them with
vocational skills but, even more important, by providing them with

access to the kinds of employment opportunities they now lack because they are excluded from the informal networks necessary to obtain jobs and move into meaningful careers.[10]

Although these arguments have merit, the employment difficulties facing young minority workers are more deeply rooted than any of them assume. First, a large body of popular and scholarly literature supports the notion that lack of skills is a major problem for many minority youth. But skills or the lack of them do not seem to be the primary consideration for many employers when they hire young workers, even for jobs in the primary labor market. A study by Paul Osterman has found that the majority of young workers in primary jobs did not know how to do their job when they were first hired, but were trained by their employers.[11] This suggests that while apprenticeship might help young minority workers build skills, it is unlikely that raising their levels of "human capital" will dramatically improve their job prospects. What apprenticeship might do is teach attention to detail, work discipline, and other work-readiness behaviors that employers believe minority youth lack. This implies, however, that the chief value of the system is "socialization, not skill building."[12]

Much recent research also supports the argument that most jobs — both in the primary and secondary labor markets — are found through personal contacts. Osterman's study of the youth labor market points out, for instance, that youth do not search for work in an "impersonal labor market" but "move through channels already traveled by people they know." In secondary jobs, friends are the most frequent source of referral, while parents and relatives are more helpful in finding jobs in the primary market. This makes sense since secondary jobs are more likely to be in small retail stores, which employ youth from the local neighborhood, or in bigger firms, which have large numbers of minimum-wage jobs and are known to hire young workers for unskilled work. By contrast, primary firms are more interested in stability, and employers believe that parents are more likely than friends to be a reliable means of control.[13]

This structure of employment undoubtedly hurts young African-Americans seeking work for two reasons. One is that they are more likely than whites to live in inner-city neighborhoods where there has been a substantial loss of the kinds of small businesses and industries that typically provide employment opportunities for young workers. The other is that even though the occupational distribution of African-Americans has improved considerably since World War II and become more similar to that of whites, African-Americans continue to be underrepresented in the most desirable sectors of the labor market. As a result, young blacks have less access to the informal job networks that help white youth find jobs and that are necessary for securing employment not only in the secondary market but in the primary labor market as well. [14]

A formal apprenticeship system will not eliminate the importance of friends and relatives in finding jobs. But by institutionalizing entry to the workplace, it might help compensate for this lack of informal job networks in the black community and thus help young African-Americans find better paying, more secure employment. Indeed, because African-Americans historically have had less access to informal job networks, they have been more dependent than whites on formal institutions such as schools and employment bureaus for finding work. Yet because schools are isolated from the workplace and employment bureaus have become little more than job referral agencies for the welfare system, these institutions typically have not done a very good job in helping minority workers find employment. [15]

But the absence of job networks and inadequate socialization are not the only reasons many African-American youth have such a hard time entering the labor market and finding better-paying, higher-status jobs. At least two others are equally, if not more, important, though there does not seem to be much apprenticeship can do about them. One is the persistence of racial discrimination. Sometimes this is explicit. Many white employers and workers, for example, resist hiring people of color — especially black men — to supervise whites. In other cases, employers equate race with characteristics that disqualify minority workers from employment, particularly in higher-level positions. As the sociologists Joleen Kirschenmann and Kathryn Neckerman discovered in their interviews with employers in Chicago, many employers associate race with inner-city schools, which in turn signifies poor education, inadequate work skills, and insufficient commitment to the work ethic. Either way, however, race compounds the employment problems facing minority youth, since it militates against hiring African-Americans and other minority workers for entry-level jobs or promoting them to more financially rewarding, higher-status positions. [16]

Youth apprenticeship advocates contend that the relationship between skilled mentors and apprentices will help combat these discriminatory practices. Because apprenticeship is not a strictly private relationship, argues Stephen Hamilton, one of the foremost supporters of youth apprenticeship in the United States, the employer must ensure that the apprentice has every opportunity to learn what is needed for certification as a skilled worker. But this hardly guarantees equal treatment on the job, as Hamilton himself acknowledged. Nor does it guarantee equal access to the most desirable apprenticeships. On the contrary, Thomas Bailey reports that in Germany, Turks and other recent immigrants, who occupy a similar position in the German labor market as African-Americans and other minorities do in the United States, are not only underrepresented in the apprenticeship system; those who do participate are also concentrated in apprenticeships in those occupations that offer the least chance for promotion and that consistently have the highest unemployment rate among students who successfully complete their apprenticeships.[17]

Employment Policies

The other problem is the absence of a full employment policy. Because young African-Americans and other minority youth are generally at the bottom of the hiring queue, tight labor markets substantially improve their employment prospects, both absolutely and relative to whites.[18] Yet once inflation began to accelerate in the late 1960s and early 1970s, successive administrations have tried to control it chiefly by letting unemployment rise. The result has been devastating for young blacks and other low-income minority youth, since they are the first fired and last hired when labor markets turn slack. Today unemployment has dropped to about 7 percent nationwide compared to 11 percent in the early 1980s, but policymakers remain convinced that lower unemployment rates would mean higher inflation, so they have avoided stimulating the economy to reduce unemployment any further even though this harms young blacks looking for work.[19]

Full employment is, of course, hardly a panacea for racial inequality in the labor market. Expanding aggregate demand will not by itself increase the availability of "good" jobs. Nor will it necessarily prevent whites from trying to monopolize them by restricting African-Americans and other people of color to the lower levels of the job hierarchy. This requires more affirmative policies that change the position of people of color in the labor queue and that intervene more directly in decisions about how to allocate workers to different jobs. But it is hard to see how policies such as apprenticeship can improve the employment prospects of those minority youth just entering the labor market without a commitment to continuous full employment as well.

While concerns about the effects of work in the youth labor market and the employment problems of minority youth have created much of the interest in apprenticeship, interest in job-based education has also been fueled by a growing concern about the skill level of the American workforce. For some, this concern stems from their belief that shifts in the occupational structure have increased the skill requirements of jobs and require reforms in the educational system in order to overcome a critical skills shortage among American workers. Others question whether skill requirements have actually changed that much but contend that an apprenticeship system is needed in order to improve the skills of future workers so that employers can move to what they call a high-productivity form of work organization. Either way, however, nearly all apprenticeship advocates maintain that by improving the skills of the workforce, an apprenticeship system will help make the economy more productive and sustain its capacity to provide a high standard of living for most American citizens.

Like most of the rhetoric surrounding proposals for apprenticeship, these concerns are badly overstated, though they are not entirely without substance. Although skill requirements are rising because of shifts in the occupational composition of jobs, for at least three reasons the overall effect of these changes on skill levels is likely to be modest. First, while the most highly skilled occupational groups are growing fastest and the growth rates of occupations such as computer programmer and electrical engineer are relatively high, because they begin from a small absolute base, the total number of these jobs remains relatively insignificant. Even by the year 2000, the importance of these occupations within the job structure as a whole will not be very large.[20] Second, whereas occupational shifts increased job-skill levels between 1960 and 1990, the rate of these changes decreased each decade. Whether these trends will persist is not certain, but Lawrence Mishel and Ruy Teixiera, two researchers at the Economic Policy Institute in Washington, D.C., estimate that future change rates will be about one-third to one-fourth the historical rate, hardly enough to support the notion that occupational changes will produce a dramatic increase in job-skill requirements.

Finally, the trend toward more high-skilled jobs and higher-skill requirements has been partially offset by the growth of relatively low-skilled jobs in the service occupations. In fact, the growth of service jobs such as cooks, waiters, household workers, janitors, and security guards may actually retard the upgrading of skill levels in the economy as a whole, since their average skill rating is below the skill rating for the entire occupational structure, and they will contribute the largest number of jobs to total employment growth between 1984 and 2000.[21]

Erroneous Assumptions

Taken together, all of this suggests that it is erroneous to assume that skill requirements are escalating rapidly and that education must be extensively reformed just because high-skill occupations and industries are growing faster than low-skill ones. Shifts in the distribution of jobs, however, are not the only way that skill levels can rise. Substantial skill upgrading can also take place because of changes in the content of existing occupations. One of the most common arguments for apprenticeship and other plans for job-based education, for example, is that the use of computers and other new technologies in factories, stores, and offices has increased the complexity of tasks that once required little technical training or sophistication but now require a better-trained workforce.[22]

Despite a considerable amount of research on the effects of technology on work requirements, it is difficult to assess this argument with certainty. Although technological innovation undoubtedly affects the content of work, its impact is seldom all in one direction. Rather, the effects vary from substantial increases to none at all to considerable skill downgrading (i.e., deskilling). Historical case studies suggest, for instance, that while new technologies have enhanced the skill levels of some jobs, they have also deskilled others, depending on the type of job, industry, and firm; the form of technology; and the dimension of skill under consideration. Whatever the particular case, however, the implication for educational policy is that we should avoid special training programs that assume that technological change automatically upgrades the skill content of work.[23]

Ironically, this is especially the case for new information technologies like computers. Although the introduction of computers has created some jobs, such as systems analyst and programmer, that require extensive computer-related training, several studies report that the use of computers has also created many relatively low-skill, data-processing jobs that require little technical training or special education. According to one study of computer use in small business, the majority of employers reported that basic skills and enthusiasm were "more important in learning to use computers than previous experience and technical training."[24]

Regardless of the impact of changes in the distribution of occupations and of technological innovation on skill requirements, it is still possible that reforms like apprenticeship are necessary because the nation needs a more skilled workforce to compete economically. This is the argument made by the Report of the Commission on the Skills of the American Workforce, *America's Choice: High Skills or Low Wages!* Although the report favors a job-based educational system such as apprenticeship, it does not contend that occupational and technological changes have dramatically upgraded skill requirements and produced a skills shortage among American workers. On the contrary, it recommends that the nation change its approach to education and work because skill levels have not gone up enough to encourage American business to adopt the less bureaucratic, more flexible forms of work organization needed to increase productivity and keep the economy competitive.

On the face of it, this is a compelling argument. But it too is a questionable one. Most important, it assumes that the organization of work reflects the skill levels of the labor force. There is not much evidence, however, that the structure of jobs is determined principally by the capacities of the people who fill them. Because of the expansion of education, American workers today are more educated and arguably more skilled than they were fifty years ago, yet with the exception of some jobs in a few "best practice" firms in certain industries, jobs have not been substantially restructured to take advantage of this rise in educational and skill levels. On the contrary, the match between workers' skills and the requirements of jobs is, in Kenneth Spenner's words, "notoriously loose" and has given rise to as much concern about the phenomenon of "overeducation" — the fact that workers have more skills than are needed for the jobs they are assigned — as to fears that workers are insufficiently skilled to perform their jobs adequately.[25] Rather than the skill levels of workers affecting the structure of work, the organization of work is shaped as much by public policy, the culture of the work environment, and the social context of worker-management relations.[26]

None of this denies that the adoption of new forms of work organization might increase productivity, or that restructuring work so that workers interact with each other as part of a team and take responsibility for independently solving technical problems requires workers with considerable skill and training. According to several studies, in those firms that have adopted less hierarchical, more decentralized forms of work organization, jobs are more likely to require skills such as intellectual flexibility and problem-solving capabilities that were seldom needed by many workers in the past.[27] But such jobs are not now the standard in American industry and business. Nor will simply raising the human capital level of the labor force — whether through educational reforms like apprenticeship or other forms of job training — make them numerically dominant in the future. Equally, if not more important, are other policies that make it inconvenient for management to rely on bureaucratic, repetitious forms of labor.[28]

Indeed, one of the chief reasons that many European and Japanese companies have adopted new, less bureaucratic forms of work organization is not just because of the higher skill levels of their workers but because national full employment policies and public support for strong unions make it in their interest to do so. Historically, in Sweden, and to a lesser extent in Germany, for example, union pressure combined with national income policies and public commitments to full employment have provided strong incentives for employers to improve productivity through investments in training and restructured forms of work. But discussion of such public policies is largely absent from the American debate, even though documents such as *America's Choice: High Skills or Low Wages!* recognize their importance.[29] Because unions in this country are weaker and our commitment to state intervention and public social provision is more limited, attention is focused instead almost exclusively on improving human capital levels through better integration of school and work.

Educational Reform and the Economy

Although there is not much evidence that technological change has dramatically raised skill requirements or that improving the skills of the workforce will by itself make the economy more productive, it is difficult to dispute much of what the advocates of apprenticeship have to say about the shortcomings of American schools and their failure to prepare high school graduates for work. High schools today do not do a very good job engaging the majority of students in academic learning. Nor, except for those headed for liberal arts colleges, is there much relationship between what happens in the classroom and the jobs students get when they enter the labor market. One result is that many students have little incentive to study hard or achieve in school. Instead, they drop out or else simply put in seat time until they graduate.[30]

For these students, a job-based education program like apprenticeship does indeed seem to offer a much-needed alternative to the academic orientation of the high school curriculum. There is some evidence, for example, that those students bored with academic work find vocational classes more appealing.[31] But despite its promise to make education more relevant and useful to noncollege-bound students, in practice it is not likely that apprenticeship will invigorate the traditional high school curriculum to accommodate either their economic needs or their diverse interests and learning styles. Rather, by channeling them into job-specific training, it seems more likely that apprenticeship will narrow their opportunities to acquire the kinds of general intellectual skills they need most both at work and in social life.

Advocates argue that apprenticeship will create a learning environment that provides for the development of both specific and general skills. But rather than broaden the character of the curriculum to meet the needs of a diverse population, the introduction of work-oriented programs has functioned over the years to fragment the curriculum and deepen the division between college and noncollege-bound students. In fact, many of those who have studied the history of vocational education contend that it has done little to unify practical and academic education or eliminate the gap between those headed for work and those headed for college. Much more often, they say, vocational education has fostered a differentiated system of schooling, with low-income and minority boys channeled into industrial education programs, low-income and minority girls channeled into traditional female courses and occupations, and white middle- and upper-class students placed in college-oriented academic programs.[32]

Despite the pleas of apprenticeship advocates, there is little reason to think that youth apprenticeship will be much different. Although advocates stress that even the most academically capable students can benefit from practical job-based education and that apprenticeship graduates will be able to go on to college, most proposals for apprenticeship make it plain that the chief raison d'être of the program is to serve working-class and minority students who they believe are not likely to pursue a baccalaureate degree. In their view, these students are not academically capable and have been poorly served by the current educational system but will benefit from a less academic, more vocationally oriented education.[33]

Indeed, some contend that this will actually make American education more democratic. They argue that making explicit provision for the noncollege-bound will promote more opportunity than the existing system, which pretends to give access to the same education to every student but in reality provides many students with little useful training at all.[34] If there is a case to be made for apprenticeship, however, it is not that it will equalize opportunities for the least advantaged. Although it comes cloaked in the rhetoric of concern for the "neglected majority" and the "forgotten half," this approach to education and work will only add "another dimension of inequality" to an already unequal system.[35]

In the end, if there is a democratic approach to changing the relationship between education and work, it is not to subordinate education even further to vocational concerns, as apprenticeship ultimately proposes to do. Despite the claims of its advocates, this will not equalize educational opportunities or improve the economic prospects of poor and minority youth; it will only reproduce the inequities that apprenticeship claims to address. A more democratic alternative for a changing economy is to provide all students with the kinds of skills they need to develop fully and manage technological change. This means offering them an education that will equip them not only with specific vocational skills but, in John Dewey's words, with the "initiative, ingenuity, and executive capacity" they need to be "masters of their own industrial fate."[36]

Such an education by itself is not sufficient, however. It is also necessary to develop policies around schooling and the economy that intervene more directly in labor markets rather than focus on schooling and training alone. Among other things, this requires policies to combat racial discrimination at work, a commitment to full employment and to macroeconomic and other pro-employment policies such as reducing the workweek and changing the pattern of government expenditures that will help sustain it, and support for unionization as well as for experiments to improve the quality of work life such as work councils and worker participation in management. This is the only way for policy to respond actively rather than reactively to the social and economic problems that apprenticeship hopes to solve and that have generated interest in job-based plans for education in the first place.[37]

Recommended Resources

Beyond the Classroom: National Policy Concerns

Center for Law and Education

955 Massachusetts Ave., 3rd Floor, Cambridge, MA 02139; 617-876-6611. Up-to-date information on vocational education legislation. See especially *NewsNotes*, the center's newsletter.

Choosing Inequality: The Case for Democratic Schooling

by Ann Bastian, Norm Fruchter, Marilyn Gittell, Colin Greer, and Kenneth Haskins, Philadelphia: Temple University Press, 1985. A concise overview of key educational policy issues that affect equity and democracy.

False Choices: Why School Vouchers Threaten Our Children's Future

edited by Robert Lowe and Barbara Miner, Milwaukee, WI: Rethinking Schools, 1992. A 40-page pamphlet critiquing school "choice" and privatization.

Savage Inequalities

by Jonathan Kozol, New York: Crown, 1991. An eloquent defense of egalitarian public schools; a modern classic.

Horace's School

by Theodore Sizer, Boston: Houghton Mifflin, 1992. An analysis of the problems of the modern-day high school with possible alternative solutions, by the founder of the Coalition of Essential Schools.

Work, Youth, and Schooling

edited by Harvey Kantor and David Tyack, Stanford, CA: Stanford University Press, 1982. Offers historical perspectives on the failure of vocational education to solve social and economic problems.

Our Schools, Our Selves

1698 Gerrard St. East, Toronto, Ontario, Canada M4L 2B2. Bi-monthly journal on education issues, focusing on Canada.

Rethinking Schools

1001 E. Keefe Ave., Milwaukee, WI, 53212–1710; 414–964–9646; fax 414–964–7220. Quarterly journal addressing both national educational policy and classroom concerns, with a focus on equity.

PART V

Building a Community:
Teachers, Students, and Parents

For children to learn well, schools must act as centers of community rather than outposts of domination. As the chapters in this section explain, building a school community is an arduous process that demands respect for all participants and a willingness to experiment with new roles for parents, teachers, and students. The editors of *Rethinking Schools* note that some schools miss the chance to build educational communities because they limit parents to fund-raising and making sure their own children are well-behaved and ready to learn. Although these traditional roles are important, the editors argue that parents should also be encouraged to help govern schools and act as advocates for all the children in the school. They challenge schools to see parents as valued resources who can help strengthen teaching and learning.

In addition to effective parent involvement, schools will only be able to act as communities if teachers receive adequate pay, supportive working conditions, and community respect. Contrary to the myth of a golden age when teachers enjoyed professional autonomy and provided top-notch academic training, historian Robert Lowe explains that teachers have typically experienced overcrowded classrooms, intrusive supervision, and low status. Despite improved training and hard-won advances in job security and professionalization, teachers still contend with bureaucratic interference, class sizes that stifle good instruction, and low public esteem. Lowe argues that teachers can only win the full creative potential of their profession by assuming increased responsibility for managerial functions and student achievement.

But an expanded role for teachers challenges old habits and traditional patterns through which teachers are prepared for their careers. In her reflections on teacher training, Cynthia Ellwood examines the difficult problem of how white, middle-class teachers can learn to educate children whose backgrounds often differ from their own. She urges teachers to be aware of how media stereotypes and discrimination can damage the children they teach, and to strive to see the world through the eyes of their students. Ellwood urges schools of education to demand strong preparation in ethnic studies of teachers-to-be and to teach them pedagogies that build a bridge between academic learning and each student's life experiences and culture.

Building schools into communities will also require a thoughtful reworking of how teacher unions function in urban settings. Bob Peterson notes that organized teachers inherit a contradictory legacy from the labor movement: unions have both championed the rights of working people and at times discriminated against women and workers of color. Because teachers are responsible for the growth of children rather than the manufacture of goods, they have an especially strong responsibility to transcend discriminatory practices that inhibit learning. Peterson urges teachers to adopt a "social justice" unionism that forges pro-education alliances with communities by balancing trade union rights with the right of all children to an effective education.

When Lola Glover first became involved in her children's school, her activities fell within traditional patterns of chaperoning and coordinating bake sales. In her interview with Barbara Miner of *Rethinking Schools,* she explains that actions that threatened the education and emotional health of children at the school prompted her to act as a parent organizer. More than three decades of experience as an activist have convinced her that even a small core of parents can make a difference, but only if they act as advocates for all the children at a school. Glover believes that effective home-school partnerships can be forged if teachers reach out to parents and if parents insist on their right to act as cooperative members of the school community.

As these articles demonstrate, building an educational community demands acts of imagination and courage. The members of such potential communities must look beyond traditional antagonisms and narrow self-interest. They must be willing to work through painful conflicts and invent new forms of cooperation. In a society that entrenches privilege and sows division, the advocates of just schools will need a vision that provides new values and practical answers.

Beyond Pizza Sales:
Parent Involvement in the 1990s

THE EDITORS OF RETHINKING SCHOOLS

Scratch the surface of parent involvement in schools and there's no telling what you'll find. In some schools it's little more than rhetoric, with involvement frozen at the level of pizza sales. In Chicago it's parents having the authority to hire principals. In some cities it's parents organizing against science courses that teach evolution.

As with many popular buzzwords in education, parent involvement can mean just about anything. *Rethinking Schools* has a particular perspective. We view parent involvement as a way to help ensure that parents act as advocates and decision makers in the schools, that they be seen as key resources working not only to improve their own children's education but the schooling of all children.

Many traditional parent involvement projects focus on the home. They try to help parents improve their parenting skills so that children come to school better behaved and prepared. While not dismissing the critical importance of parenting, we believe such an emphasis misses the broader significance of parent involvement.

All too often we hear statements like, "Schools don't need more money, what they need are better parents so kids come to school ready to learn." This mentality blames the victims and does not deal with many of the underlying causes of social and familial problems. Poverty, unemployment, racial and class inequality, and inadequate health care and housing are the real culprits at which people should aim their anger and their legislative solutions.

We believe parents have something important to offer and can help the school be a better school. In this view, parents are a strength, not a weakness. They are vital resources, not detriments, to school reform. (While we tend to use the term "parent" we realize the term's limitations in today's world; we use it as an inclusive term for any adult family members working on behalf of their children in schools.)

Why Parent Involvement?

Parent involvement in public schools is particularly important in today's world. Clearly, our society will only reluctantly provide the resources needed to solve the crisis facing our public schools, particularly urban schools attended mainly by children of color. Unless we draw on the strengths and power of parents and community members, school reform will, at best, be limited to superficial efforts designed to cover up rather than resolve the crisis in education, particularly the crisis of inequality.

Parental involvement holds many promises. It can help improve the curriculum, teaching, and learning in individual schools. It can help bridge the division between many teachers and communities they serve — a division that has tended to grow, given the overwhelmingly white composition of the teaching force and the overwhelmingly nonwhite composition of urban student bodies. Parent involvement can also help build necessary political coalitions. If teachers and parents cannot work together at their individual schools, they will be unable to forge the city- and statewide organizations necessary to counter the slash-and-burn mentality that dominates many school budget decisions.

Unfortunately, some of the most successful parent organizing projects are led by archconservatives with an agenda that runs counter to values of multiculturalism, equality, tolerance, and respect for children as people capable of learning to think critically and make their own decisions. The success of right-wing parent organizing is a chilling reminder that there is nothing inherently progressive about parental involvement.

It was parents, for example, who threw stones at buses carrying African-American children in the mid-1970s in Boston as those children tried to exercise their right to attend integrated schools. It is parents who hide behind Bibles and shout the most un-Christian epithets as they try to prevent sex education, tolerance for gays and lesbians, and measures to counter the AIDS/HIV epidemic among adolescents in many urban areas. It is parents who often are the most virulent opponents of multicultural education and who are quick to try to ban books such as *Catcher in the Rye, Of Mice and Men,* and *The Bridge to Terabithia.*

What to Do

We believe that schools should work to increase parental involvement in four areas: (1) governance and decision making, (2) organizing for equity and quality, (3) curriculum and its implementation in the classroom, and (4) home educational support. Following are some preliminary thoughts, designed to spur discussion rather than provide answers to complex issues.

GOVERNANCE

Parents should be viewed as decision makers, whether through formal or informal arrangements such as school-based councils or parent committees where their input is listened to and respected.

Key questions are: Who should serve on school councils? What should be the ratio of staff to parents to community people? How should members be selected? How can you ensure that representatives on the school council truly represent their constituents? What powers should they have? What is the relationship between school-based decisions and districtwide policies and contracts? These are complex issues that need thorough discussion.

ORGANIZING/ADVOCACY

Organized into groups, parents can advocate for children and can educate educators. This is particularly important for parents of color, who may see inequality or insensitivity from even the most well-intentioned white teachers.

Such parent groups can take various forms, from citywide advocacy organizations to ad hoc committees at individual schools. In Albany, New York, for example, parents and community activists challenged a racist tracking system. In Boston, parents are being trained to advocate for children in their individual schools through the Right Question Project.

These organizing efforts are often short-lived, hampered by funding and the many time demands on parents, especially working parents. The struggle to sustain parent advocacy groups is difficult. If such groups start receiving money from school systems, their politics might become compromised. But without funding, these efforts may die out and valuable training and experience are lost, only to be reinvented again by other parents when the next crisis erupts.

By perseverance and strong leadership, however, some organizations have managed to get funding without compromising their politics. Another approach is to have community-based organizations make parent organizing a priority and to use their resources to sustain such efforts. A third approach is to demand that local school districts, perhaps funded by state legislatures, hire parent organizers at each school.

CURRICULUM AND THE CLASSROOM

Particularly as schools try to institute multicultural curricula, parents are a valuable resource. Parents can have positive effects on curriculum, especially if their participation is organized and supported by the local school. A key step is to have the school agree on an orientation toward parental involvement, overcoming negative attitudes in either group in the process. Some parents may have to overcome a legacy of negative personal experiences with schools, while some teachers need to develop greater respect for parents.

EDUCATING AT HOME

We recognize that parents can significantly help their children at home. Many do, but others do not. Schools can encourage positive interactions between parents and children by helping the school serve as a center where parents can help one another. Support groups, parenting classes, and literacy classes can be very popular, especially when organized by or with the consultation of parents. Lending libraries of learning games, hands-on math activities, books, and tapes also help enhance education in the home.

Sometimes parents educate their children about the history and contributions of their cultures and communities – filling in gaps schools too often leave.

TEACHER TRAINING

Teachers need to be sensitized to the importance of parental involvement. At a district level this should include staff inservice. But most important, state mandates should force teacher training institutions to adequately prepare new teachers in knowing how to work with parent volunteers, conduct parent-teacher conferences, maintain ongoing communication, and overcome possible racial, class, and gender biases.

PARENTS' RIGHTS

Parents have more rights than they might imagine. They have not only legal rights, but also ethical rights, such as the right to have notes and newsletters from school come home in their native language and the right to be treated with respect by school staff, whether secretary, principal, or teacher.

People who work a nine-to-five day often have difficulty getting involved. Educators, labor leaders, and businesses would do well to follow the example initiated by the Cleveland Teachers' Union, whereby parents are allowed to take time off with pay to attend special parent-family days.

JUSTICE AND EQUALITY

It is in the long-term interests of everyone in society that schools are based on values of justice and equality. There is no way to legislate such values. In the long run, the only insurance rests with the parents and teachers who uphold these values to organize and work together.

No one has a stronger, more direct interest in good education than a parent. Educators who fail to recognize this, seeing parents instead as irrelevant, inadequate, or even obstructionist, can never fully succeed in educating young people.

Teachers Through History: The Myth of a Golden Age

ROBERT LOWE

"He was tall, but exceedingly lank, with narrow shoulders, long arms and legs, hands that dangled a mile out of his sleeves, feet that might have served for shovels, and his whole frame most loosely hung together. His head was small, and flat at top, with huge ears, large green glassy eyes, and a long snipe nose, so that it looked like a weather-cock, perched upon his spindle neck, to tell which way the wind blew. To see him striding along the profile of a hill on a windy day, with his clothes bagging and fluttering about him, one might have mistaken him for the genius of famine descending upon the earth, or some scarecrow eloped from a cornfield."

Washington Irving's unflattering portrait of Ichabod Crane, the awkward and opportunist schoolmaster from Connecticut, captured popular contempt for the calling of the country teacher in the years following the American revolution. His was a job that paid little, asked few qualifications, and occupied a short term in winter when more productive labors had come to a halt.

School reformers of widely different political views like to harken to a golden past when teaching was a true profession. Conservatives fret about the competitive position of the United States on the world market and renounce schools' responsibility for promoting equality. They imagine a time when teachers were masters of academic disciplines and provided their charges with first-rate intellectual training. On the other hand, some liberals and radicals seek to restore teachers' allegedly autonomous past when, free of the deskilling effects of bureaucratic constraints, they could devote themselves to creatively nurturing students' affective and cognitive abilities.

The historical record, however, suggests that such pasts never existed. This chapter will look briefly at what really happened with

---

This essay is based on a lecture that draws exclusively on secondary sources, especially work by David Tyack.

teaching in the United States over the last 200 years. It will dispel myths of a golden past, and in doing so, it may help us assess where we are now and what the prospects are for significant reform.

One-Room Schools

Until the middle of the nineteenth century, the one-room district school prevailed, and the typical teacher was male. Occasionally a college student earning money for the next term, the schoolmaster was more likely a local farmer, tavern keeper, or individual with no demonstrated talent for gainful employment. Basic literacy and numeracy were the general requirements for the job, plus applicants had to pass locally created, often absurd trustees' examinations that historian David Tyack has labeled "trials by trivia." Arbitrarily tested and evaluated, it was not by coincidence that the successful candidate often belonged to a trustee's family.

Only in storybooks did a teacher practice his calling in a tidy red schoolhouse nestled in a rich green meadow. In reality, Carl Kaestle has pointed out in *Pillars of the Republic,* the school typically was a crude structure of logs or a clapboard located in the swamp or other wasteland unfit for farming. In this building, the schoolmaster would find what scholar Joseph Kett has called a "promiscuous assemblage" of students ranging in age from three-year-old "a-b-c-darians" to young adults. Some fifty to sixty scholars and as many different textbooks brought from home would further perplex the tasks of the untrained teacher. Memorization backed up by corporal punishment constituted a pedagogy of repression.

Feminization of Teaching

Originally a male pursuit, the sexual composition of the teaching force first slowly and then rapidly changed during the nineteenth century. By 1870 the occupation had become 60 percent female and rose steadily to nearly 90 percent by 1920. Historians point out several reasons for this transformation. Changing conceptions of education began to stress nurturing and patience, qualities associated with women. Males enjoyed expanding opportunities in more remunerative pursuits; females did not. Women could be hired more cheaply, a matter of importance as immigration swelled the school-going population. And as public school reforms created graded classrooms and a need for supervision, it was believed that females would be more pliant subordinates.

Feminization of teaching coincided with rising entry standards. The creation of normal schools and summer institutes, as well as a lengthening school term, tended to drive men out of a job that had previously required no credentials and could be performed in the winter months when other work was scarce. Ironically, as teaching began to require formal training and occupy a greater part of the year, its identification as a female calling remanded it to a subordinate place in the occupational hierarchy. Even when men returned to teaching in large numbers after the Second World War, it did not attain the stature of an authentic profession.

The Urban Scene

By the turn of the twentieth century, women teachers predominated. Although one-room rural schoolhouses were still widespread, practices in the cities were shaping the future of teaching. Most urban elementary school teachers in 1900 had an eighth-grade education, and high school teachers, who then served a tiny percentage of the nation's youth, had attained a year or two of college. Not a single state required a high school diploma for teaching at the elementary level.

Urban teachers now benefited from facing graded classrooms with uniform texts. But in cities like New York, sixty to seventy students, speaking myriad languages, would fill dark, grim, gaslit rooms that overlooked garbage-strewn alleys or absorbed the odor of outhouses. Elementary salaries were scarcely incentives to take all this on. According to a 1905 NEA study unearthed by David Tyack, they averaged around $650 per year, generally on par with the wages of sanitation and street laborers. In addition, autonomy was absent both inside and outside the classroom. Not only did supervisors define what and how to teach, their authority spilled over into teachers' private lives. Professor Michael Kirst, for instance, located a list of rules for female teachers in Westwood, California, for the year 1915, which prohibited getting married, dating, leaving town without permission, frequenting ice cream stores, getting in an automobile with an unrelated man, dressing in bright colors, and wearing fewer than two petticoats.

Women, of course, were not always willing to play subservient roles. They dominated efforts to organize teachers early in the century. Grace Strachan led the Interborough Association of Teachers in New York City. She persistently advocated equal pay for equal work, which was achieved in most states once women gained the vote. Perhaps the most famous organizer was Margaret Haley, president of the Chicago Teachers Federation. Under her leadership, the CTF successfully forced corporations to pay taxes; it championed the rights of students to gain an education that was free of tracking, IQ testing, and other mechanisms that stratified them by social class; and it supported teacher councils, which were meant to help shape school policies. In time, however, the CTF traded efforts to control the direction of education for tenure and other bread-and-butter issues that have been the main objectives of organized teachers ever since.

Change and Continuity

Over the first half of the century, high school attendance and graduation dramatically rose. In 1900 only 3 percent of seventeen-year-olds graduated from public schools in the United States; by 1940 the graduation rate had risen to slightly over 50 percent. Qualifications for teachers rose accordingly. In 1930, for example, the average elementary school teacher had completed two years of college, and virtually all high school teachers were college graduates. Yet even by the early 1950s the majority of elementary school teachers still lacked college degrees. The educational attainments of teachers never dramatically outstripped those of the general population.

Propelled by the GI Bill and attracted by a wealth of high school positions, males began to reenter the teaching force in the 1950s. Largely of working-class origins, they struggled to ensure their rights through a trade unionist focus on wages, security, and working conditions. They furthered these interests by engaging in an unprecedented wave of strikes during the 1960s. Some of these actions, however, conflicted with the aspirations of minority people. The most prominent case involved Albert Shanker's New York–based United Federation of Teachers. The union struck in order to block Puerto Rican and black efforts to wrest community control from a system that had been notoriously unresponsive to their needs. In addition, organized teachers' narrow trade unionist orientation backfired in the 1970s. Confining their demands to those of industrial workers, they were treated as such. They, rather than supervisors, were the first to suffer layoffs when school systems were forced to retrench.

While organized teachers often acted to preserve their relatively minor privileges at the expense of groups with none, the power of the civil rights movement drew a number of idealistic and socially committed people into teaching during the 1960s. A vision of a more equal society inspired these teachers to struggle to empower their students. Yet progressive teachers generally sought change by working at the cellular level of the classroom or by joining the alternative schools movement. Insufficiently powerful to confront the elaborate bureaucratic controls that limited both teaching and learning in public schools, they failed to institutionalize their practices.

These problems aside, educational attainments of teachers continued to rise during the 1950s and beyond, and teachers today are more secure and more able to impart intellectual training than they were earlier in the century. As opposed to an eighth-grade education attainment at the turn of the century, all teachers now possess at least a bachelor's degree. Most have stayed in the occupation significantly longer than the four-year average in 1900. And state certification requirements, tenure, and grievance procedures are dramatic advances over annual rehiring, idiosyncratic qualifying tests, and arbitrary interference inside and outside the classroom. Nonetheless, teachers neither control the governance of schools nor the curricula. Teachers still have far too many students, and as historian Larry Cuban has shown, they teach out of necessity pretty much the way they did 100 years ago. Also, as in the past, they lack public esteem.

Such continuities in the history of teaching suggest that dramatic change in the status of the occupation is unlikely, despite the outpouring of major reports that advocate otherwise. Given the high demand for teachers, the interests of administrators in maintaining control and keeping their jobs, and the resistance of the public to paying for significant improvement in teachers' standard of living, it is likely that the reforms that will take hold will tighten accountability and circumscribe teachers' freedom rather than create a pedagogical profession. If teachers are to improve their opportunities to utilize their intelligence and imagination, such change will have to come from the bottom up rather than from the deliberations of corporate foundations and the deans of major schools of education. But this would mean reconceptualizing the goals of organizing teachers. Teachers collectively would have to go beyond a concern with wages and benefits to seize the prerogatives of administrators and address the quality of education students receive. Clearly there is little precedent for such action. Yet perhaps, at least, we can take sustenance and guidance from "golden" moments in the past, as when the aforementioned Chicago Teachers Federation organized not only for greater autonomy, but also to support the rights of students against a system that would stratify them by class background.

Preparing Teachers for Education in a Diverse World

CYNTHIA ELLWOOD

As a white teacher in Milwaukee's most culturally diverse high school, I believe if we are to meet the needs of urban education, we need many more teachers of color. But I cannot speak for teachers of color. Instead, I reflect here on my own experience and its particular implications for training teaching candidates of European-American descent.

At the very core of teaching is the task of helping students make connections between what they already understand and the new concepts, information, or skills. Scientists of the human mind tell us we can remember very few totally separate items at once, and all learning is a process of somehow associating new information with old. So this is my job as a teacher: to help students make connections. And to do that, I need to have a pretty good picture of what their understandings are – or I need a way to probe those understandings.

Making connections is central to my job whether I want my students to look deeply into a character in a novel we're reading; whether I'm trying to help my students write literary criticism for the first time in their lives; or whether I'm juggling the complex dynamics that automatically come into play when you put thirty teenagers in one room.

Teaching is interaction, and it demands all the resources of my being. At any moment, I have to decide whether to present information or stand back and let a student discover it. I have to know when and how to encourage, compel, accept, judge, nurture, admonish, humor, provoke, and inspire thirty individuals. Now if I am teaching your son or daughter, you undoubtedly hope that I understand your child well enough to make those decisions – so often spontaneous ones – wisely. And if I really understand your kid, if I can see into his soul a bit, or if I can figure out how his mind works when he's wrestling with a particular concept or skill, or if I can find a way to make him passionately interested in what I teach, I just might be able to inspire him to real heights. But if I don't understand, I can damage your child. I can turn him off, or set him back, or crush his feelings, or stifle his opportunities.

White Teacher

But what happens when a white teacher like myself from a Protestant, upper-middle-class family tries to teach children who are poor, or working class, or Puerto Rican, or African-American, Laotian, Mexican, Catholic, Pentecostal, Arab, or Native American? Anthropologists tell us culture and experience shape our perceptions. And there is no question that my students have all sorts of experiences and perceptions very different from my own. If the core of teaching is making connections between students' experiences and the content of the curriculum, if teaching is a series of judgment calls as I have argued, I am constantly at risk of making mistakes.

A number of scholars have shown just how easy and damaging it is for perfectly well-intentioned educators to make mistakes rooted in cultural ignorance. At worst, I am at risk of severely compromising my students' chances for success; at best I am at risk of not being very effective in my teaching if I do not understand what my students see and know — or even understand that it may rationally be different from what I see and know.

Now maybe I'm overdramatizing. If I as one teacher fail to reach, nurture, and inspire your son or daughter, it's probably not the end of the world; a child can probably recover from this single experience. But if entire educational systems repeatedly misjudge or work ineffectively with certain categories of children — if those systems test, track, and teach in such a way that creates unequal results — we have a problem of national dimensions.

Seeing Differently

I believe that race and class profoundly shape one's experiences in this country. In *Drylongso,* a collection of oral histories of black people collected by anthropologist John Langston Gwaltney, sixty-year-old Hannah Nelson reminisces:

> One time in rural Georgia a white woman and I were stranded in a ditch in her car. When some policemen came and helped us, she was relieved to see them, but I was frightened. Now, I know many other

black women who have had experiences like that and most felt just like I did. I didn't know what those policemen might do, but the white woman with me felt quite certain that they would help us. Well, I knew that they would help her, but I didn't really think they would help me.

It is not only in the rural Georgia of yesterday that people of color have reason to mistrust the police. I have a full load of bilingual classes this year, so all my students are Latino. If my students — particularly my male students — stand on a street corner in a group of three, they get a very different response from a passing patrol car than three white kids standing on a street corner in the suburbs. They could be the most clean-cut, innocent male students — and I have some real innocents, some of whom have grown up in incredibly protective environments in spite of what's going on in cities today — but the mere fact that they grew up male and Latino in the city means that they have a very different experience with the law-enforcement system.

Recently an inspirational speaker came to our school to address students about gangs, drugs, alcohol, and sex. This man, Joseph Jennings, with his "Listen hard, because I been there and I'm here to level with you" style is able to command the attention of hundreds of teenagers in an auditorium near the end of the school day in a way that I never thought possible. At the climax of his speech that day, he leaned forward dramatically and said to my students and the other students there, "You are not garbage!" and my students sat there wide-eyed as he repeated it: "You are not garbage!" Imagine — the young people I teach need to be told they are not garbage! And it's not because their families do not love them; they love their children as intensely as all parents do. Rather, if you look at media images of young people of color, if you search our national consciousness, you discover that America is afraid of these young people. I have tried imagining what it would feel like to grow up in a world that was afraid of me. What if I looked at myself in society's mirror, and I saw drug dealers, hookers, gang bangers, and welfare cheats? That feeling of being outside — of being considered garbage — could not be farther from my own experience growing up as a white person who could take certain future opportunities for granted.

It is relevant to my job that I recognize that my students may, on the basis of solid experience, respond differently to a situation than I do. And if in my English class I want my students to write from their hearts, or articulate thoughtful opinions on an issue of the day, or probe the themes in a piece of literature, if I even hope to convince them to take school and my class seriously, I have to understand something about the nature of their experience in the world.

Training Student Teachers

How, then, do we prepare teachers to teach children whose experience in the world may be very different from our own? I believe we must:

1. dramatically augment the number of faculty and students of color in colleges and universities;
2. require every teaching candidate to acquire a strong background in ethnic studies;
3. recognize that aspiring teachers need to be armed not simply with "methods" and content knowledge, but with the sensibilities and skills necessary to probe student understandings and make the connections to the curriculum.

I deal with each of these proposals briefly below.

First, I think any college or university that seriously hopes to meet the needs of multicultural urban schools must embrace significant numbers of faculty and students of color. Clearly, children in schools need more teachers that share their cultural backgrounds. But I am also contending here that we cannot train white teachers and we cannot fully explore questions of urban education if "we" is a group of white people with all the best intentions in the world who nevertheless only hear our own voices. (And having just a few students or faculty of color will not do. What happens then is that those few "culturally different" do all the adapting and then are called upon to articulate "the minority perspective.")

Ethnic Studies

Second, I propose that every teaching candidate undergo a rigorous program of ethnic studies. By ethnic studies, I don't mean learning a smorgasbord of ethnic holidays, heroes, and dates; I don't even mean studying "learning styles." I mean a series of courses that look in depth at the history, literature, and culture of particular ethnic groups.

If student teachers studied linguistics long enough to understand that, say, an African-American dialect is as rule-bound and linguistically sophisticated as the dialect that has gained prominence as

"Standard American English," they might be less inclined to judge their students as unintelligent simply because they spoke a different dialect. If they also studied African-American history and literature, gaining an appreciation for the immense love of language running through African-American culture, they might be able to recognize in their own black students skills and linguistic strengths that could be built upon in the classroom.

Similarly, if we gained an appreciation for the tenacious struggles people of color have waged historically in this country around education, it might be a little bit harder to jump to the immensely unlikely conclusion that "those parents" do not care about the education of their children.

If we want to be successful in educating urban students, this respect is essential. We need teachers who will assume absolutely that the children in front of them are worthy and capable and who will assume that parents love their children and want the best for them.

An aspiring urban teacher needs to transcend the limits of her own experience, to begin to internalize the notion that her students may see things differently, to begin to cultivate an abiding respect for the children she teaches, their parents, and their communities. A rigorous and extensive program of ethnic studies would help teachers do that.

Nor is ethnic studies needed only when we teach children of color. Even white teachers of white children need to prepare those children for a multicultural world, and teacher educators need multicultural education themselves.

Complexities

Third, I propose that teacher education programs take to heart the concept that teaching is a highly social interaction in which the teacher helps students make connections between students' prior understandings and the new material at hand.

We might make use of case studies that ask teachers to think about what's inside students' heads, or how to probe student understandings, or how to forge connections, or analyze and make use of classroom dynamics. Consider an issue I had to grapple with recently. In my English classes, I've always insisted on tossing out workbooks and anthologies of short, "basalized" readings. Instead, I have students read and write about book-length works — novels and biographies. But this year for the first time, I was teaching bilingual English classes, facing students with a great range of English and Spanish language skills. I have students who are completely bilingual, some who are English dominant, some who are Spanish dominant but intellectually extremely well trained, and a number who read and write well in neither English nor Spanish. How could all of these students proceed at the same pace in Richard Wright's autobiography, *Black Boy*? Participants in a teacher education class could gain valuable practice by articulating, debating, and imagining the outcomes of a variety of possible approaches to this dilemma.

After conducting that same dialogue in my own head and with colleagues (including my student field observer from the University of Wisconsin, Milwaukee), I decided to organize heterogeneous reading groups in which students would be expected to help one another. I came into my classes the next day and explained my thinking, telling students that I would be grading them each day on group process (these are energetic tenth graders), and they would also receive group product grades. I told them they had two class periods to read chapter two, which was forty-five pages long, and to produce one vocabulary word and one thoughtful discussion question per group member. As I anticipated, they immediately argued that they should be able to form their own groups, and after some discussion, I let them.

The results were remarkable. On the first day, nine out of twelve groups got A's in group process, and on the second, all twelve groups did. Most groups read out loud the first day, though one group divided the chapter into sections. Then they actually assigned themselves homework. On the second day, my room was abuzz with kids excitedly explaining the chapter to one another in both English and Spanish, conversing about Richard Wright's life, and sharing their own similar experiences, or pressing on with their reading. I had found a way to keep a heterogeneous group of students challenged and engaged in the business of English.

These are the kinds of dilemmas teachers constantly wrestle with. Yet too many teacher education programs fail to train teachers to address the deep complexities of human interaction that teaching really involves. When cultural differences compound these complexities, the need for sophisticated teacher training is even greater.

No teacher education program can anticipate all the complicated demands a teacher will encounter in trying to draw connections between students' understandings and the curriculum. But we can approach teaching and teacher education with the expectation that we must constantly and forever struggle to examine our own perspectives and explore the experiences of others. Then when things do not work, maybe we will be less likely to label, judge, or surrender to frustration, and more likely to search for another way.

Resources

ERICKSON, FREDERICK, AND GERALD MOHATT. (1983). "Cultural Organization of Participation Structures in Two Classrooms of Indian Students," in George Spindler (Ed.), *Doing the Ethnography of Schooling*. New York: Holt, Rinehart & Winston.

GWALTNEY, JOHN LANGSTON. (1993). *Drylongso: A Self-Portrait of Black America*. New York: The New Press.

HEATH, SHIRLEY BRICE. (1983). *Ways with Words: Language, Life and Work in Communities and Classrooms*. New York: Cambridge University Press.

LABOV, WILLIAM. (1972). *Language in the Inner City*. Philadelphia: University of Pennsylvania Press.

McDERMOTT, R. P. (1974). "Achieving School Failure: An Anthropological Approach to Illiteracy and Social Stratification," in George D. Spindler (Ed.), *Education and Cultural Process*. New York: Holt, Rinehart & Winston.

RIST, RAY C. (1970). "Student Social Class and Teacher Expectations: The Self-Fulfilling Prophecy in Ghetto Education," *Harvard Educational Review* 40(3), 411–51.

Which Side Are You On?
The Role of Teachers Unions
in School Reform

BOB PETERSON

A friend who works for a teacher union recently recounted a discussion in which an antiunion teacher asked my friend why she supported unions. My friend's reply was simple. She said that without unions, particularly the one her dad had been in, she would have grown up in poverty.

That's reason enough for many to support unions. But some poor and working people, particularly people of color and women, have had a different experience with unions: one of exclusion.

I saw that for the first time when I worked on the Milwaukee docks in the mid-1970s and witnessed the International Longshoremen's Association's resistance to allowing women into the union. The ILA was continuing a long, nefarious tradition of some sections of organized labor in Milwaukee. One of the first strikes in Milwaukee, for example, was in 1863 by typesetters at the *Milwaukee Sentinel* who struck to protest the hiring of women.

In these cases, the unions weren't just defending workers from greedy bosses but were also "defending" unionized workers from other workers. Historian Robert Allen, in his book *Reluctant Reformers,* documents how this was the case in many unions throughout much of the nineteenth and twentieth century, as white workers attempted to keep workers of color out of many jobs. As late as 1931, Allen notes, fourteen national unions prohibited African-Americans from membership.

This historic dual nature of many unions – on the one hand protecting the needs of poor and working people and on the other hand undercutting the interests of some of those very people – is now sharply manifesting itself in many teacher unions.

Teacher unions must confront this dual nature of unionism and take a stand. They must not only work to defend the rights of their members, but must also advocate for the needs of the broader community, in particular the needs of their students. When these two interests are in conflict, there has to be open debate and some difficult decisions.

Unfortunately, many teacher unionists take a different approach. Their strategy is to "circle the wagons" and to take a strictly defensive posture, concentrating on bread-and-butter issues. Such a stance is wrong for two reasons. First, it runs counter to the self-interests of teachers. Circling the wagons will cut off teachers from those with the power to ultimately save public education: parents, students, and community people.

Second, it is morally and professionally wrong. Teacher unions need to protect the rights of teachers, but they must protect the quality of teaching as well. Many teacher union constitutions acknowledge this. For example, the constitution of the Milwaukee Teachers' Education Association (MTEA) states that the "purpose of this organization shall be to develop and maintain the professional status and financial welfare of its members and to promote the cause of education through strong positive action."

If unions are to be true to such statements, they must take a fresh look at issues such as seniority, tenure, teacher evaluation, and school governance. Moreover, we must examine the role of teachers unions in addressing the broader social issues confronting the children we teach and the communities where we work.

Some people will view it as heresy even to suggest such a discussion. Within certain Milwaukee circles I will no doubt be labeled as "antiunion." But attacking the messenger instead of dealing with the message has never been a useful strategy for coping with change. A committed trade unionist should be open to such discussions.

My reflections are based on twenty-five years of political activism and fifteen years of union activism (including six years on the Executive Board of the Milwaukee Teachers' Education Association); and my involvement as co-chair of the National Coalition of Education Activists, which includes union activists from both National Education Association and American Federation of Teachers locals. It is only after many years of concern with the issues raised in this article that I have decided to write down my thoughts in the hopes of sparking a broader discussion within the pages of Rethinking Schools. It is only through an honest, thoroughgoing debate that progressive unionists will be able to clarify the issues and outline the responses needed.

I also want to underscore that I am not proposing specific solutions to the problems raised in this article. Conditions vary from district to district and so must union responses. Seniority provisions of one union local, for example, might be inappropriate for another.

What I am proposing, however, is a trade union perspective that clearly states that unions must not advance the welfare and rights of teachers at the expense of students, community people, and working people in general — that the two need not be mutually exclusive.

Public Services Under Attack

Public sector unions are simultaneously one of the strongest and yet most vulnerable sections of the labor movement. Largely because of the decline in manufacturing in the United States, coupled with incessant governmental and business attacks on the very concept of unionism, overall union membership has declined from about 31 percent of the labor force in 1970 to 17 percent in 1990. During the same period, Germany's level of unionization grew from 37 percent to 43 percent, and Canada's from 32 percent to 36 percent.

Those workers who remain unionized are increasingly public sector workers. But unionization in the public arena is also now under sharp attack. Declining social service budgets on the local, state, and national levels, combined with growing trends of privatization and contracting out, undermine the bargaining power of public sector unions.

Public sector unions face problems that private sector unions don't. First, they are paid through taxes that, unfortunately, come disproportionately from the pockets of working people. Second, their "product" is usually a public service rather than a consumer item such as a wrench or an airplane. These realities make it far more difficult for public sector unions to garner public support not only for contract demands but for work actions such as a slowdown or strike. It is far more difficult to win public support for a strike by teachers demanding higher wages than for a strike by an industrial union.

Within this context, teacher unions face special problems. Their "product," the education of children, is particularly important. (As one of my colleagues likes to say, "We are not meat cutters. We are teachers of children, and our union should keep that in mind.") Further, schools are currently the prime target of conservative forces trying to defund publicly financed social services. Finally, teacher unions in urban areas, where controversy is strongest, must confront the reality that our urban schools are increasingly populated by students of color, who are taught overwhelmingly by white teachers. In Milwaukee, for example, approximately 70 percent of the students are nonwhite, while nearly 80 percent of the teachers are white.

Thus, union politics and the tendency of some teacher union members to defend the short-term interests of their members and paid staffs at the potential expense of students and community people have clear racial implications. Anti-public education forces have been able to demagogically play on these implications and have exacerbated the divisions between white teachers and communities of color, with the purpose of further undermining support for public education.

Teacher Unions Under Attack

A common refrain from policymakers when discussing schools is that teacher unions are the main obstacle to reform. Such rhetoric is often baseless. Further, sweeping charges that unions are preventing reform mask the broader problems faced by public schools. Changes in union contracts will never overcome fundamental problems such as lack of resources, inequitable funding, and outdated curricula.

Thus, those who argue that unions prevent reform and improved student achievement are at a loss to explain the pitifully low levels of achievement in many states in the South, where teachers are not allowed to collectively bargain. Nor does it explain the alleged success of schools in other industrialized countries where teachers are unionized. Nonetheless, unions need to figure out where the truth may lie in some of those criticisms and examine options that would serve both teachers and the broader community.

When parents and community members criticize unions, the criticism usually centers on two main issues: inflexible seniority rules and union protection of "bad" teachers. It is in teachers' self-interest to take a fresh look at such issues — for teachers themselves are at times affected by inflexible rules that dictate staffing solely on the basis of seniority and by the existence of teachers who either should not be teaching, or who should be receiving support.

Seniority

One example of a questionable seniority rule is the practice, common in some large districts such as New York City, in which teachers who are put out of assignment at one school because of a closing or program shift have the right to bump teachers at another school based on seniority. (In most districts, teachers who are put out of assignment are given positions at another school only when that school has a vacancy.)

There are clearly times when this bumping policy would be at odds with the efforts of a school to build a staff committed to a common educational philosophy. Further, this bumping privilege angers parents who feel that seniority rules automatically take precedence over building a quality staff. We must ask ourselves: Is such a rule the only way to protect a teacher's job rights?

In other districts, criticisms have been raised about transfer rules that operate exclusively on the basis of seniority. In this case, when a school has an opening, teachers from other schools may request to transfer in and the decision will be made on the basis of strict seniority. Again, rigid application of such rules might harm schools — in particular, schools that are trying to ensure schoolwide reforms requiring the support of all teachers in the building. If, for example, an elementary school is trying to implement a whole language, multicultural curriculum, it harms the school if it is forced to accept teachers who, although they may have seniority, have little experience or interest in whole language or a multicultural curriculum.

At the same time, I am not arguing to eliminate the concept of seniority. It would be a disaster to hand over all staffing decisions to principals and administrators, who could easily make decisions based on favoritism and patronage.

One possible solution to this particular problem, I believe, lies in the area of school governance and reforms that give teachers more responsibility at the local school level. In some schools around the country, school-based committees of teachers, parents, and administrators make certain staffing decisions and, for example, choose between the top several senior applicants.

The purpose of this article is not to outline a specific approach, but to raise questions. Rather than blindly defending current rules, unions should take the lead in exploring how seniority work rules might be modified so that they protect the rights of teachers and support school reform. I don't believe these two purposes need to be at odds.

Another key issue is the "bad" teacher syndrome. Since almost everyone has at one time had a lousy teacher, antipublic school forces often use this issue to turn public sentiment against unions and teachers.

More often than not, such critics usually denigrate any due process rights whatsoever. Marjorie Murphy notes in her book, *Blackboard Unions: The AFT and the NEA 1900–1980,* numerous cases of arbitrary dismissal of teachers for reasons ranging from being married (for women), to being members of integrated organizations (in the South), to being, or accused of being, a communist (particularly in New York). With the growing strength of the religious right and their increasingly successful efforts to infiltrate school boards, teachers should be vigilant in their defense of basic due process rights.

Teacher Accountability

Traditionally, teacher evaluation is the responsibility of principals and administrators, who have generally done an inadequate job. Principals usually deal with failing teachers by convincing them to transfer to another school, sometimes sweetening such a "voluntary" transfer by giving a satisfactory evaluation. At the new school the problem may recur. As a result, teachers might accumulate years of satisfactory evaluations, which can be used in their defense, if they are ever confronted by a principal willing to recommend that the teacher be dismissed. A co-worker of mine refers to this problem as the "dance of the lemons."

To actually deal with this issue of "bad" teachers, we must recognize that the problem is deeply woven into the fabric of our schools. Few structures exist to help new teachers or teachers experiencing difficulties. Little time is available, particularly in elementary schools, to confer or collaborate with other adults during the work day. This isolation works against learning from one's colleagues. Virtually no on-the-job training exists once a person starts teaching. In addition, overcrowded conditions and inadequate social services exacerbate classroom problems, making teaching a highly stressful occupation.

Many teacher union activists argue that it is the administration's responsibility to deal with "problem" teachers. I agree. But the fact is most school administrations are not doing their job in this area and are unlikely to do so in the foreseeable future. As a result, teachers ultimately have to assume more responsibility on this matter.

Peer review programs such as those in Toledo and Cincinnati, Ohio, could be possible models. (See *Rethinking Schools* Vol.6,

No.3.) Such peer review programs, however, should be preceded and surrounded by nonevaluative peer coaching programs with a strong intervention component for teachers in need. Such programs would have the further benefit of changing the school culture from one of isolation and lack of accountability to one of collaboration and responsibility.

School Governance

School governance is, potentially, the most controversial issue confronting teacher unions. One obvious complexity is the relative power of teachers, parents, and community representatives on school-based councils. But even more difficult issues exist.

First, and foremost, is the relative power of such councils versus districtwide agreements between school boards and the districts' unions. Another is the scope of power of the local councils. Instead of local unions preserving all their power at the districtwide level, consideration should be given to allowing local councils, with adequate guarantees to the rights of school workers, to have more say in shaping certain work rules and policies for individual schools.

The basic question then is, Who should run our schools? Should teacher unions support the traditional hierarchies of management and workers, with occasional parent input? Or should unions consider a radical redefinition of roles in which both teachers and parents assume more power? Should schools have teams of teachers and parents assume more power? Some schools, for example, have teams of teachers running the school instead of a principal. Such approaches give teachers more power than that of any union contract, but it also means new responsibilities. Instead of rejecting such experiments outright, teacher unions should help shape them. They should view their role as more than enforcers of work rules. They should consider their ability to monitor and shape experiments in decision making that truly empower teachers.

Relations with Communities

The relations of teacher unions with the parents and communities they serve have always been a source of tension. This is particularly true when teacher unions interact with communities with large numbers of people of color.

Historically, both the AFT and NEA have at times sided with

racist practices. The NEA, for example, failed to adequately back the 1954 U.S. Supreme Court decision outlawing separate but equal schools, waiting a full seven years to actually endorse it. According to Murphy, there were still eleven segregated NEA state associations in the early 1960s, and as late as 1974 the NEA still had a segregated Louisiana Association.

The most notorious AFT example of disregarding the interests of the community occurred in 1968 in New York City. During a struggle for community control of the schools, a struggle centered in the African-American community in Ocean Hill–Brownsville, the AFT went on strike protesting the removal of several teachers who were accused of sabotaging the project of community control. Many African-American teachers and progressive whites crossed the picket lines, reopening the schools with the assistance of community organizations such as Congress for Racial Equality (CORE). The strike greatly damaged the AFT's reputation among many people in African-American communities throughout the nation.

In Milwaukee, there are more recent examples. Perhaps the most blatant one involved a controversy over the staffing at two African-American immersion schools. The administration broke the contract in 1991 when it staffed the schools with 33 percent African-American teachers. Because of court-ordered desegregation, the contract called for a maximum of 23.5 percent and minimum of 12.5 percent of African-American teachers at any one school at that time. The union immediately filed a grievance against the staffing at the African-American immersion schools, even though no teachers in the district were denied their choice because of the contract violation. For almost two years the union refused to budge or compromise, citing it as a question of principle. Within the African-American community, this intransigence was seen as a deliberate attempt to undercut the goals of the immersion schools, further alienating many in the African-American community who consider the union a stronghold of racism.

In the battle over whether public education is going to receive adequate funding and support from our society, teachers must recognize that the parents and neighbors of our students are a key ally. Instead of promoting policies that alienate the communities where our students live, we should be trying to forge alliances when possible and resolve differences when necessary. But that requires dialogue and flexibility.

Taking the Initiative

Teacher unions must do more than adequately respond to contractual controversies, however. They must take the offensive and aggressively push policies that will improve teaching and improve relations with the communities where they work, particularly communities of color.

One of the key problems facing many urban systems, for example, is the fact that predominantly white teaching staffs teach students who are mainly children of color, including an increasing number of language-minority students. A range of problems flow from this reality, from lack of understanding to low expectations to inability to communicate adequately with families of the students. Yet teacher unions seem to do little to address this problem; they should be aggressively pushing programs that ensure more teachers of color in urban schools and that train current teachers to be more culturally sensitive and antiracist. The British Columbia Teachers Federation, for example, runs an education program for its members that deals with race issues on personal, political, and pedagogical levels. That union realizes that how teachers view the issue of race is crucial to the long-term success of that union.

Ultimately, however, communities will primarily judge teacher unions on whether the union promotes quality education for their children. While most teacher unions have this as one of their goals — often written into their constitutions — too often that goal is lost amid concern for teachers' welfare. The ways that unions might be involved in school reform are innumerable. Unfortunately, finding examples of such involvement is not quite so easy. Why? Why are teacher unions sometimes at the end, creating a drag on school reform, rather than at the beginning, pushing?

Likewise, teacher unions should be at the forefront of efforts to revitalize the labor movement. Teachers need to see that their interests are connected to the rest of labor. And they should start with the people who work in the schools with them. For example, school cafeteria workers, secretaries, and school bus drivers are often paid obscenely low wages. Why aren't teacher unions helping such workers organize for the wages they deserve?

Clearly, I advocate a position that goes beyond the stance of most teacher unionists. It is only "social justice" teacher unionism that will help develop the movement we need to defend teachers' rights and to ensure quality education for all children. Social justice unionism also recognizes that it is in the interest of teachers individually, and public schools generally, to fight for equality and justice throughout society.

Internal Changes Needed

I am skeptical whether teacher unions — as they presently function — can address the issues outlined above. What befuddles teacher unions is commonplace in many unions, and in fact in most institutions in our society: they are hierarchical structures that are rarely capable of capitalizing on their biggest resource, the rank-and-file classroom teacher.

Conditions mitigate against active involvement of classroom teachers. Overwhelmed by the day-to-day task of teaching under increasingly difficult conditions, most teachers have little time to become involved in union activities. More important, however, union structures sometimes discourage rank-and-file participation. Like many other institutions in our society, power is too often concentrated in small groups whose self-interests don't always coincide with the interests of the broader membership.

The bottom line is that classroom teachers must become more central to the running of local unions, and there should be less reliance on the paid staff. The reforms necessary to do so will vary according to conditions. In the AFT, for example, that might mean putting limits on the number of terms that elected officers can serve. In the NEA, where there are term limits, often the opposite problem exists and the professional staffs essentially run the local or state association. In this case, reforms might mean letting elected officers have terms longer than a year or two. In cases like Milwaukee, key elected officials should be permitted to take a sabbatical from teaching in order to devote time to union matters.

As in many other unions, the leadership in most teacher unions has become bureaucratized. Paid staff members, some of whom have extended contracts with few provisions for accountability, dominate the union's internal life. The elected leadership is little more than a rubber stamp.

There is also a philosophy of "expertism" and "legalism" in many teacher unions, which discourages the participation of classroom teachers and justifies the inordinate power of the staff. The union people most involved are paid staff who haven't taught in a classroom for years, sometimes decades. Why not, to cite one possibility, require that union staffers teach full time at least one semester every five years? Why not also, as has been done in some AFT locals, replace some full-time paid staff with classroom teachers who work part time on such things as union publications or specific school reform projects?

Another key problem is the lack of debate, communication, and education within teacher unions. Many local union publications merely provide one-way information from the staff to the membership, without serving as a forum for discussion of key issues. At best, this fails to inform teachers about important policy issues such as school "choice." At worst, it stifles debate, leaving important policy decisions up to a few.

The Choice for the Future

My friend who works for a teacher union and who argued about the value of unions did not only talk about her father's union. She talked of how early teachers union activists were mainly women, many of whom were involved in the suffragist movement. She explained the broader labor movement's influence on social policy legislation, such as the minimum wage, unemployment compensation, and Social Security. She noted how the United Auto Workers were major backers of Dr. Martin Luther King Jr. and the civil rights movement.

I believe it is within that tradition of progressive labor that teachers should push their unions. In the past, other unions have faced difficult challenges and set ambitious goals. Today, teacher unions face a similar challenge. Only when we have a democratic teacher union movement that recognizes that its interests are bound up with the interests of the communities we serve, and with poor and working people everywhere, will we be able to gather sufficient forces to ensure that public education and teachers get the resources and support that we deserve and that children desperately need.

All Children Are Our Children: An Interview with Lola Glover

The following is condensed from an interview with Lola Glover, head of the parent and community-based Coalition for Quality Education in Toledo, Ohio. Glover is also co-chair of the National Coalition of Education Activists and board member and past chair of the National Coalition of Advocates for Students. She was interviewed in the spring of 1993 by Barbara Miner of *Rethinking Schools*.

How did you get involved in education?

I'm the mother of nine children, I started the way most parents do. That's the PTA, Mothers' Club, room mother, chaperone, chairperson for the bake sales, that kind of thing. This was thirty to thirty-five years ago.

Because I was at school at lot, I began to notice things that I felt were not conducive to the educational or emotional well-being of students. I began to realize there was a pattern to certain things, instead of something I observed for one day. I began to question those actions, or the lack thereof, and to talk more to my own children about school. It was then that I started to get involved in my children's actual schooling and in academic issues.

I always made sure, however, that I was active in such a way that all the students in that particular classroom or school would benefit, not just my child. When I advocated only for my child, not a lot changed. The teachers and administrators would just make sure that when I was on the scene or when they dealt with my child, they would do things differently.

I don't believe that we will ever get all of the parents involved in the ways that we would hope. I believe that those of us who have made a commitment to get involved must act as if all the children are our children.

Do you sense that some teachers are reluctant to have parents involved in more than homework or bake sales, a fear that parents are treading on the teachers' turf if they do so?

Absolutely. And I don't think much of that has changed over the years.

Let's say I'm a teacher, and I come in and do whatever I do in my own way, in my own time, and nobody holds me accountable in any way for providing a classroom environment conducive to learning, or for student achievement. I get pretty set in my ways – and defensive with people who might question what I do.

I've found the teachers who are reluctant to have parents involved are those who know they are not doing the best they can for their students.

Then there are some teachers whose degree gave them a "new attitude" and who question these folks who didn't graduate from high school, and surely didn't go to college. Such teachers question what these parents are doing in their classrooms. It doesn't matter that they are the parents of their students.

I also have found some really great teachers in our district. They don't have any reservations or problems about parents getting involved in their classroom or school. In fact, they welcome and encourage parent involvement.

Many parents don't necessarily have time to sit in their child's classes or visit the school on a weekly basis. How can such parents make sure their kids are getting a decent education?

Not all schools have parent organizations at their schools. But usually you find a few active parents who are great advocates for children. If you know you don't have the time and energy to be actively involved, touch base with those parents who are involved. Build an alliance with them, get on the phone with them and when you can, meet with them and talk about your concerns. Help in any way you can to assist in developing an organized parent group in your school.

You don't need all the parents in the school to be involved. Sometimes it just takes five or ten dedicated parents who care about kids, and not just their kids, to make a positive difference in what goes on in our schools.

What advice do you have for parents who want to get involved?

First of all, you have to understand that as a parent it is your right and your responsibility to be involved. You should let the school know that you would like to work together in a constructive and collaborative way if possible, but if not, you're still going to be there.

I would also find out if any parent groups exist in the school. I would try to determine whether the group is really involved in making a difference for kids, or whether it's just a rubber stamp with no voice. You also have to decide whether you want to be involved in decision making, or in things like fund-raising.

If you want to get involved in school policies, you must first know the rules. If you are interested in suspensions or expulsions, for example, you must ask for a copy of the discipline policy for the district, not just the school. Then you must find out if there is an individual school policy or practice that goes beyond the district policy.

Then you must sit down with the principal and say, "I understand that this is your policy on discipline, but this has been your practice in this building for x number of years, and these are some of the areas I'm concerned about."

It's also essential that you always try to get a neighbor or a friend or another parent to go with you when you talk to the principal or teacher. My experience has taught me, do not go alone.

Why?

Words get twisted, views get changed. People in schools are no different than anyone else. They will say, "Oh, that's not exactly what I said," or "I didn't mean it that way." If there's another person with you, they tend not to try to get away with that kind of stuff because they know more than one person will hear what they are saying.

Some schools face severe budget cuts, and teachers have larger classes and are asked to do more and more. What if the teachers and administrators say, "Parent involvement is great, and I would love to have more meetings, do parent newsletters, visit kids' homes, and have parent committees, but I barely have time to prepare lessons every day." How would you respond?

Parents have to do more than be involved in their school or district. They also have to respond to elected officials. And if more money is needed for education, let your thoughts be known. Everybody claims to be either the Education Mayor, or the Education Governor, or the Education Somebody. Parents need to lobby and fight for those funds.

Another area of concern is class size. With the kinds of problems kids bring to school today, either the classes need to be smaller or there need to be teacher aides in the classroom. And these aides should be parents or people from that school community. This allows some additional time and a resource for teachers.

How can teachers and principals make parents feel more welcome?

The district or each school should have a parent outreach program. One of the biggest mistakes that teachers make is not being in touch with parents until there's a problem. And most parents don't want to hear the problem. They would like to think that little Johnny or Mary is doing fine all the time, and if not, they don't want to hear you putting their kid down. If you start off that way with a parent, it will take some real doing to get on the right foot with them again.

It's not going to be easy to build an alliance with thirty parents, so start with one or two. Get those parents to be your liaisons. Let them know how much you care and what you are trying to accomplish in the classroom. Give them the names and addresses of parents of the kids in your classroom, and ask, "Would you help me contact these parents and explain to them that I would really like to talk to all of them personally." Find out when will be a good time for everyone to meet, and set a date.

Why is it so important to foster mutual respect between parents and teachers?

I am convinced that if students begin to see parents and people in their community and their schools working together, a lot of things would change. First of all, the kids' attitudes would change. Right now, kids' attitudes have not changed about school because they don't see any connection between home and school. They do not see any real efforts being made by either side to come together for the purpose of improving their schools or educational outcomes.

I don't think any of us have the answers to solve all of these problems. But I do believe that if we come together out of mutual respect and concern, we will make a difference in what happens in our schools and our communities. I know we'll never find the answer if we keep this division between us. For the sake of our children, public education, and our future, we can ill afford not to work together. Make the first move.

Recommended Resources

Stratification in the Classroom: Testing and Tracking

National Center for Fair and Open Testing (FairTest)

342 Broadway, Cambridge, MA 02139; 617-864-4810. Critical resources on student and teacher assessment. See especially *FairTest Examiner,* a quarterly newsletter on testing issues.

None of the Above: Behind the Myth of Scholastic Aptitude

by David Owen, Boston: Houghton Mifflin, 1985. A highly recommended exposé of the Scholastic Aptitude Test (SAT).

Crossing the Tracks: How "Untracking" Can Save America's Schools

by Anne Wheelock, New York: New Press, 1993. A critique of tracking with an emphasis on groups across America that are successfully detracking their local schools.

Keeping Track: How Schools Structure Inequality

by Jeannie Oakes, New Haven: Yale University Press, 1985. A classic work revealing how tracking hurts all students, not just the ones in lower tracks.

*Maintaining Inequality: A Background Packet on Tracking
and Ability Grouping*

by the National Coalition of Education Activists (NCEA), P.O. Box 679, Rhinebeck, NY 12572-0679; 914-876-4580. A collection of basic information on what tracking is and how it affects children.

Beyond Pizza Sales (Rethinking Schools, Vol.7 No.3)

Rethinking Schools, 1001 E. Keefe Ave., Milwaukee, WI 53212-1710; 414-964-9646; fax 414-964-7220. An expanded issue of *Rethinking Schools* focusing on parental involvement in education and reform.

Notes

Discovering Columbus: Rereading the Past

1. "The Annals of America, Vol. 1:1493–1754, Discovering a New World," *Encyclopaedia Britannica,* 1968, pp. 2, 4.

2. Quoted in Hans Koning, *Columbus: His Enterprise* (New York: Monthly Review Press, 1976) pp. 53–54. As Koning points out, none of the information included in his book is new. It is available in Columbus's own journals and letters and the writings of the Spanish priest, Bartolomé de las Casas, and other observers.

3. Ibid., pp. 84–85.

4. Ibid., pp. 85–87.

5. It's useful to keep in mind the distinction between cynicism and skepticism. As Norman Diamond writes, "In an important respect, the two are not even commensurable. Skepticism says, 'You'll have to show me, otherwise I'm dubious'; it is open to engagement and persuasion....Cynicism is a removed perspective, a renunciation of any responsibility." See Norman Diamond, "Against Cynicism in Politics and Culture," *Monthly Review,* Vol. 28, No. 2, June 1976, p. 40.

6. Edna McGuire, *The Story of American Freedom* (New York: Macmillan, 1964) p. 24.

7. Ibid., p. 26.

8. See Paulo Freire, *Pedagogy of the Oppressed* (New York: Continuum, 1970).

9. Paulo Freire and Donaldo Macedo, *Literacy: Reading the Word and the World,* (South Hadley, MA: Bergin & Garvey, 1987).

What Should Children Learn?

1. *Robinson Crusoe* is especially endearing to E. D. Hirsch and is routinely listed in publications associated with his "core knowledge" project. The resource guide published by Hirsch's Core Knowledge Foundation specifically recommends that fourth graders read the version of *Robinson Crusoe* published by Usborne/ Hayes Picture Classics, as retold by Angela Wilkes and illustrated by Peter Dennis. Making ample use of color drawings accompanied by short blocks of type, the version could be described as a cross between a comic book and a novel.

   It could also be described as unabashedly racist. It has numerous references to "savages" and "cannibals," accompanied by ugly-looking people eating human flesh.

   One typical block of copy, referring to Crusoe's discovery that other humans had been on the island recently, reads: "Another year passed and Crusoe did not see anyone. Then one morning, as he walked along the beach, he stopped in horror. On the ground were the remains of a fire and round it were human bones. Crusoe felt sick. Cannibals, man-eating savages, had been there." The picture accompanying the text shows burnt wood and several skulls.

Interestingly, the book distorts the reason that Crusoe set sail on the fateful voyage that led to his shipwreck, perhaps because young children would have thought less of Crusoe had they known he was sailing to Africa to capture slaves. The Wilkes retelling merely says that Crusoe set sail for Africa "to trade for gold and ivory."

The Perils of School Vouchers

1. Milton Friedman, "The Role of Government in Education," in Robert A. Solow, ed., *Economics and the Public Interest* (New Brunswick: Rutgers University Press, 1955).

2. The most notorious instance of this occurred in Prince Edward County, where public schools were closed for five years. Blacks, too, were offered vouchers, but committed to desegregation. They refused, and many children received no formal education during that period. See J. Harvie Wilkinson III. *From Brown to Bakke: The Supreme Court and School Integration, 1954–1978* (New York: Oxford University Press, 1979) pp. 98–100.

3. See Charles Murray, *Losing Ground: American Social Policy, 1950–1980* (New York: Basic Books, 1984); Diane Ravitch, *The Troubled Crusade: American Education, 1945–1980* (New York: Basic Books, 1983).

4. See especially National Commission on Excellence in Education, *A Nation at Risk: The Imperative for Educational Reform* (Washington, DC: Government Printing Office, 1983).

5. John E. Chubb and Terry M. Moe, *Politics, Markets, and America's Schools* (Washington, D.C.: Brookings Institution, 1990).

6. See, for instance, *Milwaukee Journal,* July 23, 1990.

7. *Milwaukee Sentinel,* October 20, 1990, p.7; October 22, 1990, p.8.

8. *New York Times,* June 12, 1991, p.B9.

9. Wisconsin *DPI Bulletin* 2 (August 16, 1991):3. The most dramatic drop in returning students took place at the Harambee Community School, where only nineteen of the seventy-nine nongraduating participants returned. See *Milwaukee Journal,* October 2, 1991, p.A21.

10. *A Nation at Risk.*

11. See Lawrence C. Stedman and Carl F. Kaestle, "The Test Score Decline Is Over: Now What?" *Phi Delta Kappan* (November 1985): 204–10; Lawrence C. Stedman and Marshall S. Smith, "Weak Arguments, Poor Data, Simplistic Recommendations," in Beatrice and Ronald Gross, eds. *The Great School Debate* (New York: Touchstone, 1985) pp. 83–105.

12. Stedman and Smith, "Weak Arguments," p. 90.

13. See, for example, Peter H. Rossi and James D. Wright, "Best Schools – Better Discipline or Better Students? A Review of High School Achievement," *American Journal of Education* 91 (November 1982): 82; comments on John Witte's unpublished paper presented at the 1990 meeting of the American Political Science Association, *Education Week,* November 14, 1990, p.20.

14. *Milwaukee Journal,* August 1, 1991, pp. 1,8.

15. Gene V. Glass and DeWayne A. Matthews, "Are Data Enough?" *Educational Researcher* 20 (April 1991):26.

16. Ibid., p.25.

17. On this issue, see Richard Murname, "Evidence, Analysis, and Unanswered Questions," *Harvard Educational Review* 51 (November 1981):485–87.

18. *Education Week,* November 14, 1990, p. 20. See also Douglas Williams, "Do Private Schools Produce Higher Levels of Academic Achievement?" in Thomas James and Henry M. Levin, eds., *Public Dollars for Private Schools: The Case of Tuition Tax Credits* (Philadelphia: Temple University Press, 1983) pp.230–31.

19. See Peter W. Cookson Jr. and Caroline Hodges Persell, *Preparing for Power: America's Elite Boarding Schools* (New York: Basic Books, 1985) pp.84–93.

20. David Tyack, *The One Best System: A History of American Urban Education* (Cambridge, MA: Harvard University Press, 1974) p.4.

21. Thomas J. Peters and Robert H. Waterman, Jr., *In Search of Excellence: Lessons from America's Best Run Corporations* (New York: Harper & Row, 1982) p.318.

22. Richard Elmore and Associates, *Restructuring Schools: The Next Generation of Educational Reform* (San Francisco: Jossey-Bass, 1990).

23. Tyack, pp. 132–33.

24. Chubb and Moe, pp.221–22.

25. James Anderson, *The Education of Blacks in the South, 1861 to 1935* (Chapel Hill: University of North Carolina Press, 1988).

26. W. E. B. Du Bois, "Pechstein and Pechsniff," *The Crisis* 36 (September 1929):314.

27. Policies have included federal highway subsidies, segregationist FHA loans, zoning ordinances, and legal standing for restrictive covenants. See Kenneth T. Jackson, *Crabgrass Frontier: The Suburbanization of the United States* (New York: Oxford University Press, 1985) p.293; Ira Katznelson and Margaret Weir, *Schooling for All: Class, Race and the Decline of the Democratic Ideal* (Berkeley: University of California Press, 1985) p.217.

28. Robert Weisbrot, *Freedom Bound: A History of America's Civil Rights Movement* (New York: Plume, 1991) p. 302.

29. Jackson, pp. 297–303.

30. See, for instance, Robert B. Reich, "Secession of the Successful," *New York Times Magazine,* January 20, 1991, p. 42.

31. See *Chronicle of Higher Education,* July 3, 1991, p. A17.

32. Reich, pp. 43,44.

33. Jonathan Kozol, *Savage Inequalities: Children in America's Schools* (New York: Crown, 1991).

34. From advocacy of choice programs with redistributive goals, see John E. Coons and Stephen D. Sugarman, *Education by Choice: The Case for Family Control* (Berkeley: University of California Press, 1978) p.31; Henry M. Levin, "Educational Choice and the Pains of Democracy," in James and Levin, eds., *Public Dollars for Private Schools* (Philadelphia: Temple University Press, 1983) pp.27–36.

35. The Landmark Legal Center is funded in part by the Bradley Foundation. See *Milwaukee Journal,* July 23, 1990, pp.1, 4; for its opposition to the 1990 Civil Rights Act, see *New York Times,* October 21, 1990, p.15.

36. *Education Week,* September 18, 1991, p.1.

The Hollow Promise of Youth Apprenticeship

1. For a summary of the Clinton plan, see Lynn Olson, "Creating Apprenticeship System Will Be Tough, Advocates Admit," *Education Week* 12 (March 3, 1993): 1, 29–30.

2. William T. Grant Foundation Commission on Work, Family and Citizenship, *The Forgotten Half: Non-College Youth in America* (Washington, D.C.: William T. Grant Foundation, 1988); Commission on the Skills of the American Workforce, *America's Choice: High Skills or Low Wages!* (Rochester, N.Y.: National Center on Education and the Economy, 1990); Jobs for the Future, *Youth Apprenticeship, American Style: A Strategy for Expanding School and Career Opportunities* (Somerville, MA: Jobs for the Future, 1990); Robert I. Lerman and Hillard Pouncy, "The Compelling Case for Youth Apprenticeships," *The Public Interest* 102 (Fall 1990): 62–77; Kit Lively, "Maine's Month-Old Apprenticeships Show How a National Plan Might Work," *Chronicle of Higher Education* 39 (March 31, 1993): A20–21, 23.

3. In addition to the sources cited in note 2, see also Stephen Hamilton, "Apprenticeship as a Transition to Adulthood in West Germany," *American Journal of Education* 95 (Fall 1987): 314–45; Robert Lerman, "Reversing the Poverty Cycle with Job-Based Education," in Roberta Wollons, ed., *Children at Risk in America: History, Concepts, and Public Policy* (Albany, N.Y.: SUNY Press, 1993) pp. 230–58; Robert W. Glover and Ray Marshall, "Improving the School-to-Work Transition of American Adolescents," *Teachers College Record* 94 (Spring 1993): 588–610.

4. W. Norton Grubb, "Preparing Youth for Work: The Dilemmas of Education and Training Programs," in David Stern and Dorothy Eichorn, eds., *Adolescence and Work: Influences of Social Structure, Labor Markets, and Culture* (Hillsdale, N.J.: Lawrence Erlbaum, 1989) pp. 27–28; Joseph Kett, "The Adolescence of Vocational Education," in Harvey Kantor and David Tyack, eds., *Work, Youth, and Schooling: Historical Perspectives on Vocationalism in American Education* (Stanford, CA: Stanford University Press, 1982) pp. 98–100.

5. Paul Osterman, *Getting Started: The Youth Labor Market* (Cambridge, MA: MIT Press, 1980) chap. 2; Grubb, "Preparing Youth for Work," esp. pp. 23–26; Peter B. Doeringer and Michael J. Piore, "Unemployment and the 'dual labor market,'" *The Public Interest* 38 (Winter 1975): 67–79; W. Norton Grubb and Marvin Lazerson, "Education and the Labor Market: Recycling the Youth Problem," in Kantor and Tyack, eds., *Work, Youth, and Schooling*, pp. 110–41.

6. Thomas Bailey, "Can Youth Apprenticeship Thrive in the United States?" *Educational Researcher* 22 (April 1993): 6.

7. Bailey, "Can Youth Apprenticeship Thrive?" p. 7; Paul Osterman, *Employment Futures: Reorganization, Dislocation, and Public Policy* (New York: Oxford University Press, 1988) p. 112; Hamilton, "Apprenticeship as a Transition to Adulthood," p. 336.

8. Bailey, "Can Youth Apprenticeship Thrive?" p. 7.

9. On racial differentials in the youth labor market and the deterioration of the labor market position of black youth, see Richard B. Freeman and James L. Medoff, "The Youth Labor Market Problem in the United States: An Overview," in Richard B. Freeman and David A. Wise, eds., *The Youth Labor Market Problem: Its Nature, Causes and Consequences* (Chicago: University of Chicago Press, 1982) pp. 35–74; Richard B. Freeman and Harry Holzer, eds., *The Black Youth Employment Crisis* (Chicago: University of Chicago Press, 1986);

Harvey Kantor and Barbara Brenzel, "Urban Education and the 'Truly Disadvantaged': The Historical Roots of the Contemporary Crisis," in Michael B. Katz, ed., *The 'Underclass' Debate: Views From History* (Princeton: Princeton University Press, 1993) pp. 366–402.

10. See especially, Glover and Marshall, "Improving the School-to-Work Transition," p. 593; Lerman, "Reversing the Poverty Cycle with Job-Based Education," p. 248; Lerman and Pouncy, "Compelling Case for Youth Apprenticeships," p. 72.

11. Osterman, *Getting Started,* p. 33.

12. Osterman, *Employment Futures,* p. 112.

13. Osterman, *Getting Started,* chap. 2.

14. On the deterioration of employment opportunities in the inner city, see William Julius Wilson, *The Truly Disadvantaged: The Inner City, The Underclass, and Public Policy* (Chicago: University of Chicago Press, 1987); Gary Orfield and Carol Ashkinaze, *The Closing Door: Conservative Policy and Black Opportunity* (Chicago: University of Chicago Press, 1991). On the employment distribution of black and white workers, see Reynolds Farley, "The Common Destiny of Blacks and Whites: Observations about the Social and Economic Status of the Races," in Herbert Hill and James E. Jones, Jr., eds., *Race in America: The Struggle for Equality* (Madison: University of Wisconsin Press, 1993) pp. 197–233.

15. On the historical importance of formal institutions for African-Americans seeking work, see Walter Licht, *Getting Work, Philadelphia, 1840–1950* (Cambridge, MA: Harvard University Press, 1992) chaps. 2–4.

16. Joleen Kirschenman and Kathryn M. Neckerman, "'We'd Love to Hire Them But...': The Meaning of Race for Employers," in Christopher Jencks and Paul E. Peterson, eds., *The Urban Underclass* (Washington, D.C.: Brookings Institution, 1992) pp. 203–24. On the persistence of racial discrimination in the labor market and the reluctance of employers to hire blacks to supervise whites, see Norman Fainstein, "The Underclass/Mismatch Hypothesis as an Explanation for Black Economic Deprivation," *Politics and Society* 15 (1986/87): 403–51; Raymond Franklin, *Shadows of Race and Class* (Minneapolis: University of Minnesota Press, 1991) chap. 4.

17. Stephen Hamilton, "Prospects for an American-Style Youth Apprenticeship System," *Educational Researcher* 22 (April 1993): 13–15; Bailey, "Can Youth Apprenticeship Thrive?" pp. 8–9.

18. On the benefits of full employment for young minority workers, see Richard B. Freeman, "Employment and Earnings of Disadvantaged Young Men in a Labor Shortage Economy," and Paul Osterman, "Gains From Growth? The Impact of Full Employment on Poverty in Boston," both in Jencks and Peterson eds., *The Urban Underclass,* pp. 103–21, 122–34; Christopher Jencks, *Rethinking Social Policy: Race, Poverty, and the Underclass* (Cambridge, MA: Harvard University Press, 1992) pp. 124–25; Osterman, *Getting Started,* chap. 7.

19. Many conservative and some liberal economists argue that high unemployment is the necessary price we must pay to prevent inflation. But the level of inflation and unemployment is not dictated solely by the laws of the market. As the sociologists Seymour Bellin and S. M. Miller have pointed out, it also reflects what the government is willing to do to control prices and promote employment. The argument that little can be done to create jobs and that prices can be kept under control only by letting unemployment rise is

based on the belief that the government should not intervene actively in the market. However, more interventionist policies such as limiting price increases in industries that are rapidly raising their prices, subsidizing the cost of producing vital commodities and services, and limiting pay increases in high-wage industries and occupations can also reduce inflationary pressures, while other measures such as shortening the workweek and shifting government spending away from military research and development (which produces fewer jobs than spending for civilian purposes) can help expand employment. See Seymour S. Bellin and S. M. Miller, "The Split Society," in Kai Erikson and Steven Peter Vallas, eds., *The Nature of Work: Sociological Perspectives* (New Haven: Yale University Press, 1990) pp. 173–91.

20. For instance, Henry Levin and Russell Rumberger report that between 1982 and 1995, computer systems analysts, computer programmers, and electrical engineers, three of the fastest growing occupations, have estimated growth rates of 65 percent. Yet each occupation will generate fewer than 100,000 jobs during this period. By contrast, custodians, cashiers, and sales clerks, three traditional occupations, will grow relatively slowly compared to the three technical occupations, but will still generate more than 600,000 jobs. See Henry Levin and Russell Rumberger, "Educational Requirements for New

Technologies: Visions, Possibilities and Current Realities," *Educational Policy* 1 (1987): 339.

21. See Lawrence Mishel and Ruy A. Teixeira, *The Myth of the Coming Labor Shortage: Jobs, Skills, and Incomes of America's Workforce 2000* (Washington, D.C.: Economic Policy Institute, 1991) pp. 13–22; David R. Howell and Edward N. Wolff, "Trends in the Growth and Distribution of Skills in the U.S. Workplace, 1960–1985," *Industrial and Labor Relations Review* 44 (April 1991): 486–502; Bill J. Johnson, "The Transformation of Work and Educational Reform Policy," *American Educational Research Journal* 30 (Spring 1993): 39–65.

22. See, for example, Glover and Marshall, "Improving the School-to-Work Transition," pp. 589–92.

23. For reviews of the research on the effects of technological innovation on skill requirements, see Kenneth I. Spenner, "Technological Change, Skill Requirements, and Education: The Case for Uncertainty," in R. M. Cyert and D. C. Mowery, eds., *The Impact of Technological Change on Employment and Economic Growth* (Cambridge, MA: Ballinger, 1988) pp. 131–84; Kenneth I. Spenner, "The Upgrading and Downgrading of Occupations: Issues, Evidence, and Implications for Education," *Review of Educational Research* 55 (Summer 1985): 125–54: Russell Rumberger, "The Potential Impact of Technology on the Skill Requirements of Future Jobs," in Gerald Burke and Russell Rumberger, eds., *The Future Impact of Technology on Work and Education* (London: Falmer, 1987) chap. 5; Levin and Rumberger, "Educational Requirements for New Technologies."

24. Levin and Rumberger, "Educational Requirements for New Technologies," p. 344. On the mixed effects of computers and other technological innovations on work, see also Spenner, "Technological Change, Skill Requirements and Education," pp. 131–84; Paul Attewell, "The Deskilling Controversy," *Work and Occupations* 14 (August 1987): 323–46; Shoshana Zuboff, *In the Age of the Smart Machine: The Future of Work and Power* (New York: Basic Books, 1984).

25. Spenner, "Technological Change, Skill Requirements, and Education," p. 137. On overeducation and the mismatch between workers with given skills and jobs with given skill requirements, see Iver Berg, *Education and Jobs: The Great Training Robbery* (New York: Praeger, 1970).

26. Zuboff, *In the Age of the Smart Machine;* Spenner, "Technological Change, Skill Requirements, and Education"; Levin and Rumberger, "Educational Requirements for New Technologies."

27. Spenner, "Technological Change, Skill Requirements, and Education,: p. 171; Mishel and Teixeira, *Coming Labor Shortage,* p. 23.

28. Mishel and Teixeira, *Coming Labor Shortage,* pp. 23, 40; Johnston, "The Transformation of Work," p. 65.

29. Commission on the Skills of the American Workforce, *America's Choice,* pp. 61–64; Osterman, *Employment Futures,* chap. 6.

30. This is the message of several recent reports on the American high school. See especially Arthur G. Powell, Eleanor Farrar, and David K. Cohen, *The Shopping Mall High School* (Boston: Houghton Mifflin, 1985); John Goodlad, *A Place Called School* (New York: McGraw-Hill, 1984).

31. Grant Commission on Work, Family, and Citizenship, *The Forgotten Half,* p. 50; Lerman, "Reversing the Poverty Cycle," p. 240.

32. Marvin Lazerson and W. Norton Grubb, introduction to *American Education and Vocationalism: A Documentary History, 1870–1970* (New York: Teachers College Press, 1974); W. Norton Grubb and Marvin Lazerson, "Rally 'Round the Workplace: Continuities and Fallacies in Career Education," *Harvard Educational Review* 45 (November 1975) pp. 461–62; Paul Violas, *The Training of the Urban Working Class: A History of Twentieth Century Urban Education* (Chicago: Rand-McNally College Publishing, 1978) chaps. 6–7; Samuel Bowles and Herbert Gintis, *Schooling in Capitalist America* (New York: Basic Books, 1976).

33. See especially Lerman, "Reversing the Poverty Cycle" pp. 230–58; Lerman and Pouncy, "Compelling Case for Youth Apprenticeship." The experience of German and Turkish youth in German secondary schools bears out the connection between apprenticeship and educational stratification. The German secondary system has three levels of schooling. The highest level is focused on academic preparation for higher education; the middle level includes both college and vocational preparation; the lowest level is limited predominantly to preparation for manual occupations. In the mid-1980s, only 28 percent of Turkish youth but 65 percent of German youth were enrolled in the two highest levels. See Bailey, "Can Youth Apprenticeship Thrive?" p. 8; Hamilton, "Apprenticeship as a Transition to Adulthood," pp. 318–21, 333.

34. Hamilton, "Apprenticeship as a Transition to Adulthood," pp. 333-34. Lerman and Pouncy also take this position in "Compelling Case for Youth Apprenticeship," p. 72.

35. Bailey, "Can Youth Apprenticeship Thrive?" p. 9.

36. John Dewey, "Education vs. Trade-Training," *New Republic* 3 (May 15, 1915): 42.

37. The same point is made by Norton Grubb in "Preparing Youth for Work," p. 41. Also see, Bellin and Miller, "Split Society," pp. 183–88.

Contributors

Ann Bastian is a senior program officer at the New World Foundation, a college history teacher, and co-author of *Choosing Equality: The Case for Democratic Schooling*.

Bill Bigelow is an editorial associate at *Rethinking Schools* and a teacher at Jefferson High School in Portland, Oregon.

Linda Christensen is a *Rethinking Schools* editorial associate and an English teacher at Jefferson High School in Portland, Oregon.

Harvey Daniels teaches at National-Louis University in Evanston, Illinois, where he directs the Center for City Schools. He is the author and co-author of a number of books, the latest of which is *Best Practice: New Standards for Teaching and Learning in America's Schools*.

Lisa Delpit holds the Benjamin E. Mays Chair of Urban Educational Leadership at Georgia State University in Atlanta. She is the author of *Other People's Children: Cultural Conflict in the Classroom*.

Louise Derman-Sparks is on the faculty at Pacific Oaks College in Pacific Oaks, California. She is the author of *Anti-bias Curriculum: Tools for Empowering Young Children*, and producer of the *Anti-bias Curriculum Video* from Pacific Oaks.

Cynthia Ellwood is a former bilingual English teacher at South Division High School in Milwaukee, Wisconsin. She is now director of the Department of Educational Services for Milwaukee Public Schools.

Henry Louis Gates Jr. is chair of Afro-American Studies at Harvard University.

Lola Glover is head of the parent and community-based Coalition for Quality Education in Toledo, Ohio. Glover is also co-chair of the National Coalition of Education Activists and co-director of the National Coalition of Advocates for Students.

Suzan Shown Harjo is president and director of the Morning Star Foundation in Washington, D.C.

Lenore Gordon is a teacher, consultant, and writer.

Harvey Kantor is an associate professor at the University of Utah who specializes in educational history and policy.

Stan Karp, an editorial associate at *Rethinking Schools,* teaches English and Journalism at JFK High School in Patterson, New Jersey.

Enid Lee is an education consultant and the former supervisor of race/ethnic relations for the North York Board of Education in metropolitan Toronto. She was born and raised in the Caribbean, and has been working in the field of language, culture, and race for more than fifteen years in Canada and the United States.

David Levine is an editor at *Rethinking Schools* and a former high school English teacher. He is currently a graduate student in the Department of Educational Policy Studies at the University of Wisconsin, Madison.

Robert Lowe teaches at National-Louis University in Evanston, Illinois, and is an editor at *Rethinking Schools.*

Foyne Mahaffey teaches at the 38th St. School in Milwaukee.

Elizabeth Martínez is a San Francisco-based writer, educator, and activist who has written extensively on Latino issues. Her most recent book is the bilingual volume, *500 Years of Chicano History in Pictures.*

Terry Meier is an associate professor in the graduate school at Wheelock College in Boston. Her areas of specialty are assessment, language development, and cross-cultural communication.

Barbara Miner is the managing editor at *Rethinking Schools.*

Pedro Noguera is president of the Berkeley School Board and a professor in the School of Education at the University of California, Berkeley.

Bob Peterson is an editor at *Rethinking Schools* and a bilingual fifth-grade teacher at La Escuela Fratney in Milwaukee, Wisconsin.

Howard Zinn is a historian, professor, and author of *A People's History of the United States.*

Index